*The Bible of Compounding Money*

**The Complete Guide to Investing with World Class Money Managers**

# Disclosure
### Limit of Liability/Disclaimer of Warranty:

While the author has used his best efforts in preparing this book, he makes no representations or warranties with respect to the accuracy or completeness of the contents of this book and specifically disclaims any implied warranties of merchantability or fitness for a particular purpose. No warranty may be created or extended by sales representatives or written sales materials. The advice and strategies contained herein may not be suitable for your situation. You should consult with a professional where appropriate. Neither the publisher nor author shall be liable for any loss of profit or any other commercial damages, including but not limited to special, incidental, consequential, or other damages.

**Past performance is not necessarily indicative of future performance**. The risk of loss in trading futures contracts, commodity options or forex can be substantial, and therefore investors should understand the risks involved in taking leveraged positions and must assume responsibility for the risks associated with such investments and for their results. You should carefully consider whether such trading is suitable for you in light of your circumstances and financial resources.

**This publication contains references to hypothetical trading results**.

HYPOTHETICAL PERFORMANCE RESULTS HAVE MANY INHERENT LIMITATIONS, SOME OF WHICH ARE DESCRIBED BELOW. NO REPRESENTATION IS BEING MADE THAT ANY ACCOUNT WILL OR IS LIKELY TO ACHIEVE PROFITS OR LOSSES SIMILAR TO THOSE SHOWN. IN FACT, THERE ARE FREQUENTLY SHARP DIFFERENCES BETWEEN HYPOTHETICAL PERFORMANCE RESULTS AND THE ACTUAL RESULTS SUBSEQUENTLY ACHIEVED BY ANY PARTICULAR TRADING PROGRAM. ONE OF THE LIMITATIONS OF HYPOTHETICAL PERFORMANCE RESULTS IS THAT THEY ARE GENERALLY PREPARED WITH THE BENEFIT OF HINDSIGHT. IN ADDITION, HYPOTHETICAL TRADING DOES NOT INVOLVE FINANCIAL RISK, AND NO HYPOTHETICAL TRADING RECORD CAN COMPLETELY ACCOUNT FOR THE IMPACT OF FINANCIAL RISK IN ACTUAL TRADING. FOR EXAMPLE, THE ABILITY TO WITHSTAND LOSSES OR TO ADHERE TO A PARTICULAR TRADING PROGRAM IN SPITE OF TRADING LOSSES ARE MATERIAL POINTS WHICH CAN ALSO ADVERSELY AFFECT ACTUAL TRADING RESULTS. THERE ARE NUMEROUS OTHER FACTORS RELATED TO THE MARKETS IN GENERAL OR TO THE IMPLEMENTATION OF ANY SPECIFIC TRADING PROGRAM WHICH CANNOT BE FULLY ACCOUNTED FOR IN THE PREPARATION OF HYPOTHETICAL PERFORMANCE RESULTS AND ALL OF WHICH CAN ADVERSELY AFFECT ACTUAL TRADING RESULTS
** THE MATERIAL DISPLAYED IN THIS PUBLICATION IS INTENDED FOR EDUCATIONAL PURPOSES ONLY

*To my family,*

*Ruthie, Gabrielle, Ariel, Micael, my mother, and all those who supported me along this marathon of investing.*

*Thank you.*

# Contents

FOREWORD ............................................... 1

PREFACE .................................................. 3

CHAPTER 1: Are You Sure You Want to Invest with Warren Buffett? ........................ 25

CHAPTER 2: Compounding is the Key ............. 37

CHAPTER 3: Investing with World Class Commodity Trading Advisors ...................... 51

CHAPTER 4: Inflation ............................... 91

CHAPTER 5: Trend Followers Lead the Pack ..... 117

CHAPTER 6: Why Invest in Managed Futures? .... 123

CHAPTER 7: World Class Trading Program ....... 141

CHAPTER 8: Money Manager Blow Ups ........... 155

CHAPTER 9: Common Investor Mistakes ......... 163

CHAPTER 10: Doing the Uncomfortable: Buying the Drawdown ........................ 183

CHAPTER 11: Transparency and Liquidity ......... 189

CHAPTER 12: Buying the Drawdowns of Commodity Trading Advisors ................... 199

CHAPTER 13: Due Diligence ...................... 203

**CHAPTER 14:** The First Question: Are the Returns REAL? ........................... 213
**CHAPTER 15:** Risk Management ................. 227
**CHAPTER 16:** How to Find the World Class Trend Followers ......................... 243
**CONCLUSION** .................................... 251

*The Bible of Compounding Money*

# Foreword

**M**ost people think diversifying is having a basket of stocks with some bonds mixed in. Yet when the markets crash, as we've experienced, stocks have a tendency to move in unison. These portfolio mixes have been lackluster at best.

How do you truly diversify and give yourself the best chance to grow your assets overtime? How do you hire a professional money manager that invest in the items we use every day like gasoline to drive our cars, heating oil to keep us warm in the winter, wheat and meat to dine on, coffee and orange juice to drink, gold and silver for our jewelry (or teeth), currency exchange when we travel, interest rates for our bank accounts, cotton for our cloths, and lumber for our homes?

With nearly two decades of investment management experience, Andy Abraham's ***Bible of Compounding Money*** is a must read for anybody who is serious about increasing their assets long term. Stocks have gone down to sideways. Real Estate has cave dived. Interest Rates are abysmal. However, Andy shows you how to find professional money managers (CTA's) who invest in diverse items through managed futures programs. Andy is not only a money manager himself, but successfully manages a family office that invests with these professional money managers. He's able to present the industry from both sides of the equation and put it into terms that the non-professional can grasp and understand.

Andrew shares:
- The keys to compounding
- How to find the world class money managers
- How to profit from the coming inflation attack
- Why choose Trend followers
- Common and easy mistakes to avoid
- The best time to invest
- How much to allocate to each program
- Risk management

From personal experience Andy shows you how, despite the best minds in the business doing otherwise, he was able to avoid being burned by Bernie Madoff. By applying the books "10 Commandments for Compounding" you too can have a chance, just like author has done, to compound your investments over time.

Robb Ross
Commodity Trading Advisor
Owner/Manager - White Indian Trading Company Limited

*The Bible of Compounding Money*

# Preface

Paul Singer, the principle of Elliott Associates L.P., started in 1977 with $1.3 million from proverbial friends and family investors. Today Singer's firm has more than $16 billion in assets under management. Elliott's principal investment strategy is buying distressed debt cheaply and selling it at a profit or suing for full payment. It is clear that he has seen many different financial cycles and is a world class money manager.

Before the crisis of 2007 he presented his concerns and fears to numerous world finance ministers—that a systemic financial collapse could occur from securitizations of mortgage obligations and collateralized debt obligations. **This warning fell on deaf ears.** Singer recently gave a speech called "The Shape of the Next Crisis". In this speech he stated "There are a number of elements that are in play, some of which are novel, completely new in virtually the human landscape". He stated:

*The thing that scares me most is significant inflation, which could destroy our society.*

Andy Abraham

Excerpts of the speech;

*Let's talk about financial institutions and the financial system. The major message that I want to give you (and I've invited challenge on both parts of my thesis here and I've never had anybody challenge it):* **The major financial institutions in the US and around the globe are utterly opaque; and the next financial crisis will happen faster, more suddenly.**

*We cannot (I have 110 investment professionals), and I surmise that* **you cannot, understand the financial condition of any bank, major financial institution.** *You can't see the actual size of the balance sheet. You have no idea what that derivatives section means…it's 10 to 100 times the size of the actual balance sheet.*

**So when people say, "Well, it used to be 40x leveraged," (some of them were 90x leveraged) "but now they're 15 to 20 times leveraged."** *Well that's just great. Except you go to the derivatives and see numbers in the trillions and trillions and trillions and there is no clue, you have no clue, no understanding, of what that is actually composed of. Is that composed of trades that are basically unwound where all you have is counterparty risk? Is that composed of actual hedges of upper tranches the way we would have in an admitted hedge fund?*

**So you are looking at balance sheets without any real understanding of how the balance sheets and the companies would perform in the event of a crisis.** *Which of these trades or trillions of dollars of trades, which in normal times oscillate like this [very small motion] and that's why they're so big, would in really bad times start going like this [large motion].*

And if you actually have capital of only half a percent, or one percent or five percent of your actual footings, not just unwound trades that happen to still be on balance sheet, but actual footings, you're in trouble.

**The kind of thing that wound up the financial system three years ago is expected to be different** in form than the kind of things that would unwind the financial system the next time. But I'm going to argue that the **next time will be faster**. If you think back to '07 and '08, it was episodic. It wasn't just suddenly that in the second or third week in September that Lehman goes under and that's the crisis and the whole world collapsed. No, there were several episodes leading up to that.

After that, what kept the entire financial system from coming to a grinding halt was quite simple. It wasn't that all of the other firms were in much better shape than Lehman. **It's very simple; it's that governments, here and in Europe, underwrote the entire system.** Ben Bernanke, of whom I'm not a fan... at all, has been quoted as saying that in the absence of the government guarantee and underwriting, 12 of the 13 biggest banks in the world would have gone out of business following Lehman. Whether it's 12/13, or 13/13, or 6 or 8 of 13, is completely imponderable, but the point is actually well-taken. **In the absence of that guarantee there would have been a cascading collapse because of the opacity.**

There are people in this room that are on trading desks or manage trading operations at investment banks. You know for a fact that you knew nothing about the financial condition of your five biggest counterparties. **And so your relationships and your willingness to trade with those counterparties were dependent on rumor or credit spreads widening or not**

***widening**. And that's a very terrible place for the financial system to be in.*

*So take the opacity, take the fact that you can't really understand the financial condition, and take the fact that the leverage hasn't really been rung out.* ***And what you realize is that the lessons of '08 will actually result in a much quicker process, a process that I would describe as a "black hole" if and when there is the next financial crisis.***

*The next financial crisis obviously can only happen if, believably, the governments either cut loose the major financial institutions—believably and credibly unwound the guarantee—or even more difficult and scary, if the government guarantees were not enough. And that's one of the next elements in the shape of the next crisis.* ***As you know, risk has migrated upward; it's migrated from lenders and borrowers really to governments.*** *It's gone on the balance sheet of the US, the ECB (the various countries of Europe, particularly Germany, France, etc.). That the credit of Europe, the credit of America, is being called into question in the starkest way is part of what will shape the next crisis.*

*But before I get to that part, and explain how I think that impacts, I want to come back to the trader and trading part of this.* ***The lesson of '08, which is indelibly stamped upon every hedge fund forehead and trading desk head, is: Move your assets first, stop trading first, sell the paper first, and ask questions later.*** *Those that moved from Lehman days or weeks before the end were happy. Those that sat there thinking that they were protected in prime brokerage accounts or protected in some other ways, or that firms like Lehman wouldn't be allowed to go under were stuck in the company (of course Lehman is still in bankruptcy) with claims trading at 20-something cents*

*The Bible of Compounding Money*

on the dollar, depending on where you are in the capital structure.

Paul Singer, one of the best and smartest investors in the world, is most terrified by the one thing that every leading economist says will never happen: **High Inflation!**

*This book that you have been lucky enough to pick up could be what differentiates between success and failure!*

## MY STORY

During University I began to take notice of and witnessed the investment manias and the delusions of the crowds and their hype. I witnessed what transpired to gold. This so-called bastion of stability fell nearly 70% from the 1980s through the early 2000s. Interest rates were running close to 18% and the stability of the financial system was questioned. However fortunes could have been made by buying these rejected bonds. Nothing changed as I was growing up. Stocks that everyone had to own—called the greatest investments in 2000—ended up imploding. I remember being instructed by a colleague that *I should buy tech stocks before there were no stocks left*. We all know what happened to the NASDAQ. The story sadly continued with real estate, an investment that also was considered safe.

Investing is risky. Bad things can happen and eventually do happen to *all* assets. There are no safe havens. Valuations get out of whack, industries change, managers screw up, politicians make terrible decisions, and things don't always work out as expected. In order to survive we must have the ability to ignore crowds and hype. In order to provide for our families we need to have a complete plan. The vast majority of investors spend less time planning their investment future than deciding what to eat for dinner. It is easier for them to buy whatever the so-called professionals feed us or to simply, "Buy and Hold". This book is different—my goal is to give you a different perspective on how to invest with world class money managers with somewhat of a margin of safety.

Many of my friends and colleagues are overwhelmed by the prospect of managing their own money as well as being skeptical of the so-called professional money managers. There are so many complex investing products, opinions and strategies flying around that they don't know where to begin, so they capitulate and end up hiring someone else to look after their cash. That's unfortunate. The truth is that *no individual* could possibly keep up with—let alone understand—all the arcane financial products out there. But here's the good news: You don't have to. Nor do you have to know which way the market is heading (NEWS FLASH: NOBODY DOES!) to be a successful investor.

***In fact, the more you can tune out the noise,
the better off you'll be.***

I started investing in 1994. I wrote this book because I wanted to separate the snake oil from reality when investing. More so, I never found a book that expressed the points that I wanted to present as my way of giving back. The lessons that I have shared in this book I have also shared with my children in order for them to perpetuate financial freedom for themselves and their families in the future. The ideas and lessons are timeless and often forgotten when the markets are healthy. I learned from the onset that the majority of the people on Wall Street did not have my interests at heart. I learned that the fastest and most reliable way to get rich on Wall Street isn't to become the next Warren Buffett. It's to find people gullible enough to pay outrageous fees and commissions on products that rarely beat a basic index fund.

I had made our families money by a business which I started in college. I sold the business in 1994 and sought out a way to make our money work for us. I avidly saved during the years I was making a lot of money. We enjoyed life, yet we lived below our means. We would buy luxury cars, but buy them used with 10,000 or less miles. It was very clear to me that saving was more important than investing. I had to have resources to invest with. I saw my peers who were more interested in having the latest gadgets and not saving for a rainy day or even investing. They would have been better off if they devoted that energy to figuring out how to save more money than live for the moment.

Most financial problems are caused by debt. I witnessed a colleague of mine, who I went to college with, who earned several hundred thousand dollars a year as a specialist in an advanced field. He declared bankruptcy in 2009 and will probably need to work well into his 70s. There are people in my mother's condo who never made a lot of money throughout their lifetime, however they avoided debt, invested and are living a comfortable retirement.

Investing and trading first started out as an interest. This interest grew into a passion, or as my wife would say at times—an obsession. I love the possibilities the markets can offer. I wake in the mornings at 5am or many times earlier. Even worse, I will wake in the middle of the night with a trading idea to test out on my mechanical system. I write it down and first thing in the morning I start to test it out. I wake up early because I am anxious to know what has already occurred in Asia. Beside this strong fascination and passion for the markets, I have a strong respect for the markets. I believe in the complete uncertainty of the markets. I know at any moment I can lose money. This basis of belief builds the necessity of strong risk measures to be constantly in place when investing.

Upon the sale of my business, I did not know what to do with the proceeds. I asked my accountant and my attorney for suggestions. I asked who their most successful client was. I was given a name, a phone number and was told he had made money for decades yet they did not exactly understand what he did. I found out, to my shock, that he was not a Wharton or Harvard graduate, nor a professional money manager. He was a dentist. He was down to earth and especially humble.

He started in 1979 with slightly under $200,000—a lot of money at that time—with a strategy called trend following, with a diversified basket of commodities, interest rates and currencies. He experienced the 1973-74 stock market crash and thought there had to be a better way. He made himself available to whichever market generated a buy or sell signal. He would go long as much as he would go short. He did not trade his opinions. He looked for trends. He based his trading on the principles of Richard Donchian, with breakouts of the highest highs over X periods or breakdowns of the lowest lows over X periods. This trend following strategy is very simple in concept to do, however very hard emotionally to do.

Most investors like to buy low and sell high. The vast majority of investors want to be right or smart. I have no desire to be right. My way of being smart is to **try** to compound money over long periods of time for myself and my family. My desire is to *try* to mitigate big losses. The dentist's thoughts were to buy high with the possibility of high going higher or sell lows with the thought of lows going lower. This trend following strategy is the anti-thesis of most investors. The trends the dentist sought could be in the grain markets, energy markets, metals, interest rates or even the currencies; each of these markets have their bull and bear runs. He was totally systematic without any emotion. This lack of emotion gave him the ability to compound money to the tune of $18 million dollars. He did not use any magical system. He was not a guru or genius. He had countless losses and long periods of time he did not make money (yet he complained about them).

## THE TEN-YEAR RULE

The dentist understood the Ten-Year Rule and transformed it into a lifetime strategy. Money is made by being patient. Warren Buffett stated, "If you aren't willing to own a stock for ten years, don't even think about owning it for ten minutes." The same connotation was used by the dentist. He was patient and he even took the ten year rule and turned it into the lifetime investing rule.

There are those from the school of fundamental analysis and those from a technical background. The dentist was from the technical analysis He understood the concept of robust trading systems. The dentist's concepts resonated with me. I did not completely buy into the concept of just buying bonds or stocks (as did the masses). More so, I had a very hard time simply buying into the proverbial "Buy and Hold". As the markets became my passion I spent countless hours studying market history. I knew that there were periods in which "Buy and Hold" actually lost money. I learned that stocks markets did not only go up. There were periods in which really nothing happened. During these periods in which the stock market did not go anywhere I would not be able to make money. This was an option I wanted to try to avoid. I learned there were always opportunities.

*I learned the concept of compounding money!*

Through the dentist I learned the power of reasonable returns, time, and compounding of money can lead to extreme wealth.

I internalized these principles in the management of my family's net worth.

## REASONABLE RETURNS + TIME + COMPOUNDING OF MONEY = EXTREME WEALTH.

Pretty simple formula but not especially easy to do!

In 2003 Marhedge featured an article in which they featured a trend following commodity trading advisor Tom Shanks, the principle of Hawksbill. It was a short piece, however on page three what hit me was Tom had an investor who started with him in 1988. This investor allocated $300,000 in his trading program. By the article's date in 2003, it stated that this investor's account was up to $18,000,000 plus he took out $1,000,000. I read this article much later on, probably in 2010 or even later. All I could think about was the compounding over the years. For easy numbers I assumed a 10% rate of return on this money. Playing the numbers, 10 years at 10% on 18,000,000 this sum would compound to approximately $45,000,000 dollars.

For full disclaimer, I have also invested in Hawksbill, but this is not a recommendation of any sort. I purchased one of his recent drawdowns (which are one of my rules). All managers will have drawdowns and this is one of the strategies I use to allocate. I was fascinated of another example of wealth created by allocating to trend followers who were commodity trading advisors. I called the marketing people to chat regarding what I read. To my absolute shock this same investor invested with two other commodity trading advisors in 1988. He invested with Bill Eckhardt from Turtle fame, as well as Howard Siedler from Saxon (another original Turtle). What made the hair stand up on the back of my neck was the fact that this investor—who was a trader himself—invested a total of $900,000 in 1988 with these traders and the account, as of 2012, was pushing close to $100,000,000. Again this is not an endorsement of these managers, rather an example that it is possible. I asked the marketing person who other clients were who succeeded. He explained to me that there was another investor who would buy the drawdowns of these traders as well as scale out when they had good periods. This clearly was more difficult to replicate as it required a great deal of discretion.

These managers are not GD or gurus. These money managers jointly went through steep downs and long periods in which they did not make money. What enabled their perspective investors to succeed to such magnitudes was how they themselves thought. These investors had patience, discipline and fortitude. They were not interested in, ***"How did you do last month or how was last year".*** They believed in the managers. They understood that there were no gurus or magical managers. However these commodity trading advisors all had long records, understood risk and were unique. Most commodity trading advisors are not world class and close within 5 years.

**I strongly believe in buying money managers who have been around for 10 years or more (that have compounded annual rates of returns in excess of 15%) and then buying their drawdowns.**

However, in investing, there is no perfect. I can and *have* missed the upside in numerous managers by investing in this strategy. Later I will present concepts which can offset this pitfall to some degree.

The money managers in which I invest in are not typical of all money managers. Actually, statistically most money managers do not survive for more than 5 years. The same can be said for the vast majority of hedge fund managers. I only want to invest in the best of the best. I do not want to settle. The money managers who have survived more than 10 years, have learned that various bear and bull markets are unique. It takes a lot to survive in the markets for more than 10 years.

## INVESTING STRATEGY FOR LIFE

I invest utilizing two concepts. I build and trade my own systematic trend following trading programs in my money management firm and I allocate to money managers, hedge fund managers and commodity trading advisers. The goal was and is—to be diversified and compound money over long periods of time—something I learned along the way and initially probably made every mistake possible. Due to liquidity and transparency concerns I mostly focus on managed accounts with commodity trading advisers.

I believe by investing in managed futures, I make myself available for bull and bear markets in virtually every aspect of my life. When one looks at managed futures, every aspect of our life is addressed. For example, I wake in the morning. I have coffee (a traded market), I eat my cereal (wheat and corn both traded markets) or I might drink an orange juice (another traded market, thin however). After having my breakfast I get into my car. I use gasoline in my car (a traded market). I need to pay for the gasoline and I use a credit card (another traded market). The rest of my day continues and everything from getting dressed (cotton is a market) to what I digest and how I live my life is a market. All of these markets go through bull phases and bear phases.

*During these phases these markets trend and can offer investment opportunity.*

The vast majority of my family's net worth is invested in the managed futures arena. I believe in this concept due to the influences of mentors as well as with managed futures; you are available to any and all bull markets and bear markets. I am not just limited to the stock market. More so, with all the money that has been printed by the central banks throughout the world, I believe that managed futures might be the only haven to survive strong inflation. I participate in the broader indexes of the stock markets.

The basic premise is trend following based on buying the strongest markets or selling the weakest markets—if I or if the managers I invest with deem it a low risk trade. An example of a low risk trade is risking 1% or less of my allocated equity on any trade. For example, if my account size is $200,000 in a particular allocation, my max risk is $2,000. Managing the risks is one of the paramount issues of staying in the investment game. Jack Schwager wrote various versions of his *Market Wizards* book. All of these wizards traded differently. However the bottom denominator was the attempt to keep losses small.

*The only certainty is uncertainty.*

**There is no free lunch with investing.** Our goal has to be to limit our losses. This way we stay in the marathon. I want to reiterate marathon. Trading and investing is a lifetime strategy and endeavor. Those that are seeking 'get rich quick schemes' or no drawdowns are deluding themselves or were Madoff clients.

Truly, investing is tough. There are no short cuts. Grind it out over many long years and stay out of trouble.

As I believe anything can actually occur, I invest only 1-5% of my family's money in any one manager. I truly believe diversification will keep me in the game of investing. As well, as much as I believe very strongly in trend following and commodity trading advisors, I will equally invest with money managers who understand risk and offer diversification as well as offer liquidity.

One of my main tenants that I used, in my business that I sold and later in my investing career, was to always surround myself with the most successful people. I learned from the traders I invested with, as well as from the money managers. I wanted to invest with only the best money managers. In 1994 I invested through feeder funds Monroe Trout who were featured in Market Wizards and Julian Robertson. I understood the power of compounding even in 1994. I had invested $200,000 with both Monroe Trout and Julian Robertson. At the time I believed in gurus and market wizards. One of the best lessons of my investment career was made with these two investments.

Julian Robertson had compounded money in the 20% range in the 1980s. I knew the rule of 72 and was already counting the profits. The rule of 72 is a method for estimating an investment's doubling time. The rule number is divided by the interest percentage per period to obtain the approximate number of periods (usually years) required for doubling.

Concerning Julian Robertson, approximately every 3 years I would double my money. Great…get out the yacht and the new sports car (Ha-ha). However, as reality would have it, in 1998 Julian Robertson ran into big issues and I experienced an unimaginable drawdown.

The guru lost his magic touch! What was explained to me afterwards, Julian Robertson (like so many other Hedge fund managers) borrowed Japanese Yen and purchased US 30 year bonds. This was great while the Yen was weak. However the Yen spiked and blew this trade out. Combining

*The Bible of Compounding Money*

this situation was the tech stock boom that Robertson stated he did not understand. I did not lose money from the investment however I did give back a lot of open profits. What I learned was *there are no magic managers* and more important *ANYTHING CAN HAPPEN*. The **only certainty is uncertainty** and to focus my attention on diversification. I learned firsthand—there are no gurus!

Monroe Trout on the other hand taught me valuable lessons. Investing with Trout was relatively stress-free. He did not have big peak to valley drawdowns. It was rather a smooth ride. Not a great deal of volatility. I put in $200,000 in 1994. I made additions as well as had withdrawals, however by the time I took the money out in 2006, the money compounded close to the tune of 7 times or $1,400,000. Sometimes luck is better than brains. I can honestly say this was the case with him. I left him when he retired and gave the reigns of his company to one of his colleagues.

Through Trout I learned the concept of compounding money over long periods of time. I did not feel comfortable after he retired. I was not sure if the passion of the firm would be the same after Trout's retirement. I believe that passion is a valuable component of success. I always want the money managers I invest with to have passion and a strong desire to succeed

I use three letters to accentuate this: **PHD**

I utilize PHD in a different context rather than the traditional definition. I look for managers that have passion, that are hungry and driven. This is much different to the tradition PHD concept such as those who throw money at the PHDs of Long Term Capital who almost brought down the financial system.

Many times the managers I invest with are sports addicts. That same competiveness in sports is exemplified in their trading. There is that goal of winning and succeeding.

I have tremendous enthusiasm for my trading and would easily say trading is my passion. I look for money managers who share my passion. I believe very strongly that passion brings greater results. This can be seen in anything from sports to trading. My personal passion is to have for my family a world class trading program. The only way I can do that is work hard. However it is not hard for me to work hard. I love what I do. I even wake in the middle of the night thinking of trading ideas and test them out the next morning.

My programmer is as passionate as me. He loves thinking of systematic trading programs. Due to the fact we love what we do; we have probably tested thousands of concepts over the years (maybe even many more).

I truly believe those that are passionate and work harder than most, achieve greater success. I have a simple example of one of my neighbor's children (actually he is 17 now). His passion is soccer. He kicks the ball into the net, 25 hours a day. I usually wake up at 5am and he is practicing before school. I go to sleep at 10pm and he is still kicking that ball into the net. If I compare him to other kids who play soccer, I would bet that I would be hard-pressed to find another child who is as dedicated or passionate as him. Others might want to be professional soccer players, however they do not put in the work nor do they have the passion.

## WORK + PASSION = WORLD CLASS RESULTS

This is not just with sports or investing, it is with *everything* in life.

Due to my experience and success trading a large basket of commodities, interest rates, currencies, energies, grains, metals etc... I am biased as to my belief that this is one of the best ways to compound money over long periods of time. This is not the *only way* to compound money. **One of the most important issues when investing is that it fits your personality and risk profile**. There are others who have compounded money via real estate, their own business or countless other venues. When trading commodities in managed accounts or even in a fund context, in most cases there is greater liquidity and transparency than virtually any other investment. Taking liquidity and transparency and potential for profit into context, the advantages begin to stand out.

Money is important, but for me it is not the prime objective. Having a fulfilling, interesting and happy life is my objective. In other words—the driver has to be passion.

*Passion for what I do, passion for a cause and passion for my life.*

# THE GOAL OF THIS BOOK

I have 19 years of experience in investing with money managers as well as running my own money management firm. My goal from the onset was to be able to compound money over long periods of time. The only way for you to compound money is to surround yourself with the best and invest with the best. It was clear to me from the onset that there were superior money managers that could assist me in my investment goals. I did not want to settle with mediocre money managers. I would have never achieved the goals I sought with meritocracy. I have sat on both sides of the table. I am the principle of a money management firm called Abraham Investment Management which has given me the insight to what has the possibility to succeed over long periods of time as well as what does not. The goal of this book is my personal way of giving back

By investing with world class money managers I have compounded money and thus been able to live my dreams and enjoy this with my family. I have a complete set of rules for investing in and identifying world class money managers. It is both a quantitative approach as well as qualitative approach full of due diligence. I want to "try" to buy the best managers, diversify among them and make sure they are liquid and transparent. Nothing is held back. Everything is disclosed.

*My goal is to give family offices, banks, pension funds, fund of funds as well as high net worth investors an "Aha" experience from this book!*

Investing pension funds, endowment funds and family offices requires a special approach. Clearly family offices, pensions and endowments need to perpetuate wealth and need to overlook short term performance. They need to focus on long term results. They want compounded returns far into the future. Conversely fixed income securities offer certainty, but low returns. Even the stock market has only averaged less than several percent over the last decade and *who knows* what will be, with all the money printing throughout the world.

In order to compound money and beat inflation you want money managers who will beat the market, protect you from inflation, provide liquidity and transparency and who will give you at least a +15% or more compounded annual rate of return over time. It is not easy, but there are world class managers who can provide this service.

# INVESTMENT ALLOCATION RULES

*The Bible of Compounding Money*

In order to "try" to compound money over long periods of time you want to invest with world class money managers who have been around at least 10 years, in which they have seen various cycles that have generated at least a 15% compounded annual rate of return (on average) while at the same time offer complete liquidity and complete transparency.

You have to be ready to endure drawdowns. They are inevitable. The only money managers who did not have drawdowns are Bernie Madoff and Alan Stanford with their Ponzi schemes. You need to monitor and be in contact with your managers.

### Sounds too good to be true?

The fact is that these money managers are unique and you have probably never heard of them. They do exist. I have been investing with these money managers since 1994 and I have been fortunate to be a client.

One of my tools that has served me over time and created a margin of safety is I look to buy the drawdowns of these world class managers. As there is nothing perfect in life I might miss the upside in the money managers returns by waiting for a drawdown however my goal is to try as best as possible to have a smooth, ever-increasing equity curve of returns without too much emotional energy wasted on drawdowns.

There are money managers who are world class but they are far from being perfect and will always have trades that do not work and periods of drawdowns.

**You need a wide margin of time and over-performance to tell skill from luck.**

Murphy's Law comes into play as nothing is perfect in the real world. Your managers may do worse after you hire them. You might go through a period of time this world class manager whose record falls to 9%. I promise you it will happen. It has happened to me.

## SAFETY FIRST

*"The first rule of investment is don't lose money or at least try not to. The second rule of investment is: don't forget the first rule. And that's all the rules there are."*

*--Warren Buffett*

We all have seen managers with several years of good performance that raise lot of money and then their performance falls off. Everyone is looking for the next genius.

There is a strong dichotomy between genius and simple luck. That is why I strongly suggest 10 years. 10 years shows all types of market cycles. It can be luck or whatever you want to call it however over 10 years (as a minimum) it is not luck anymore. There is skill. We seek skill and the best of the best. This plan is contrary to what many investors do. They chase returns without fully doing their due diligence. Chasing returns leads to disasters. By chasing returns, which in itself seems prudent, has left many investors simply buying the highs of money managers only to sell the money manager's lows. Everything should be planned out exactly. We are dealing in uncertainty when we invest. Anything can happen. We must prepare for this uncertainty.

It is not easy and it took me a long time to learn. I made many mistakes along the way. Investing with world class managers *does exist in reality* and can be taught. World class money managers very often do not hold themselves out and are hard to find. I will teach you how to find them and the appropriate questions when you do your due diligence.

### Due diligence is imperative!

Even after you find the world class managers, the next issue is: they might not want you as an investor. Some of these world class money managers and some other funds have problematic policies. Preferably you will want a managed account, as you will have full transparency and liquidity, but some have high minimums; $5 million is quite common, and some have $10 million minimums. Some are only open to tax-exempt investors, some to non-U.S. citizens. Some are closed to new investors because the partnership has too many members or too much money. The general partner of a partnership has the right to restrict entry for any reason. Similar problems occur with individual accounts.

Surprising as it seems, it can be hard work just to get your money under the management of some of the great investors. It is always a balance between seeking managers who have survived more than 10 years and then determining if they will take you as a client. Believe it or not, I have actually been interviewed by a manager to see if they would take my allocation.

### Why most managers don't beat the market?

### Which managers do beat the market?

## THIS IS THE GOAL OF THIS BOOK.

I will give you all the tools and if I can assist you personally, I am available to help you. I have been helped and this is a way of giving back. The vast majority of investors have never heard of the strategies encompassed in this book; and many do not have the appropriate investment psychology to succeed. There are some investors who are not aware of the potential of high inflation—which might be on our horizon.

Successful investing is not easy but hopefully you will find that many of the chapters of this book give you an "AHA" experience.

*Andrew Abraham*

*Andrew Abraham can be reached at:*

Abraham Investment Management

www.AbrahamCTA.com

Andrew@AbrahamCta.com

## CHAPTER 1

# Are You Sure You Want to Invest with Warren Buffett?

There are countless investors who have been blessed to be investors of Warren Buffett. All of us who have ever even considered investing know that Warren Buffett is the world's third richest man with an estimated fortune of over $52 billion. He has made a career of being right when the rest of Wall Street was wrong. Buffet has stated he doesn't view the purchase of shares in a company as *buying a stake in that business*, but believes that he is *actually buying that business outright and owning it*. This is the antithesis of most stock investors. Buffett has made millions for countless investors over the years. Columbia Business School magazine introduced "Warren Buffett, who got an A + from Ben Graham at Columbia in 1951, never stopped making the grade." On the surface it seems very easy to have made money along with Warren Buffett.

## *But was it really?*

## *In the following paragraphs I will present you with some thought evoking ideas.*

Like many, Buffett has been a hero of mine for decades. One of my favorite statements from Buffett, "Only buy something that you'd be perfectly happy to hold if the market shut down for 10 years." In Buffett's case this meant Coca Cola or Wells Fargo, however you can apply the same concept to investing with a money manager in which you have done all of your due diligences. You do not want to regret your investment in a month or even in a couple years during the first inevitable drawdown. You understand this is a long term marathon and fully understand the concept of compounding money. There is no jumping around from last quarter's or last year's hot new Hedge Fund manager or CTA (Commodity trading adviser).

We all know that Buffett made his money through identifying companies that he believed were worth more than their market value, investing in them and holding that investment for the long-term (actually almost forever). Actually, Buffett's strategy is remarkably simple, but given the ups and downs of the stock market, **it takes a high level of discipline, nerve and conviction in your decisions—** *which the vast majority does not have*.

Everyone seems to want it now. Compounding is a very strange concept to them. The words discipline and patience are somehow forgotten along the path; we will speak about later on in this chapter. Investors want 15-20% or more returns without any period of drawdown. At the slightest drawdown—investors run. They look for the next so-called guru who will lead them to the 'Promised Land'.

> *They want positive returns without the pain of drawdowns.*

In the real world this does not exist. I have to take that back; it existed in the warped dreams of the investors of Madoff and Alan Stanford.

There is a quest to find the new guru managers that make money without drawdowns. This also does not exist. All one has to do is look at the last bear market and realize even the famous gurus also bled profits. At one point in my career I was an NFL financial advisor. I saw what these rookie football players went through. The coaches and the staff were seeking the new upcoming marquee players and magically talented sportsmen. Out of hundreds of players, maybe one would survive his career and become a marquee player. He was a marquee player until he was hit one too many times and some bone broke. There is a great many similarities between investing and sports. I want to invest with marque players however I realize they are not perfect and that they will have periods of drawdowns. Look for experience and a proven track record!

> *10 years real time returns and*
> *15% plus returns minimums.*
> *This is a marquee Player!*

Returning to Buffett, there are those who hang on every word he says. With his countless admirers he is almost an idol to worship. Counting their riches before time, they buy whatever Buffett does. However these scores of admirers who mimic his methods and purchases are still wannabees. The vast majority don't have the needed skills (patience, discipline, dedication and knowledge of compounding) such as basketball pro LeBron James has of dunking a basketball shot.

Buffett has another major advantage over mortal investors and hedge fund managers. Berkshire will keep going long after Buffett dies, and the corporation will never retire. It will always have a source of investment capital from its many companies. The companies Buffett has invested in throw off cash—at times lots of cash! Buffet's job is to allocate that cash and have it compound. Berkshire does not need to look for new investors or markets. This allows Buffett to dollar-cost-average virtually forever with basically no time horizon. They can do this indefinitely as long as the underlying companies in which they invest in are managed appropriately by honest people (which are one of Buffett's criteria).

Comparing this to us or even hedge fund managers, they get old and retire and even die. More so, our job is to mathematically and qualitatively determine who is honest and a worthy steward of our investment. Hedge funds have marketing people to bring in assets. Berkshire does not care when stockholders leave, as the cash flow generated by their underlying companies just keep on generating new monies to be invested. Very interesting difference!

Buffett has another leg up on other mortal investors. Just Buffett's reputation assures success. He has become an activist investor to some degree, as well as in times of crisis, he is the proverbial go-to guy. The power of Berkshire Hathaway gives the stamp of good housekeeping. Whatever Buffet buys is considered worthy of investing in. With all of his admirers they bid up the stocks merely because he buys them. Due to his immense capital Buffett can go to public companies and even negotiate the purchase of shares at prices unavailable to us mortals and hedge fund managers.

The Class A shares in Buffett's company Berkshire Hathaway were $15 when he first took over in 1965 and they were valued at $83,500 per share by the end of July 2012. However the story started even earlier.

*So the simple question is why isn't everyone rich?*

*All you have to do is invest with Buffett and find an island to buy right?*

*Big wrong!*

*How easy it wasn't (as you will soon see).*

What I alluded to previously was Buffett's unique mental outlook. He does not buy shares—he buys ownership. He doesn't look or care about how much money he made last month or last year. He totally understands compounding of money and as already stated he has the cash flow from the underlying companies as an ever-producing spring of cash. Buffet is disciplined and patient more than any mortal investor. Looking at the next couple of charts proves my point and introduces an interesting question you will need to ask yourselves.

How many of you would love to generate the rates of return that Buffett has over the long decades? Foolish question right! However if you look at the chart of the BRKA it becomes a lot more complicated. I remember vividly in 1998, many thought Warren Buffett was a has-been and all one needed to do was invest in tech stocks (this time it really is different) however there have been other examples in which we will delve into.

It was shocking to many Buffet fans that he was experiencing such a big drawdown (almost 50%)

Chart Created in Thomson Reuters MetaStock. All rights reserved. Past Performance is not necessarily indicative of future performance.

The following are questions you really need to ask yourself. Here is the world's most successful investor, yet you will see from the following examples how hard it really was/is to have invested with him, as well as you will be shocked at the compounded returns.

*The question will arise—if you cannot invest in one of the world's greatest investors, how will you really succeed in investing period? I explain to my investors in my managed accounts what to expect.*

I do not want them to have false expectations. I want them to truly realize what is possible and how hard it really is to achieve. I have first-hand experience seeing investors' compound money to shocking amounts. However what most people forget was how hard it really was. They went through long drawdowns and periods of time of elusive profits.

## HOW EASY IT REALLY WASN'T!

Let's go back to 1995. The tech stock boom was just taking off. You were going to cocktail parties and everyone was making all kinds of money on *this tech* and *that tech* stock. Let's assume you had invested with BRKA (Berkshire Hathaway) in March of 1996. You did not want to follow all the so-called hype of tech stocks and were a meat and potatoes type of investor. You probably did as most investors; you purchased the high of BRKA and felt it could only go up. You paid approximately $37,000 for a share and maybe you even went to the annual Buffet pilgrimage to hear Warren's thoughts and magical insights. A year goes by, fast as usual and you have not made any money. It is May 1997 and all of your cocktail party friends have made a killing on *dot this* and *dot that* and you did not make any money. How do you really feel? Probably like an old fart. You were not cool. You did not buy the latest and coolest stocks. You bought a stock that probably your grandfather would have bought. You bought BRKA.

*Andy Abraham*

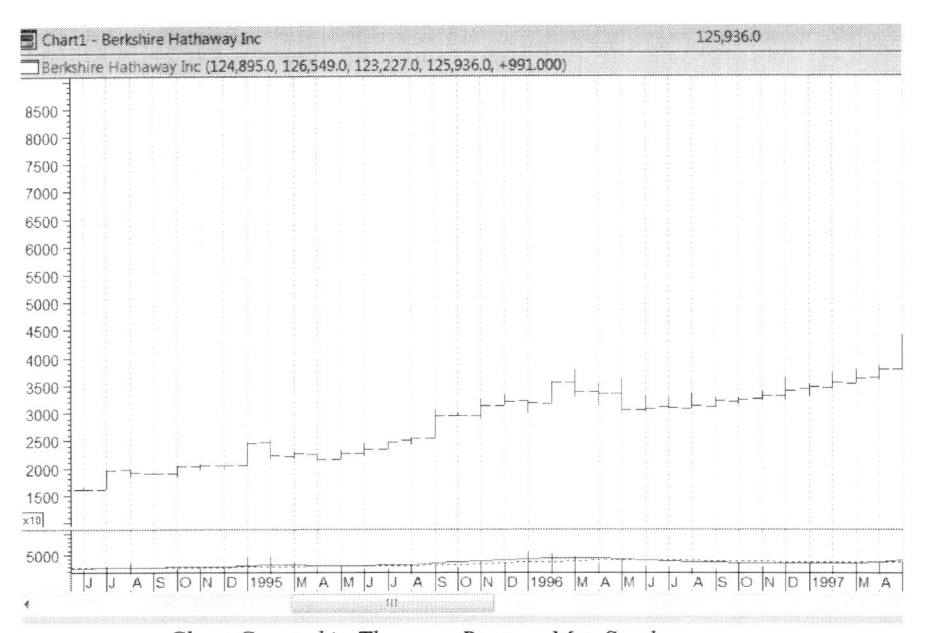

*Chart Created in Thomson Reuters MetaStock.
All rights reserved. Past Performance is not necessarily indicative of future performance*

Finally you are somewhat relieved and BRKA starts moving up, albeit not as quick as all of your cocktail party friends. However you are feeling pretty good. By 1998 you are hitting new great highs. In June of 1998 you hit a great new peak of $55,320. You are counting that money. You are looking great. You wife is telling you everything that she wants to buy. If you are managing money for clients—you are a genius.

However reality sets in and you will shortly be in for a shock you never imagined. By 2000 you had an open drawdown of 50%. That surely is uncomfortable. You probably heard the nagging of your wife asking you what you did. Your clients, if they are a family office or a registered investment adviser might even consider leaving you. It was not until 2006 you recovered from this drawdown. Now in all honesty, you invested in the world's greatest investor; you had an open drawdown of approximately 50% and it took you 8 years to recover to the levels of 1998. How do you really feel? Do you feel smart? Do you think you worked in your client's best interest?

My point is very simple. Here is the world's greatest investor and you see firsthand how hard it really is. There is no 'get rich quick'. There is no consistent 1% per month or painless "All Weather Funds" or even any fund of fund which negates some of the pain. The reality is plain and clear. This is a marathon. I doubt very many of you reading this right now would have waited 8 years to get back to break even. I doubt many of you would have the mental fortitude to withstand a 50% drawdown. Buffett was not alone.

He was joined by other stock market gurus.

Ken Heebner (CMG Fund) -56%

Harry Lange (Fidelity Magellan) -59%

Bill Miller (Legg Mason Value) -50%

The reality is this was not a $6^{th}$ sigma or rare event. In 2007 BRKA had a high of $101,202. This was also short lived. By March of 2009 BRKA was at a low of $45,000. UGH!!!!

*Another 50%+ draw down from the World's Best Investor.*

*Chart Created in Thomson Reuters MetaStock.
All rights reserved. Past Performance is not necessarily indicative of
future performance.*

What are you saying to yourself? What are you thinking at this point? The stock market has been terrible. The real estate market has been terrible. How do I make money on my money? The icing on the cake is that the highs of 2007 have not been surpassed again now, at the time of this writing (July 2012). Five more years of nothing—even with the world's greatest investor! If you take into account the compounding of money since 1996 you have not really done that great. It is hard to consider this world class.

Here is the world's greatest investor with celebrity status with masses that listen to every word he states, yet he has not made a very high CAGR since 1996.

The share price of BRKA went from $37,000 to $87,000 after 16 years.

*Impressive?????????*

There are many other unknown money managers that have surpassed him. This accentuates one tenant that is engrained in my psyche. Anything can happen. Be available for any situation. There are no gurus or genius—including Warren Buffett. There are no magic systems. Investing is not retirement in a box.

*Investing is a marathon!*

## CHAPTER 1 SUMMATION

Even the greatest investors struggle at times. Warren Buffett, the world's greatest investor, has endured periods that the vast majorities are not aware of or have considered. Many value investors simply buy BRKA shares and are swayed by the media. Do your homework and be independent.

*Andy Abraham*

## CHAPTER 2

# Compounding is the Key

**M**ost of you reading this book are very aware of the long term results of various asset classes. Treasury bills and bonds on average have returned less than 5%. Stocks have returned approximately 9% yet one had to go through multiple 50% drawdowns. Most mutual funds as well as hedge fund managers underperformed even these abysmal returns in the last decade. Actually, many went out of business.

The goal is to do better than this and with less drawdown. The goal is to invest with world class money managers that understand risk and offer liquidity and transparency.

Following is an equity curve that reflects the S&P 500 stock index. As this graph clearly shows, it would have been difficult to compound a portfolio during the last 10 years being invested in the S&P 500. That is not to say the next 10 years will not be better, but my plan aims to avoid long periods where we are unable to compound our portfolios.

To the contrary, some established and unique commodity trading advisors who traded futures compounded money in the mid-teens. Managed futures looks at a large basket of markets of products we use in our daily existence.

*Managed futures are not an exotic concept.*

*Managed futures are products we use in our daily life.*

We all eat wheat, use crude oil for our cars, use credit cards and eat meat. There are always bull markets and bear markets which offer us the potential for profit and the possibility of compounding money.

We **must avoid large losses** or we will not be able to compound our way to wealth.

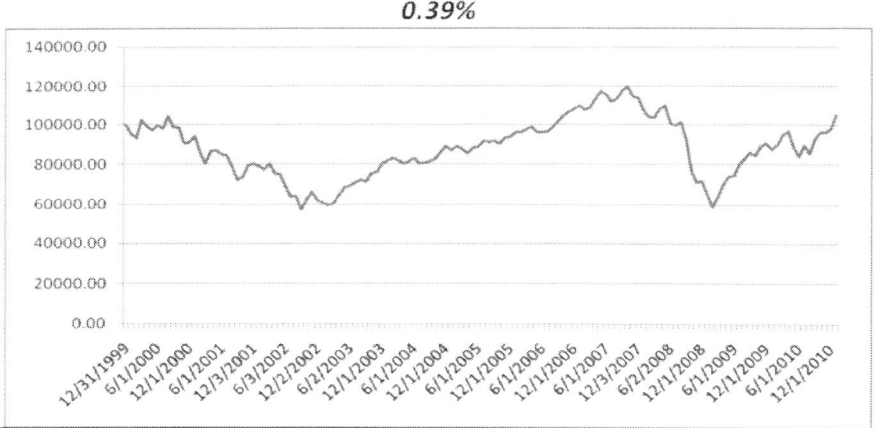

*Equity Curve of the S&P 500 with a compound annual rate of return of 0.39%*

# LUNCH CONVERSATION

I recently went to lunch with a buddy from college. He has been trading commodities as a trend follower since 1983. He understands trading and risk management. He is disciplined and is very successful.

At lunch he confided that he was giving his son, who just finished college, $200,000 to trade. This was not a blind gift. He had taught his son the principles of developing a

## The Bible of Compounding Money

trading plan that matched his personality, money and risk management and how to have a winning trading mentality. He told me depending on the markets he thought by the time his son was close to 50 this $200,000 should compound into about $6,000,000 dollars.

If I asked you to raise your hands if you believed this was possible, how many of you would raise your hands? Probably not that many....however I did some quick thinking and figured that his son had approximately 30 years to compound money and I assumed it would compound at 10-12%.

Not to completely embarrass myself I listened and agreed it was definitely possible. Once I returned to my office I went and checked a compounding money calculator.

| Inputs | |
|---|---|
| Current Principal: | $ 200,000.00 |
| Annual Addition: | $ 0 |
| Years to grow: | 30 |
| Interest Rate: | 12 % |
| Compound interest | 1 time(s) annually |
| Make additions at | ● start ○ end of each compounding period |
| | Calculate |
| **Results** | |
| Future Value: | $ 5,991,984.42 |

Albert Einstein called the power of compounding "the greatest mathematical discovery of all time" and deemed it to be the eighth wonder of the world.

Richard Russell of the famed Dow Theory Letters declared that compounding is the "**Royal road to riches and fortunately, anybody can do it**".

*To compound successfully you need the following:*

**Perseverance** in order to keep you firmly on the savings path

**Intelligence** in order to understand what you are doing and why

**Knowledge** of the mathematics tables in order to comprehend the amazing rewards that will come to you if you faithfully follow the compounding road

**Time** to allow the power of compounding to work for you

*Remember, compounding only works over time.*

Ben Franklin echoed that thought, saying, "Money can beget money, and its offspring can beget more." Warren Buffett's partner Charlie Munger expressed a similar sentiment about money, "Never interrupt it unnecessarily."

Warren Buffett understands compounding extremely well. In Buffett's biography by Alice Schroeder she wrote: "Since Warren looked at every dollar as $10 *someday*, he wasn't going to hand over a dollar more than he needed to spend." Buffett apparently was so cheap; he only washed his car when it rained so he wouldn't have to pay for the water. Another example was the *Washington Post* heir and publisher Katherine Graham who once asked Buffett for a dime to make a phone call (before the advent of cell phones, people had to use phone booths). Buffett only had a quarter, so the

## The Bible of Compounding Money

billionaire first went to get change. Buffett's calculation of 'a dollar today being $10 someday' was way off. From 1965 through 2009, Berkshire Hathaway stock returned an average 20.3% annually, turning $1 into $4,341. Makes you think twice? This exemplifies compounding.

***Combining realistic annual returns with the power of compounding is a powerful recipe for building wealth- But How????***

Unfortunately, most investors are unable to consistently achieve the investment returns necessary to compound their accounts. Most investors never even think of what their compounded annual rate of returns is. The problem is that most investors simply do not understand how to formulate a plan that will accomplish this.

- If you don't know where you're going, how are you going to get there?
- It is synonymous to having a trading plan. If you do not have an exact trading plan you are destined to fail.
- Forget about how was last month or last year. Take a long term perspective. My trading is a lifetime strategy
- My children have 60-70 years of compounding.
- This is how Family offices and pensions think!

Pension funds will be paying benefits long into the future. Family offices' goal is generational wealth transfer. Both of these must provide growing long term income. After 18 years investing with a set of rules to invest in great managers that offer liquidity and transparency I have survived various investment debacles. I had the chance to invest with Madoff however passed due to transparency and it did not make sense to me that he never lost money. I lose money trading all the time.

I avoided the Asian contagion in 1998 as well as 2000, and the stock market crash of 2008. Most people do not even consider investing in great managers. They are placated by the concept of buy and hold. People are content investing in mutual funds. They might buy last year's winners only to be disappointed the following year. Many investors have no plan whatsoever. They spend less time contemplating their investments than planning dinner. People do not have patience to hold an investment for a long period of time. People have unrealistic expectations and do not have the discipline to go through eventual drawdowns that occur with every money manager. They jump around looking for the "hot" new upcoming manager. They chase returns that in the short run that are intriguing.

*Long term compounding takes patience, discipline, fortitude, passion and knowledge.*

Your job as an investor is to find a level of risk that you can live with and then structure an efficient portfolio and trading plan accordingly. You want to invest only with world class money managers. The secret to getting rich slowly is the miracle of compounding money overtime. Compounding money over time is the reason why it is a lot easier to stay rich than it is to become rich. The more money you have the more you can compound. Even modest returns can generate real wealth given enough time and dedication. Then you must let the law of compound returns work its magic. In the short-term, it doesn't make a huge difference, but on the slow, sure path to wealth, we take the long view. Short-term results are not as important as what will happen over the course of twenty or thirty years.

**Start early.** The younger you start, the more time compounding has to work in your favor, and the wealthier you can become. *The next best thing to starting early is starting now. Think of your children. As I stated above my children have 60-70 years of compounding.*

**Be patient.** Do not touch the money. Compounding only works if you allow your investment to grow overtime! Understand your investments before you make them. The results will seem slow at first, but persevere. Most of the magic of compounding returns comes at the very end.

Lack of time, taxes, investment fees, and underperformance interrupt the law of compound returns and lower the money you will have in the future. The "law of 72" helps us understand compounding. Divide your yearly return by 72. The result is the number of years it will take for your money to double. Actually my trading programs are called, Formula 72 L (low volatility), Formula 72 M (mid volatility) and Formula 72 H (high volatility). Each of these program targets a different type of investor. Every investor has different investment goals and risk tolerances.

## THE DARTH OF INFLATION

Inflation is the dark side of the law of compound returns and determines how your savings deteriorate over time. Assuming real inflation is 4 percent per year, with the law of 72 that means every 18 years prices double, and your money will buy half of what it did before. As an investor you fight the reality that 20 years after you retire your money will lose 50 percent of its buying power. The law of compound returns is a slow, powerful, and largely invisible force that you can't ignore. Because of how it operates with inflation, in 18 to 24 years your money will be worth half of what it is today. But if you can reduce your fees, taxes, and increase your returns by just 2 to 3 percent per year, you'll double your savings in 24 years.

There are two catches in the compounding process. The first is clear; compounding involves sacrifice (you can't spend it and still save it). Second, compounding is boring. George Soros once stated successful investing is boring. Boring is good. Successful investors do not seek action nor do they chase results.

## *Boring over a period of ten years compounds to a lot of money*

Then, clearly compounding becomes very interesting. In fact, it becomes downright fascinating.

A very simple rule of compounding is:

**DON'T LOSE MONEY:** This may sound simplistic, but believe me it isn't. If you want to be wealthy, you must not lose money, or I should say you must not lose BIG money. Keep your losses small. There are only four possible outcomes.

Big Losses

Small Losses

Small Profits

Large Profits

Avoid the large losses; the small losses and small profits offset each other and overtime you will stumble into some rare big profits. Using simple math we also learn that it is exceptionally difficult to compound money over a long period of time after suffering a large decline in our portfolios.

*The Bible of Compounding Money*

## *Below is a table reflecting the mathematics of recovering from losses:*

| Starting Portfolio Value | If Your Portfolio Drops | New Value of Portfolio | % Gain Needed to Recover |
|---|---|---|---|
| $100,000 | 10% | $90,000 | 11% |
| $100,000 | 20% | $80,000 | 25% |
| $100,000 | 30% | $70,000 | 43% |
| $100,000 | 40% | $60,000 | 67% |
| $100,000 | 50% | $50,000 | 100% |

This table actually shows us that the less you lose, the more you have when things get better. The lesson we learn is that it is very difficult to recover from large losses. While "come from behind" victories are exciting in the athletic arena, compounding wealth after suffering large losses is exceedingly difficult.

Below is a hypothetical example of an investment that suffered a 50% decline. This chart indicates just how difficult it is to recover from large losses. A positive 8% compounded return for 8 years will only bring your account back to even after initially suffering such a large loss. It is simply not easy to recover from large losses, and yet all markets will likely suffer 50% declines at some point in time. The power of compounding can work for you only if you do not suffer large losses.

~ 45 ~

You'll need 10 years at an 8% return to recover from a 50% loss
**HYPOTHETICAL EXAMPLE**

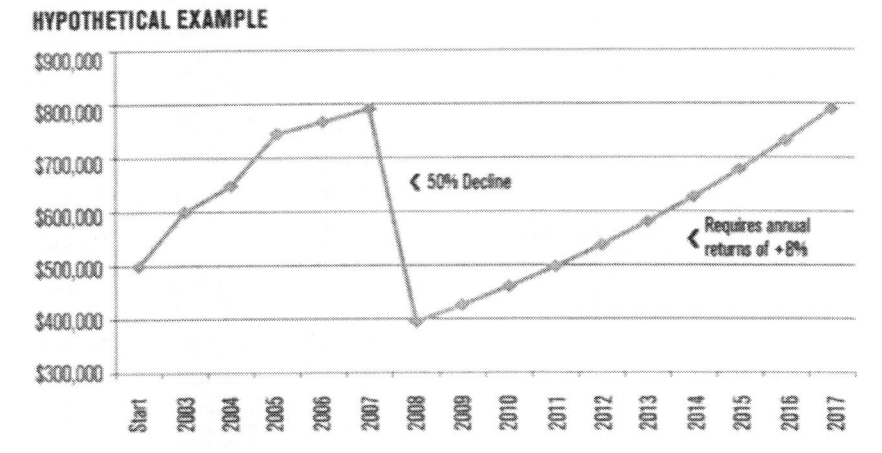

Nothing gets a point across as well as a picture. Putting compounding into perspective the below chart demonstrates the growth of $100,000 over 10 years at 15% as it grows into $404,000 dollars

*$100,000 over 15 years generating 15%*

*grows into $813,000*

| Current Principal: | $ 100,000.00 |
| --- | --- |
| Annual Addition: | $ 0 |
| Years to grow: | 15 |
| Interest Rate: | 15 % |

Compound interest 1 time(s) annually

Make additions at ● start ○ end of each compounding period

Calculate

**Results**

| Future Value: | $ 813,706.16 |
| --- | --- |

*The Bible of Compounding Money*

### *$100,000 over 20 years generating 15% grows into $1,636,000*

| | | |
|---|---|---|
| Current Principal: | $ | 100,000.00 |
| Annual Addition: | $ | 0 |
| Years to grow: | | 20 |
| Interest Rate: | | 15 % |

Compound interest 1 time(s) annually

Make additions at ⦿ start ◯ end of each compounding period

[Calculate]

**Results**

| | | |
|---|---|---|
| Future Value: | $ | 1,636,653.74 |

### *$100,000 over 25 years generating 15% grows into $3,291,000*

| | | |
|---|---|---|
| Current Principal: | $ | 100,000.00 |
| Annual Addition: | $ | 0 |
| Years to grow: | | 25 |
| Interest Rate: | | 15 % |

Compound interest 1 time(s) annually

Make additions at ⦿ start ◯ end of each compounding period

[Calculate]

**Results**

| | | |
|---|---|---|
| Future Value: | $ | 3,291,895.26 |

# COUNTLESS WAYS TO LOSE MONEY

Most **PEOPLE LOSE MONEY** in disastrous investments, gambling, rotten business deals, greed, and poor timing. The tenants in this book will direct you and put the odds of compounding over many long decades in your reach by investing with only the top money managers that offer liquidity and transparency.

*Do not think that compounding is out of your reach.*

There are managers who have been around for decades and have compounded money for themselves and their investors. I am a big believer in managed futures and trend following however there are traders who trade stocks, mortgages and bonds as well as other vehicles. There are equity managers that have great long term track records however it is very difficult to make money in a single market during a bear market.

I prefer managed futures and commodity trading advisors because they look at numerous markets around the world and there is always a bull market or bear market somewhere. Regardless of inflation, deflation, bull market or bear market, there can be trends. Trends are what drive profits for commodity trading advisors.

For sake of disclosure I am a commodity trading advisor specializing in trend following; the vast majority of my investments over the last 18 years have been with commodity trading advisors who are trend followers. However do not think that this type of investing is retirement in a box. You will always go through ugly drawdowns and periods of losing trades.

*The Bible of Compounding Money*

Trend following is natural and not that complicated. Trend following entails following the markets when they go up as well as following them when they go down!

*Markets can only do several things.*

*Markets only go up, down, or sideways.*

However complicated and easy are a misnomer. Trend following probably has to be one of the *hardest easiest* things to do because of our emotional baggage.

Let's keep it simple: money is made if you buy when the market is going up and sell when the market is going down. An uptrend is present when prices make a series of higher highs and higher lows. A downtrend is present when prices make a series of lower highs and lower lows.

**Trading can be simple: you buy when the market is going up and you sell when the market is going down. That's how money is made.**

*Trend followers do the hard thing!*

*Trend followers buy the highs and sell the lows.*

This is clearly counterintuitive as virtually all market participants want to be smart and buy the low and sell the highs right? In the real world this is impossible. Only liars & people at parties with a lot of drinks in them can call tops and bottoms consistently.

Trend following is the antithesis of what we are taught in school. We are taught to rely on intelligence. We want to prove we are smart. Trend followers take responsibility for their trades and do not need to prove anything. Trend followers are committed to compounding money over long periods of time. Trend followers are committed to the plan.

I cannot reiterate enough the importance of liquidity and transparency however. Managed futures offer this as well as the possibility of profitability with measured risks.

In the following chapter I highlight a handful of managers that are examples of longevity, transparency and liquidity. These money managers are not the norm. They are the exception. They have been around for decades. Many aspiring commodity trading advisors blow up within the first 5 years.

## CHAPTER 2 SUMMATION

We all know the concept of compounding however very few attendees at any of the lectures I have given know their compounded rate of return over the last 5 or even 10 years. The concept of compounding is a compass which keeps on track to accomplish your financial goals.

**CHAPTER 3**

# Investing with World Class Commodity Trading Advisors

The following commodity traders have exceptional track records over the decades. They are not risk junkies or cowboys. Actually they approach risk much more prudently than many mutual fund managers who burned their investors with worthless tech stocks.

Trades are analyzed by risk per trade, risk per sector as well as open trade risk on the whole portfolio. The same cannot be easily said for fundamental managers who trade their opinions. Most of the commodity trading advisors I consider world class (15% CAROR on average with over at least a 10 year period) have developed and trade systematic trend following systems. These systematic trend following systems trade multiple markets that are diversified.

I will not allocate into a niche sector such as energies, currencies or even agricultural traders even if they are trend followers. As in everything, I want to be diversified. These sectors can get very quiet at times and my goal is to compound money. These systematic trading systems can even contain various models that could offset each other as well non correlated markets. There are traders that encompass multiple time periods even for the same type of system. These systems are not the Holy Grail and there is nothing perfect. No magic manager and no magic system. **They will all have drawdowns at some point.**

Mentioning some of the following commodity trading advisors is not an endorsement of any of them and they are a unique group. Out of 2000 commodity trading advisors in the universe, there might be only 40 to 50 that are world class and understand risk and that I would consider investing in or have invested with. Many commodity trading advisors do not survive more than 5 years from their onset. Due to this fact I look to invest with commodity trading advisors who have a track record of at least 10 years. These commodity trading advisors have seen various cycles and they have overcome the inherent drawdowns and tough periods.

The managers listed are not representative of all commodity trading advisors. Do not be swayed by the positive compounded annual rate of returns as these managers have also gone through ugly drawdowns at points in their careers. Many of these managers whom I consider world class have gone through 30% drawdowns or more. My goal is to identify and invest with world class money managers when they have drawdowns. When managers of this caliber have drawdowns you are enhancing the possibility of safety. The only thing we are really dealing with however when we invest is uncertainty. The length of their record gives some margin of safety because they have proven their ability to overcome various market environments. This is far from absolute and the proverbial statement "Past performance is not necessarily indicative of future performance" is an absolute given.

*All we are trying to do is make a best bet in an uncertain world.*

# ABRAHAM TRADING GROUP

Abraham Trading Group has been trading since 1988. They have a CAROR of 18.31% and a worst peak to valley draw down of 31.96%. They have returned over 6,100% over all of these years. If you had invested $100,000 with Abraham Trading Group in 1988, it would be worth $5,656,071.68 today.

Salem Abraham's fascination with commodity trading started with his years in Notre Dame University in 1984. His family in Texas had been in the commodity markets and ranching for 100 years. Salem's passion was researching technical approaches and systematic trading. His research included back-testing the profitability of numerous trading theories.

Salem graduated cum laude in Finance in December of 1987 and moved back to Canadian Texas, where in January of 1988, he began to manage customer accounts using his systematic approach. He attributes his success of commodity trading by managing the inherent risks while trading. He traded money for Commodity Corporation as well as pension funds and high net worth investors throughout the world.

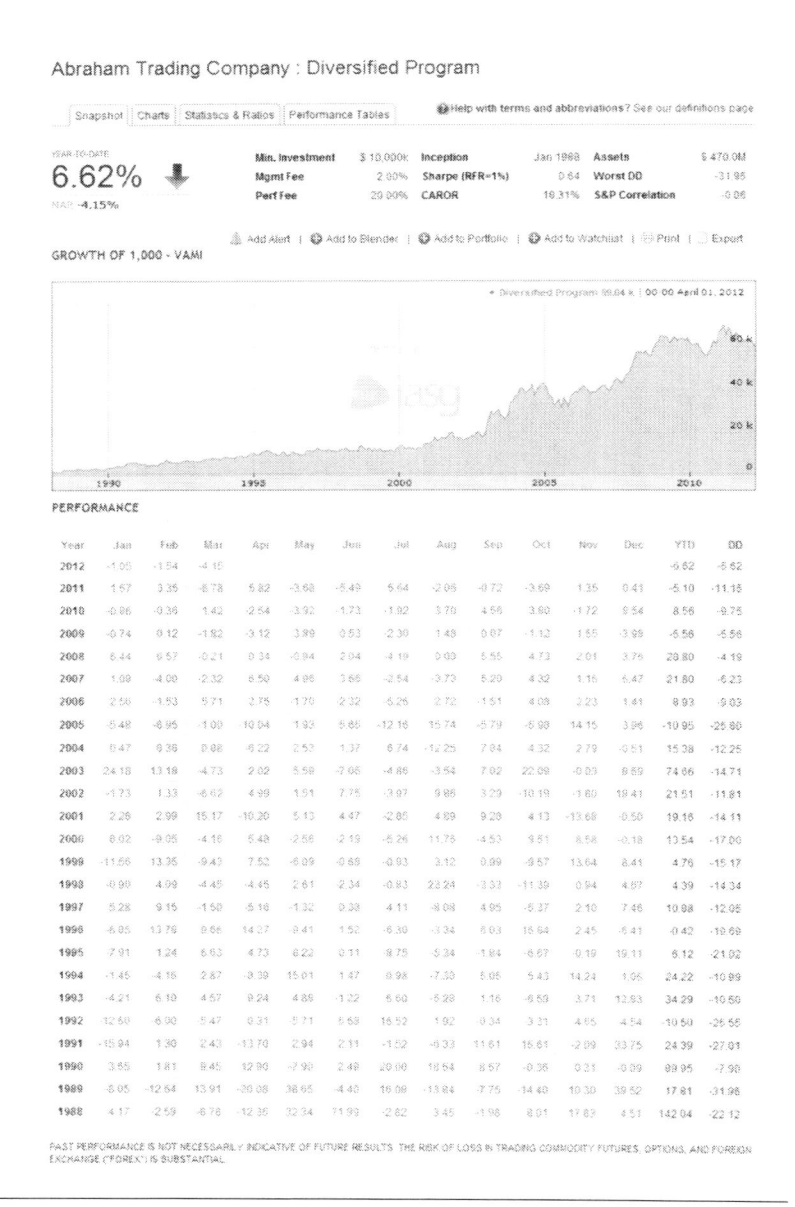

## Abraham Trading Company : Diversified Program

| | | | |
|---|---|---|---|
| YEAR-TO-DATE **6.62%** NAV -4.15% | Min. Investment $10,000k | Inception Jan 1988 | Assets $470.0M |
| | Mgmt Fee 2.00% | Sharpe (RFR=1%) 0.64 | Worst DD -31.95 |
| | Perf Fee 20.00% | CAROR 19.31% | S&P Correlation -0.06 |

### GROWTH OF 1,000 - VAMI

### PERFORMANCE

| Year | Jan | Feb | Mar | Apr | May | Jun | Jul | Aug | Sep | Oct | Nov | Dec | YTD | DD |
|------|-----|-----|-----|-----|-----|-----|-----|-----|-----|-----|-----|-----|-----|-----|
| 2012 | -1.05 | -1.54 | -4.15 | | | | | | | | | | -6.62 | -6.62 |
| 2011 | 1.57 | 3.35 | -8.78 | 5.82 | -3.68 | -5.49 | 5.64 | -2.06 | -0.72 | -3.69 | 1.35 | 0.43 | -5.10 | -11.15 |
| 2010 | -0.96 | -0.36 | 1.42 | -2.54 | -3.92 | -1.73 | -1.92 | 3.70 | 4.56 | 3.90 | -1.72 | 9.54 | 8.56 | -9.75 |
| 2009 | -0.74 | 0.12 | -1.92 | -3.12 | 3.89 | 0.53 | 2.30 | 1.48 | 0.07 | -1.12 | 1.55 | -3.99 | -5.56 | -5.56 |
| 2008 | 6.44 | 6.57 | -0.21 | 0.34 | -0.94 | 2.04 | -4.19 | 0.60 | 5.55 | 4.73 | 2.01 | 3.76 | 20.80 | -4.19 |
| 2007 | 1.09 | -4.08 | -2.32 | 6.50 | 4.86 | 1.66 | -2.54 | -3.73 | 5.20 | 4.32 | 1.16 | 6.47 | 21.80 | -6.23 |
| 2006 | 2.56 | -1.53 | 9.71 | 2.75 | -1.70 | -2.32 | -5.26 | 2.72 | -1.51 | 4.08 | 2.23 | 1.41 | 8.93 | -9.03 |
| 2005 | -5.48 | -6.95 | -1.00 | -10.04 | 1.93 | 5.66 | -12.16 | 15.74 | -5.79 | -5.99 | 14.15 | 3.96 | -10.95 | -25.89 |
| 2004 | 6.47 | 9.36 | 0.08 | -6.22 | 2.52 | 1.37 | 6.74 | -12.25 | 7.64 | 4.32 | 2.79 | -9.51 | 15.38 | -12.25 |
| 2003 | 24.18 | 13.19 | -4.73 | 2.02 | 5.58 | -7.65 | -4.85 | -3.54 | 7.02 | 22.09 | -0.03 | 8.69 | 74.66 | -14.71 |
| 2002 | -1.73 | 1.33 | -6.62 | 4.99 | 1.51 | 7.75 | -3.97 | 9.86 | 3.29 | -10.19 | -1.60 | 19.41 | 21.51 | -11.81 |
| 2001 | 2.26 | 2.99 | 15.17 | -10.20 | 5.13 | 4.47 | -2.85 | 4.89 | 9.20 | 4.13 | -13.68 | -0.50 | 19.16 | -14.11 |
| 2000 | 8.02 | -9.05 | -4.16 | 5.48 | -2.56 | -2.19 | -5.26 | 11.76 | -4.53 | 9.51 | 8.58 | -0.18 | 13.54 | -17.00 |
| 1999 | -11.56 | 13.35 | -9.43 | 7.52 | -6.89 | -0.88 | -0.93 | 3.12 | 0.99 | -9.57 | 13.64 | 8.41 | 4.76 | -15.17 |
| 1998 | -0.99 | 4.09 | -4.45 | -4.45 | 2.61 | -2.34 | -0.83 | 23.24 | -3.33 | -11.39 | 0.94 | 4.87 | 4.39 | -14.34 |
| 1997 | 5.28 | 9.15 | -1.50 | -5.18 | -1.32 | 0.33 | 4.11 | -8.06 | 4.95 | -5.27 | 2.10 | 7.46 | 10.88 | -12.05 |
| 1996 | -6.05 | 13.76 | 9.66 | 14.27 | -9.41 | 1.52 | -6.30 | -3.34 | 6.03 | 15.64 | 2.45 | -5.41 | -0.42 | -19.69 |
| 1995 | 7.91 | 1.24 | 6.63 | 4.73 | 8.22 | 0.11 | 8.75 | -5.34 | -1.84 | -8.67 | 0.19 | 19.11 | 6.12 | -21.02 |
| 1994 | -1.45 | -4.18 | 2.87 | -0.39 | 15.01 | 1.47 | 0.98 | -7.33 | 5.05 | 5.43 | 14.24 | 1.05 | 24.22 | -10.99 |
| 1993 | -4.21 | 6.19 | 4.67 | 9.24 | 4.89 | -1.22 | 5.60 | -5.28 | 1.16 | -6.59 | 3.71 | 12.93 | 34.29 | -10.59 |
| 1992 | -12.60 | -6.00 | 5.47 | 0.31 | -5.71 | 5.59 | 16.52 | 1.92 | -0.34 | 3.31 | -4.65 | 4.54 | -10.50 | -26.55 |
| 1991 | -15.94 | 1.30 | 2.43 | -13.70 | 2.94 | 2.11 | -1.52 | -0.33 | 11.61 | 15.61 | -2.09 | 33.75 | 24.39 | -27.01 |
| 1990 | 3.65 | 1.81 | 9.45 | 12.90 | -7.90 | 2.48 | 20.06 | 18.54 | 8.57 | -0.36 | 0.21 | -0.39 | 89.95 | -7.98 |
| 1989 | -8.05 | -12.64 | 13.91 | -20.08 | 38.65 | -4.48 | 16.08 | -13.84 | -7.75 | -14.40 | 10.30 | 39.52 | 17.81 | -31.96 |
| 1988 | 4.17 | -2.59 | -6.76 | -12.35 | 32.34 | 71.99 | -2.82 | 3.45 | -1.98 | 8.01 | 17.83 | 4.51 | 142.04 | -22.12 |

PAST PERFORMANCE IS NOT NECESSARILY INDICATIVE OF FUTURE RESULTS. THE RISK OF LOSS IN TRADING COMMODITY FUTURES, OPTIONS, AND FOREIGN EXCHANGE ("FOREX") IS SUBSTANTIAL.

## CHESAPEAKE CAPITAL

Chesapeake Capital has been trading since 1988. Chesapeake has a CAROR of 12.60% over these years. Chesapeake's worst peak to valley drawdown of 35% is occurring as of this writing. Chesapeake has returned over the years 1750%. If you had invested $100,000 with Chesapeake in 1988, it would be worth $1,725,525.46 today.

Jerry Parker was one of fortunate turtle students of William Eckhardt and Richard Dennis. Many have considered him one of the most successful of the turtles. When the turtle program ended in 1988 after almost five years of trading proprietary capital, Mr. Parker decided to continue his professional money management career by forming Chesapeake.

Jerry did not swing for the fences. He took more of an institutional approach and has tried to temper down the inevitable drawdowns. At his peak in 2008, Chesapeake had a little under $2 billion dollars of assets under management. However, as I earlier mentioned we are only dealing with uncertainty and currently he is in his worst drawdown in the mid 35% range.

Jerry's approach is systematic and he looks at over 90 markets. He can go long or short in markets ranging from coffee to German bonds. The concept is to be available for any opportunity that arises.

He, like other commodity trading advisors takes a trend following approach. The system, on average generates 200 trades per year, of which some six will pay for losses and generate the positive returns for the year.

Jerry has stated, "One would not want to invest too much negative emotion in the 194 losers; you likely won't be around for the six big winners."

*Andy Abraham*

## Chesapeake Capital : Diversified

| Snapshot | Charts | Statistics & Ratios | Performance Tables |

Help with terms and abbreviations? See our definitions page

YEAR TO DATE
**4.11%** ⬇
MAR 0.72%

| | | | |
|---|---|---|---|
| Min. Investment | $ 10,000k | Inception | Feb 1988 | Assets | $ 775.1M |
| Mgmt Fee | 2.00% | Sharpe (RFR=1%) | 0.62 | Worst DD | -27.84 |
| Perf Fee | 20.00% | CAROR | 12.60% | S&P Correlation | 0.12 |

Add Alert | Add to Blender | Add to Portfolio | Add to Watchlist | Print | Export

**GROWTH OF 1,000 - VAMI**

### PERFORMANCE

| Year | Jan | Feb | Mar | Apr | May | Jun | Jul | Aug | Sep | Oct | Nov | Dec | YTD | DD |
|---|---|---|---|---|---|---|---|---|---|---|---|---|---|---|
| 2012 | 2.16 | -2.69 | 0.72 | | | | | | | | | | -4.11 | -4.79 |
| 2011 | 1.62 | 6.07 | 0.77 | 5.54 | -9.27 | -8.15 | 3.51 | -1.03 | -14.09 | -1.61 | 5.58 | 1.04 | -11.75 | -27.84 |
| 2010 | -5.90 | 2.47 | 6.40 | 3.71 | -18.29 | -3.85 | -1.54 | 3.50 | 8.80 | 10.93 | -6.11 | 13.89 | 10.85 | -22.00 |
| 2009 | 0.50 | -0.89 | -1.04 | -3.13 | -3.12 | -1.38 | -0.32 | 4.80 | 3.20 | -4.68 | 4.15 | 2.81 | 0.38 | -9.52 |
| 2008 | 2.35 | 17.15 | -7.49 | 0.63 | 2.07 | 9.48 | -9.39 | -7.50 | -7.20 | 7.29 | 6.44 | 4.14 | 15.38 | -22.22 |
| 2007 | 2.63 | -2.33 | -1.27 | 4.53 | 5.48 | 0.80 | -8.30 | -16.42 | 11.42 | 10.64 | -6.73 | 5.52 | 2.28 | -23.36 |
| 2006 | 5.54 | -0.70 | 5.37 | 3.19 | -1.50 | -0.74 | -2.13 | -4.66 | -1.53 | 1.38 | 3.38 | 3.36 | 10.88 | -10.17 |
| 2005 | -3.82 | 0.46 | 0.92 | 3.62 | -1.25 | 3.40 | 0.48 | 4.70 | -1.10 | -4.75 | 4.33 | 1.97 | 1.14 | -7.19 |
| 2004 | 1.63 | 5.05 | -2.70 | -6.05 | -0.50 | -2.90 | -1.86 | -3.23 | 3.50 | 2.32 | 8.89 | 1.53 | 4.84 | -16.12 |
| 2003 | 8.52 | 3.61 | -8.76 | 0.29 | 5.35 | -5.65 | -1.95 | 2.42 | -2.78 | 15.48 | 1.91 | 6.61 | 23.08 | -11.11 |
| 2002 | -2.11 | -1.79 | 2.43 | -3.27 | 2.26 | 4.19 | 2.84 | 2.55 | 3.81 | -2.63 | -1.56 | 4.31 | 11.07 | -4.75 |
| 2001 | -0.43 | 3.75 | 4.98 | -7.50 | -1.43 | 0.16 | -3.06 | -3.40 | 7.15 | 5.01 | -10.09 | -1.92 | -7.98 | -15.15 |
| 2000 | -0.87 | 0.92 | 1.88 | -3.80 | 0.63 | -0.99 | -3.71 | 3.90 | -7.30 | -0.62 | 7.42 | 9.80 | 5.23 | -11.66 |
| 1999 | -2.76 | 1.90 | -2.65 | 8.42 | -8.71 | 3.57 | -4.80 | 3.37 | 1.98 | -7.83 | 4.15 | 8.49 | 3.30 | -12.59 |
| 1998 | -1.29 | 6.06 | 3.65 | -2.16 | 3.82 | -0.87 | 3.03 | 7.27 | -0.59 | -3.21 | -1.68 | 1.80 | 16.31 | -5.40 |
| 1997 | 1.86 | 5.48 | -1.24 | -2.41 | -2.28 | 1.44 | 6.24 | -7.88 | 5.06 | -2.34 | 1.70 | 4.88 | 9.94 | -7.88 |
| 1996 | 1.69 | -4.26 | 0.28 | 10.16 | -3.04 | 3.27 | -7.64 | 0.57 | 6.47 | 5.92 | 6.57 | -4.30 | 15.05 | -7.64 |
| 1995 | -3.23 | -4.39 | 9.60 | 1.45 | 6.84 | 0.88 | -3.09 | -2.66 | 0.29 | -1.11 | 1.76 | 9.18 | 14.09 | -7.48 |
| 1994 | -3.33 | -4.88 | 0.09 | -0.60 | 9.06 | 7.82 | -1.70 | -2.98 | 3.49 | 1.97 | 4.83 | 2.86 | 15.87 | -8.52 |
| 1993 | 0.42 | 15.99 | 5.86 | 7.38 | 0.40 | 0.99 | 9.49 | 5.88 | -2.63 | -0.06 | 1.03 | 5.77 | 61.82 | -2.69 |
| 1992 | -10.98 | -2.86 | 0.53 | -0.44 | -3.66 | 6.52 | 12.96 | 3.16 | -6.78 | 5.21 | 2.27 | -1.93 | 1.81 | -16.62 |
| 1991 | -1.29 | 4.84 | 2.32 | -2.80 | 0.27 | -1.25 | -1.75 | -3.32 | 4.39 | 4.21 | -4.68 | 12.08 | 12.51 | -8.58 |
| 1990 | 0.49 | 3.37 | 8.62 | 4.37 | -4.61 | 1.77 | 6.25 | 15.15 | 0.80 | 1.86 | -0.25 | 0.11 | 43.12 | -4.61 |
| 1989 | 4.93 | -5.42 | 6.64 | -8.82 | 22.38 | -8.28 | 11.55 | -11.75 | -2.82 | -7.40 | 3.90 | 28.56 | 28.30 | -20.58 |
| 1988 | | -2.63 | -6.88 | -10.71 | 6.93 | 32.42 | -9.41 | 6.85 | 2.03 | 10.65 | 11.06 | 7.04 | 48.91 | -19.05 |

PAST PERFORMANCE IS NOT NECESSARILY INDICATIVE OF FUTURE RESULTS. THE RISK OF LOSS IN TRADING COMMODITY FUTURES, OPTIONS, AND FOREIGN EXCHANGE ("FOREX") IS SUBSTANTIAL

*The Bible of Compounding Money*

# CLARK CAPITAL

Clarke Capital has been trading since 1996. Clarke Capital Worldwide program has returned CAROR of 15.76% over the years. The worst peak to valley draw down was 26.06%. They have returned over 830% over the years. If you had invested $100,000 with Clarke Capital in 1996, it would be worth $2,239,554 today.

Michael Clarke, the principle of Clarke Capital Management runs various programs which are a combination of traditional trend followers at times, and the newer shorter term trades at other times. All of Clarke Capital's programs have the basic premise of systematic multi-market strategy specializing in medium to long-term trend following.

The Clarke programs are designed to identify a trend as early as possible, get in line with it, and then ride it as long as possible. Michael was successful in his trading in the beginning focusing on arbitraging equity options before he started trend following. His strategy was to be a disciplined buyer of volatility sensitive options when they were extremely cheap and hedge them with overvalued options or stock.

In the late 1980s the nature of the equity options business changed and it became less attractive to Michael. Starting in 1989 he started researching and verifying whether he could write computer algorithms that would be based on his knowledge and previous trading experiences in the markets. Clarke started with ten mechanical trading models in 1993. He developed them for 3 years before they were traded with client assets.

Clarke is a volatile investment which rotates back and forth between run up, drawdown, and recovery periods. I have been invested with Clarke for years. I sell all positions after substantial run ups and buy his drawdowns. This smooths out my returns from him yet it is far from perfect.

Clarke also does a few things which are a little out of the norm for most commodity trading advisors. The biggest negative is that he doesn't compound capital for you or increase positions as equity increases or decreases; instead Clarke relies on the investor to provide instructions on when to increase or decrease treading levels. Investing with Clarke is not retirement in a box.

In order to diversity Michael has seven different programs. The programs are called:

Orion with a minimum investment of $200,000,

Worldwide with a minimum investment of $250,000,

Millennium with a minimum investment of $1,000,000,

Jupiter with a minimum investment of $3,000,000,

Global Basic with a minimum investment of $50,000,

Global Magnum with a minimum investment of $100,000,

FX Basic with a minimum investment of $1,000,000.

Over the years Michael's hard work and efforts paid off. Michael has been awarded many accolades including:

- 1993 Futures Magazine "Top Trader"
- 2000 Futures Magazine "Top Trader"
- 2007 Futures magazine "Top Trader"

*The Bible of Compounding Money*

## Clarke Capital Management : Worldwide

Snapshot | Charts | Statistics & Ratios | Performance Tables    ⊕Help with terms and abbreviations? See our definitions page

YEAR-TO-DATE
**0.96%** ↑
MAR **-4.62%**

| | | | |
|---|---|---|---|
| Min. Investment | $ 250k | Inception | Jan 1996 | Assets | $ 26.2M |
| Mgmt Fee | 1.80% | Sharpe (RFR~1%) | 0.64 | Worst DD | -27.15 |
| Perf Fee | 25.00% | CAROR | 13.83% | S&P Correlation | -0.16 |

⚑ Add Alert | ⊕ Add to Blender | ⊕ Add to Portfolio | ⊕ Add to Watchlist | 🖨 Print | 📄 Export

GROWTH OF 1,000 - VAMI

### PERFORMANCE

| Year | Jan | Feb | Mar | Apr | May | Jun | Jul | Aug | Sep | Oct | Nov | Dec | YTD | DD |
|---|---|---|---|---|---|---|---|---|---|---|---|---|---|---|
| 2012 | -1.79 | 7.78 | -4.62 | | | | | | | | | | 0.96 | -4.62 |
| 2011 | -8.43 | -1.22 | -9.13 | 12.55 | -8.49 | -2.40 | 5.97 | 1.00 | 2.64 | -19.12 | 2.07 | -1.01 | -25.82 | -26.59 |
| 2010 | 5.90 | -4.63 | 1.41 | 5.45 | 3.95 | 3.16 | 2.86 | 9.15 | 4.23 | 4.24 | -3.53 | 3.96 | 41.69 | -4.63 |
| 2009 | -4.22 | 0.81 | -6.02 | -4.84 | 19.16 | -4.46 | -1.76 | -2.03 | 6.20 | -4.04 | 6.90 | -13.74 | -11.09 | -13.74 |
| 2008 | 4.88 | 12.24 | 5.85 | -7.57 | 5.42 | 3.22 | -12.34 | 3.96 | 9.15 | 11.53 | 9.46 | 7.04 | 62.90 | -12.34 |
| 2007 | -0.46 | -1.77 | -2.33 | 3.69 | 1.40 | 3.61 | 6.48 | -3.57 | 30.57 | 0.59 | 2.61 | -0.12 | 43.79 | -4.50 |
| 2006 | -3.72 | -1.99 | 3.64 | 18.95 | 2.62 | -5.39 | -6.75 | -3.03 | -3.76 | -3.75 | 6.56 | -8.05 | -7.32 | -22.36 |
| 2005 | -1.83 | -0.18 | -4.26 | -1.06 | 7.40 | 0.13 | -5.47 | -1.80 | -3.32 | -1.48 | 1.40 | 0.09 | -10.42 | -11.74 |
| 2004 | 0.03 | 6.82 | 4.88 | -9.11 | 1.31 | -3.48 | 0.12 | -2.37 | 4.73 | 0.89 | 6.15 | -4.29 | 4.51 | -13.13 |
| 2003 | 2.62 | 6.21 | -7.42 | 3.69 | 14.59 | -3.99 | -0.55 | -0.03 | 2.75 | 3.49 | -1.48 | 5.27 | 26.21 | -7.42 |
| 2002 | -1.31 | -3.63 | 4.00 | -2.94 | 2.52 | 6.11 | 3.96 | 2.01 | 3.90 | -7.87 | -2.40 | 16.57 | 20.50 | -10.08 |
| 2001 | -1.32 | -2.65 | 5.25 | -9.00 | 3.83 | -5.58 | 0.20 | -2.16 | 0.51 | 4.49 | -5.98 | -0.62 | -13.32 | -14.27 |
| 2000 | 2.85 | -4.57 | -2.94 | 2.96 | 9.52 | 2.45 | -7.83 | 9.73 | 0.47 | -9.34 | 4.68 | 10.48 | 17.25 | -9.34 |
| 1999 | 0.87 | 6.84 | 0.61 | -1.84 | -5.99 | 5.08 | 4.61 | 1.04 | 0.01 | -4.57 | 6.29 | 1.69 | 14.64 | -7.72 |
| 1998 | 5.91 | -0.36 | -0.41 | -3.22 | 6.40 | -3.17 | -0.56 | 21.67 | 11.35 | -6.10 | 1.33 | -0.77 | 33.31 | -6.10 |
| 1997 | 3.81 | 8.56 | -1.14 | 0.55 | -0.13 | 0.76 | 4.88 | -3.53 | 6.11 | -3.88 | 1.61 | 5.57 | 24.66 | -3.88 |
| 1996 | -4.38 | -0.90 | 1.79 | 9.10 | -7.33 | 6.87 | 0.17 | -1.11 | 22.07 | 9.10 | 15.64 | -8.64 | 45.26 | -8.64 |

PAST PERFORMANCE IS NOT NECESSARILY INDICATIVE OF FUTURE RESULTS. THE RISK OF LOSS IN TRADING COMMODITY FUTURES, OPTIONS, AND FOREIGN EXCHANGE ("FOREX") IS SUBSTANTIAL.

# ECKHARDT TRADING

Eckhardt Trading has been active since 1991. The CAROR of Eckhardt is 15.16%. The worst peak to valley draw down was 27.11%. Eckhardt has returned a little less than 2000% over these years. If you had invested $100,000 with Eckhardt in 1991, it would be worth $2,231,703.20 today.

In conjunction to Eckhardt's Standard fund he has a greater leveraged version. The Standard Plus fund has a CAROR of 20.70% with a worst peak to valley drawdown of -40.39%. If you had invested $100,000 with Eckhardt in his Standard Plus fund 1991 it would be worth $6,285,668.87 today.

In March of 2011 Futures magazine featured William Eckhardt. They called the article "The Man Who Launched 1,000 Systems".

Besides this title, William Eckhardt is considered to be the father of the famous "Turtle Traders". He and Richard Dennis taught a group of non-traders trend following and created extreme wealth.

Ironically Eckhardt *lost* a bet with Dennis; he did not think the turtles could be trained.

Some of the commodity trading advisors I am mentioning are either Turtle traders or people who have worked at one of the firms based on the tenants of turtle trading.

Eckhardt's background is based in mathematical logic and interestingly he gave up on his PHD to further trading and developing trading systems. What is more interesting about his background is that the turtle experiment proved that you did not need a PHD degree in mathematical logic to take money out of the markets.

This is just another proof for me; if Richard Donchian could successful trade for 50 years, my dentist buddy can trade for

## The Bible of Compounding Money

almost 25 years and a group of turtle traders can trade—so can I and so can you.

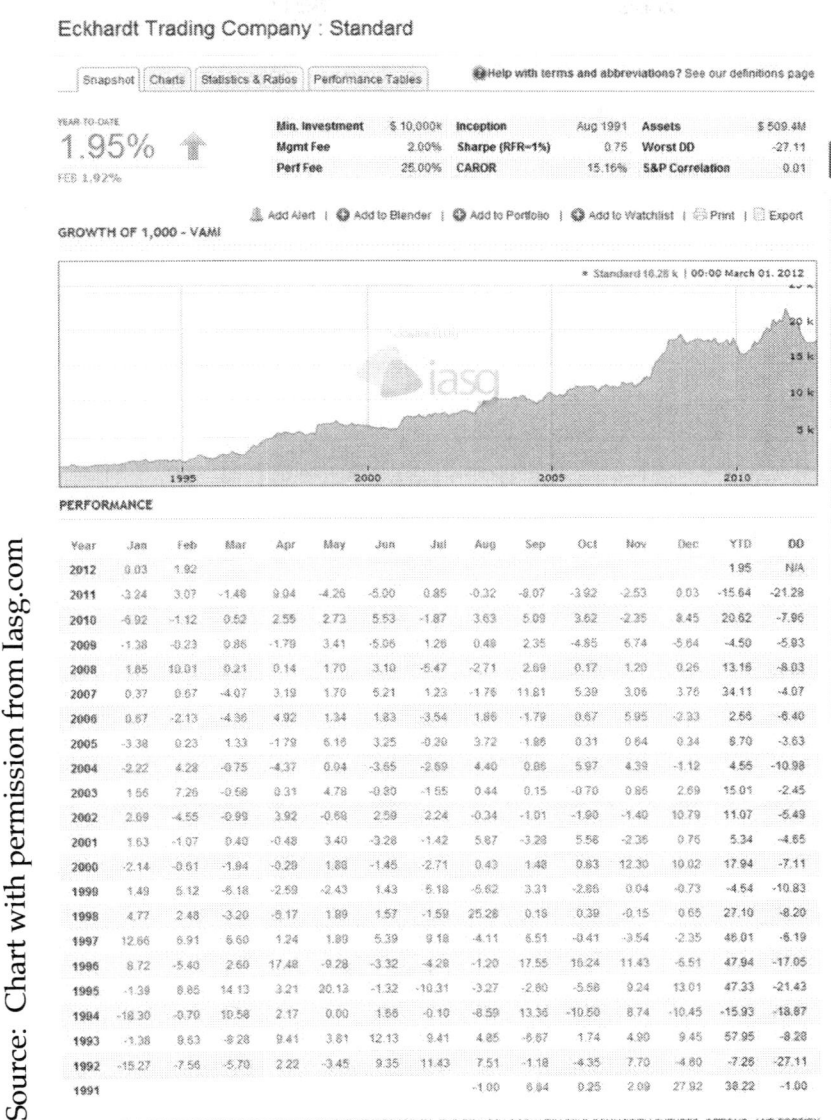

**Eckhardt Trading Company : Standard**

| | | | |
|---|---|---|---|
| YEAR-TO-DATE **1.95%** ↑ FEB 1.92% | Min. Investment $10,000k<br>Mgmt Fee 2.00%<br>Perf Fee 25.00% | Inception Aug 1991<br>Sharpe (RFR=1%) 0.75<br>CAROR 15.16% | Assets $509.4M<br>Worst DD -27.11<br>S&P Correlation 0.01 |

GROWTH OF 1,000 - VAMI

Standard 16.28 k | 00:00 March 01, 2012

### PERFORMANCE

| Year | Jan | Feb | Mar | Apr | May | Jun | Jul | Aug | Sep | Oct | Nov | Dec | YTD | DD |
|---|---|---|---|---|---|---|---|---|---|---|---|---|---|---|
| 2012 | 0.03 | 1.92 | | | | | | | | | | | 1.95 | N/A |
| 2011 | -3.24 | 3.07 | -1.48 | 9.04 | -4.26 | -5.00 | 0.85 | -0.32 | -8.07 | -3.92 | -2.53 | 0.03 | -15.64 | -21.28 |
| 2010 | -6.92 | -1.12 | 0.52 | 2.55 | 2.73 | 5.53 | -1.87 | 3.63 | 5.09 | 3.62 | -2.35 | 8.45 | 20.62 | -7.96 |
| 2009 | -1.38 | -0.23 | 0.86 | -1.79 | 3.41 | -5.95 | 1.26 | 0.48 | 2.35 | -4.85 | 6.74 | -5.64 | -4.50 | -5.93 |
| 2008 | 1.85 | 10.01 | 0.21 | 0.14 | 1.70 | 3.10 | -5.47 | -2.71 | 2.69 | 0.17 | 1.20 | 0.25 | 13.16 | -8.03 |
| 2007 | 0.37 | 0.67 | -4.07 | 3.19 | 1.70 | 5.21 | 1.23 | -1.76 | 11.81 | 5.39 | 3.06 | 3.76 | 34.11 | -4.07 |
| 2006 | 0.67 | -2.13 | -4.36 | 4.92 | 1.34 | 1.83 | -3.54 | 1.86 | -1.79 | 0.67 | 5.95 | -2.33 | 2.56 | -6.40 |
| 2005 | -3.38 | 0.23 | 1.33 | -1.79 | 6.16 | 3.25 | -0.39 | 3.72 | -1.85 | 0.31 | 0.64 | 0.34 | 8.70 | -3.63 |
| 2004 | -2.22 | 4.28 | -0.75 | -4.37 | 0.04 | -3.65 | -2.69 | 4.40 | 0.86 | 5.97 | 4.39 | -1.12 | 4.55 | -10.98 |
| 2003 | 1.56 | 7.26 | -0.58 | 8.31 | 4.78 | -0.80 | -1.85 | 0.44 | 0.15 | -0.76 | 0.85 | 2.69 | 15.01 | -2.45 |
| 2002 | 2.69 | -4.55 | -0.99 | 3.92 | -0.68 | 2.59 | 2.24 | -0.34 | -1.01 | -1.90 | -1.40 | 10.79 | 11.07 | -5.49 |
| 2001 | 1.63 | -1.07 | 0.40 | -0.48 | 3.40 | -3.28 | -1.42 | 5.87 | -3.28 | 5.56 | -2.35 | 0.75 | 5.34 | -4.65 |
| 2000 | -2.14 | -0.61 | -1.94 | -0.29 | 1.88 | -1.45 | -2.71 | 0.43 | 1.48 | 0.63 | 12.30 | 10.02 | 17.94 | -7.11 |
| 1999 | 1.49 | 5.12 | -6.18 | -2.59 | -2.43 | 1.43 | 6.18 | -5.62 | 3.31 | -2.85 | 0.04 | -0.73 | -4.54 | -10.83 |
| 1998 | 4.77 | 2.48 | -3.20 | -6.17 | 1.89 | 1.57 | -1.59 | 25.26 | 0.15 | 0.39 | -0.15 | 0.65 | 27.10 | -8.20 |
| 1997 | 12.66 | 6.91 | 5.60 | 1.24 | 1.89 | 5.39 | 9.18 | -4.11 | 6.51 | -0.41 | -3.54 | -2.35 | 48.01 | -6.19 |
| 1996 | 8.72 | -5.40 | 2.60 | 17.48 | -9.28 | -3.32 | -4.28 | -1.20 | 17.55 | 18.24 | 11.43 | -6.51 | 47.94 | -17.05 |
| 1995 | -1.38 | 8.85 | 14.13 | 3.21 | 20.13 | -1.32 | -10.31 | -3.27 | -2.60 | -5.58 | 9.24 | 13.01 | 47.33 | -21.43 |
| 1994 | -18.30 | -0.70 | 10.58 | 2.17 | 0.00 | 1.55 | -0.10 | -8.59 | 13.36 | -19.50 | 8.74 | -10.45 | -15.93 | -18.87 |
| 1993 | -1.38 | 8.63 | -8.28 | 9.41 | 3.81 | 12.13 | 9.41 | 4.85 | -6.67 | 1.74 | 4.90 | 9.45 | 57.95 | -8.28 |
| 1992 | -15.27 | -7.56 | -5.70 | 2.22 | -3.45 | 9.35 | 11.43 | 7.51 | -1.18 | -4.35 | 7.70 | -4.80 | -7.26 | -27.11 |
| 1991 | | | | | | | -1.00 | 6.84 | 0.25 | 2.09 | 27.92 | 38.22 | -1.00 |

PAST PERFORMANCE IS NOT NECESSARILY INDICATIVE OF FUTURE RESULTS. THE RISK OF LOSS IN TRADING COMMODITY FUTURES, OPTIONS, AND FOREIGN EXCHANGE ("FOREX") IS SUBSTANTIAL.

Source: Chart with permission from lasg.com

## Eckhardt Trading Company : Standard Plus

| | | | |
|---|---|---|---|
| **YEAR-TO-DATE** | Min. Investment $10,000k | Inception Oct 1991 | Assets $181.0M |
| **13.67%** ↑ | Mgmt Fee 2.00% | Sharpe (RFR=1%) 0.75 | Worst DD -40.39 |
| SEP -1.05% | Perf Fee 25.00% | CAROR 20.70% | S&P Correlation 0.03 |

**GROWTH OF 1,000 - VAMI**

Standard Plus 52.03 k | 00:00 October 01, 2012

### MONTHLY PERFORMANCE

| Year | Jan | Feb | Mar | Apr | May | Jun | Jul | Aug | Sep | Oct | Nov | Dec | YTD | DD |
|---|---|---|---|---|---|---|---|---|---|---|---|---|---|---|
| 2012 | 1.65 | 1.93 | -3.19 | 1.72 | 9.27 | -7.49 | 9.29 | 1.91 | -1.05 | | | | 13.67 | -7.49 |
| 2011 | -3.87 | 3.64 | -1.72 | 10.88 | -5.23 | -6.04 | 0.91 | -0.29 | -9.47 | -4.58 | -2.35 | 0.00 | -18.37 | -24.81 |
| 2010 | -8.11 | -1.27 | 0.50 | 2.83 | 3.41 | 6.41 | -2.37 | 4.31 | 5.97 | 4.37 | -2.92 | 10.12 | 24.23 | -9.28 |
| 2009 | -1.60 | -0.28 | 1.01 | -2.19 | 4.02 | -5.05 | 1.23 | 0.47 | 2.60 | -5.43 | 3.14 | -6.70 | -5.52 | -7.06 |
| 2008 | 2.16 | 11.42 | 0.39 | 0.23 | 1.96 | 3.48 | -6.54 | -2.93 | 3.09 | 0.12 | 1.38 | 0.18 | 14.76 | -9.33 |
| 2007 | 0.35 | 0.84 | -4.54 | 3.71 | 2.10 | 5.81 | 1.48 | -2.80 | 13.33 | 6.04 | 3.36 | 4.18 | 39.28 | -4.54 |
| 2006 | 0.68 | -2.64 | -5.29 | 5.63 | 1.29 | 2.06 | -4.21 | 2.09 | -2.22 | 0.71 | 7.09 | -3.10 | 1.30 | -7.79 |
| 2005 | -4.09 | 0.29 | 1.54 | -2.16 | 7.22 | 3.85 | -0.38 | 4.87 | -2.25 | 0.31 | 0.72 | 0.40 | 10.01 | -4.44 |
| 2004 | -2.43 | 5.10 | -0.91 | -5.27 | 0.06 | -4.19 | -3.08 | 5.11 | 1.03 | 6.92 | 5.28 | -1.19 | 5.64 | -12.78 |
| 2003 | 2.00 | 8.82 | -0.44 | 0.46 | 5.70 | -0.75 | -1.33 | 0.70 | 0.44 | -0.70 | 1.29 | 3.35 | 20.21 | -2.57 |
| 2002 | 3.22 | -5.27 | -1.10 | 4.68 | -0.62 | 3.07 | 2.65 | -0.33 | -1.14 | -2.41 | -1.41 | 13.20 | 14.23 | -6.31 |
| 2001 | 2.08 | -1.01 | 0.65 | -0.38 | 4.11 | -3.54 | -1.49 | 7.03 | -3.39 | 6.54 | -2.53 | 1.00 | 8.70 | -4.98 |
| 2000 | -2.48 | -0.59 | -2.15 | -0.14 | 2.44 | -1.50 | -3.01 | 0.71 | 1.65 | 1.03 | 15.98 | 11.28 | 23.75 | -7.29 |
| 1999 | 2.01 | 6.42 | -6.89 | -3.07 | -2.74 | 1.87 | 6.30 | -6.42 | 4.11 | -3.23 | 0.41 | -0.79 | -3.05 | -12.22 |
| 1998 | 6.74 | 3.70 | -4.75 | -8.55 | 2.28 | 2.04 | -2.02 | 32.07 | 0.28 | 0.57 | 0.00 | 1.20 | 35.81 | -10.99 |
| 1997 | 18.53 | 8.97 | 7.72 | 1.48 | 2.47 | 6.35 | 11.08 | -4.64 | 8.00 | -0.46 | -5.08 | -2.91 | 61.47 | -8.27 |
| 1996 | 13.92 | -8.27 | 4.31 | 26.29 | -14.51 | -5.92 | -9.23 | -1.95 | 26.88 | 24.25 | 16.81 | -7.64 | 67.60 | -28.42 |
| 1995 | -2.59 | 14.63 | 20.81 | 3.46 | 26.71 | -2.03 | -16.91 | -5.95 | -4.79 | -9.45 | 15.16 | 21.57 | 63.41 | -34.00 |
| 1994 | -28.85 | 0.11 | 16.36 | 6.06 | 9.48 | 2.01 | 1.21 | -13.18 | 19.93 | -17.61 | 14.47 | -15.90 | -17.94 | -28.65 |
| 1993 | -1.85 | 12.16 | -9.22 | 11.39 | 8.03 | 15.00 | 16.09 | 8.66 | -7.72 | 2.90 | 7.71 | 14.52 | 101.40 | -9.22 |
| 1992 | -19.25 | -12.70 | -12.52 | 6.65 | -9.37 | 17.89 | 25.69 | 11.22 | 0.50 | -4.51 | 9.76 | -4.14 | -0.98 | -40.39 |
| 1991 | | | | | | | | | -6.09 | 3.25 | 48.70 | 44.18 | -6.09 | |

*The Bible of Compounding Money*

# TACTICAL INVESTMENT MANAGEMENT

Tactical has been trading since 1993. They have a CAROR of 18.87%. The worst peak to valley draw down has been 32.94%. If you had invested $100,000 with Tactical in 1993, it would be worth $3,172,818.68 today.

David Druz started out as an emergency room doctor however his passion was trading. While working in medicine he was researching ideas for trading. Dave learned under Ed Seykota, a famous trend follower. He actually stayed in his house for an extended period of time and began an intense learning process. This learning process was more of a self-introspection as a pose to learning trading indicators or systems. In 1981, he setup his first futures fund Tactical, while practicing as an emergency doctor in Fairbanks, Alaska.

As a side note, I have been invested with him for years. He wrote the forward of my first book *"The Bible of Trend Following"*. He came out with some interesting points in the forward. Over 30 years of real time trading, Dave has really seen it all—bull and bear markets, inflation and deflation.

Quoting Dave in the foreword he states, "Even after you've learned how to do it, you still take your hits. To succeed you just need to stand up every time you get knocked down. You need to have the confidence that standing up is the right thing to do. You need to know how to stand back up and how. And just by standing up again and again and staying standing as long as you can before you get hit again, you will actually make more money than you lose over the long run in trend trading. Very few people succeed in this process. The learning curve is too steep and the correct psychology is too hard to implement. If you have any attachment to making money (and who doesn't?), it is very tough to trade correctly."

*Andy Abraham*

What Dave is saying is applicable to not just traders, but the investors in traders. It is not easy nor is it possible to avoid drawdowns. There is no magic; rather the correct mindset is what separates success and failure for both traders and investors.

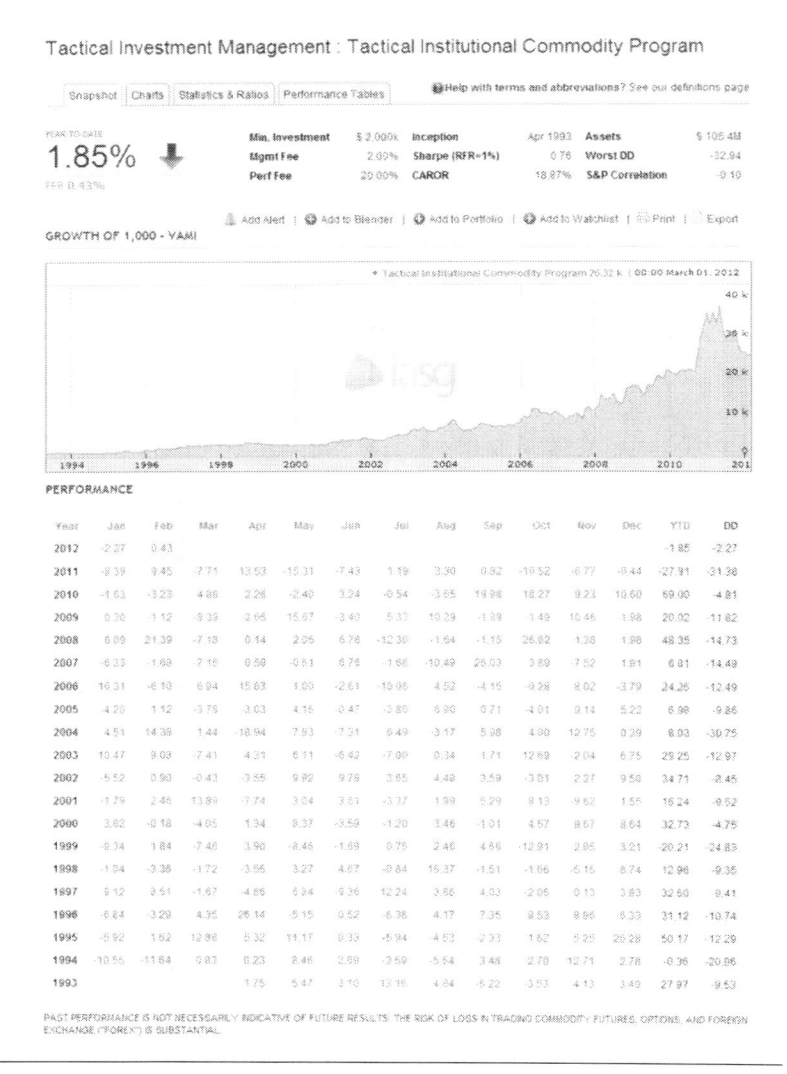

### Tactical Investment Management : Tactical Institutional Commodity Program

| | | | |
|---|---|---|---|
| YEAR TO DATE **1.85%** ↓ FEB 0.43% | Min. Investment $2,000k<br>Mgmt Fee 2.00%<br>Perf Fee 20.00% | Inception Apr 1993<br>Sharpe (RFR=1%) 0.76<br>CAROR 18.87% | Assets $105.4M<br>Worst DD -32.94<br>S&P Correlation -0.10 |

GROWTH OF 1,000 - VAMI

*[Chart showing growth from 1994 to 2012, peaking around 40k with Tactical Institutional Commodity Program 26.32 k | 00:00 March 01, 2012]*

### PERFORMANCE

| Year | Jan | Feb | Mar | Apr | May | Jun | Jul | Aug | Sep | Oct | Nov | Dec | YTD | DD |
|---|---|---|---|---|---|---|---|---|---|---|---|---|---|---|
| 2012 | -2.27 | 0.43 | | | | | | | | | | | -1.85 | -2.27 |
| 2011 | -8.39 | 9.45 | -7.71 | 13.53 | -15.31 | -7.43 | 1.19 | 3.30 | 0.32 | -10.52 | -6.77 | -0.43 | -27.93 | -31.38 |
| 2010 | -1.63 | -3.23 | 4.86 | 2.28 | -2.40 | 3.24 | -0.54 | -3.65 | 19.98 | 18.27 | 9.23 | 19.60 | 69.00 | -4.81 |
| 2009 | 0.20 | -1.12 | -9.33 | -2.65 | 15.67 | -3.40 | 5.32 | 10.29 | -1.39 | 1.49 | 10.46 | 1.98 | 20.02 | -11.82 |
| 2008 | 6.09 | 21.39 | -7.18 | 0.14 | 2.05 | 6.78 | -12.38 | -1.54 | -1.15 | 26.82 | 1.38 | 1.98 | 48.35 | -14.73 |
| 2007 | -6.33 | -1.68 | -7.15 | 0.59 | -0.51 | 6.76 | -1.66 | -10.49 | 26.03 | 3.89 | -7.82 | 1.81 | 6.81 | -14.49 |
| 2006 | 16.31 | -6.13 | 6.94 | 15.83 | 1.00 | -2.61 | -10.96 | 4.52 | -4.15 | -0.28 | 8.02 | -3.79 | 24.26 | -12.49 |
| 2005 | 4.20 | 1.12 | -3.75 | -3.03 | 4.16 | -0.47 | -3.80 | 6.90 | 0.71 | -4.01 | 9.14 | 5.22 | 6.98 | -9.86 |
| 2004 | 4.51 | 14.39 | 1.44 | -18.94 | 7.93 | -7.31 | 6.49 | -3.17 | 5.98 | 4.00 | 12.75 | 0.39 | 8.03 | -30.75 |
| 2003 | 10.47 | 9.03 | -7.41 | 4.23 | 6.11 | -6.82 | -7.00 | 0.34 | 1.71 | 12.69 | -2.04 | 6.75 | 29.25 | -12.97 |
| 2002 | -5.52 | 0.90 | -0.43 | -3.55 | 9.92 | 9.78 | 3.65 | 4.48 | 3.59 | -3.81 | 2.27 | 9.58 | 34.71 | -2.45 |
| 2001 | -1.79 | 2.46 | 13.89 | -7.74 | 3.04 | 3.51 | -3.37 | 1.99 | 5.29 | 9.13 | -9.62 | 1.55 | 16.24 | -9.52 |
| 2000 | 3.82 | -0.18 | -4.05 | 1.34 | 8.37 | -3.59 | -1.20 | 3.46 | -1.01 | 4.57 | 8.67 | 8.64 | 32.73 | -4.75 |
| 1999 | -9.34 | 1.84 | -7.46 | 3.96 | -8.46 | -1.69 | 0.75 | 2.46 | 4.56 | -12.91 | 2.05 | 3.21 | -20.21 | -24.83 |
| 1998 | -1.94 | -3.38 | -1.72 | -3.56 | 3.22 | 4.67 | -0.84 | 15.37 | -1.51 | -1.86 | -5.15 | 8.74 | 12.96 | -9.35 |
| 1997 | 9.12 | 2.51 | -1.67 | -4.86 | 6.34 | -9.36 | 12.24 | 3.66 | 4.03 | -2.85 | 0.13 | 3.83 | 32.60 | -9.41 |
| 1996 | -6.84 | -3.29 | 4.35 | 26.14 | -5.15 | 0.52 | -6.36 | 4.17 | 7.35 | 9.53 | 8.96 | -6.33 | 31.12 | -10.74 |
| 1995 | -5.92 | 1.62 | 12.86 | 5.32 | 11.17 | 0.33 | -5.94 | -4.53 | -2.33 | 1.62 | 5.25 | 26.28 | 50.17 | -12.29 |
| 1994 | -10.55 | -11.84 | 9.83 | 8.23 | 2.46 | 2.59 | -3.59 | -5.54 | 3.48 | 2.70 | 12.71 | 2.78 | -0.36 | -20.96 |
| 1993 | | | | 1.75 | 5.47 | 3.70 | 13.19 | 4.84 | -5.22 | -3.53 | 4.13 | 3.49 | 27.97 | -9.53 |

PAST PERFORMANCE IS NOT NECESSARILY INDICATIVE OF FUTURE RESULTS. THE RISK OF LOSS IN TRADING COMMODITY FUTURES, OPTIONS, AND FOREIGN EXCHANGE ("FOREX") IS SUBSTANTIAL.

*The Bible of Compounding Money*

## SAXON INVESTMENT MANAGEMENT

Saxon has been trading the Diversified Program since 1988. They have a CAROR of 14.26%. The worst peak to valley draw down has been 41.55%. If you had invested $100,000 with Saxon in 1988, it would worth $2,145,690 today.

Saxon also has an aggressive Diversified Program. This program has returned a CAROR of 20.37% with its worst peak to valley drawdown of -65.86%. If you had invested $100,000 with Saxon's aggressive Diversified Program in 1988 it would be worth $7,110,825.02 today.

You would have had to suffer greater drawdowns however in the same period of time you would have more than tripled your results. I had the pleasure to sit with Howard Siedler in the last Alphametrix convention. I strongly suggest events like Alphametrix and the CTA Expos. This is the best way to actually feel the managers and get to know them. Quantitative numbers are not the whole picture. I like getting to know managers before investing with them.

Seidler graduated from the MIT in 1980 with a B.S. in chemical engineering and management science. By 1983 he began his full-time intensive study of the futures markets. In December 1983 he was hired and became one of the turtles in the experiment of Richard Dennis and Bill Eckhardt.

Upon the closure of the turtle program in 1988, Howard opened his trading company, Saxon, in order to manage other accounts for multiple clients as a registered commodity trading advisor. He runs a small boutique trading shop and keeps it in the family. He works with his sister as well as his brother, I believe based out of Coral Springs Florida. Howard is solely responsible for the trading decisions and strategies of Saxon, and for directing its ongoing research and development of trading and money management principle. As of this writing Howard is implementing new changes to his programs that have a greater bias to the long side which he feels will lead to improvement. Howard has developed multiple systems and uses them in a synergistic approach. There is some discretion and judgment over certain trades depending on market conditions.

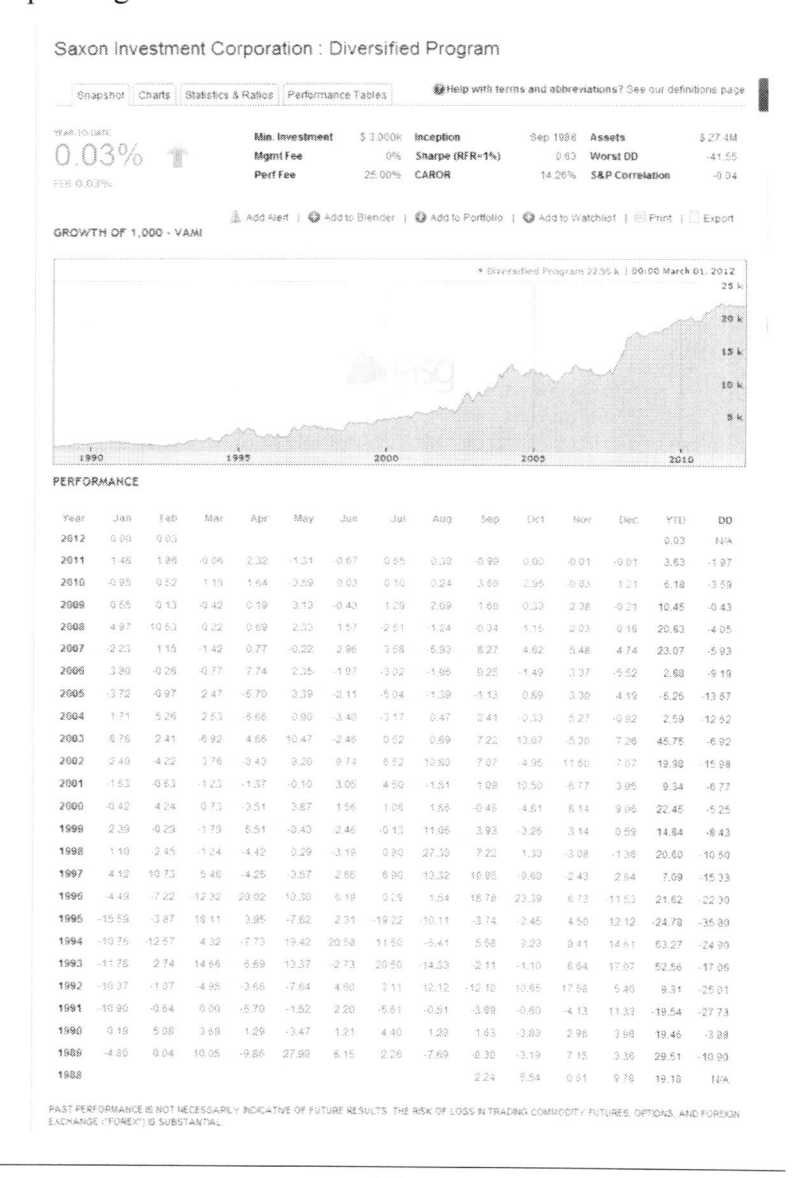

**Saxon Investment Corporation : Diversified Program**

YEAR-TO-DATE: 0.03%
FEB 0.03%

| | |
|---|---|
| Min. Investment | $3,000k |
| Mgmt Fee | 0% |
| Perf Fee | 25.00% |

| | |
|---|---|
| Inception | Sep 1988 |
| Sharpe (RFR=1%) | 0.63 |
| CAROR | 14.26% |

| | |
|---|---|
| Assets | $27.4M |
| Worst DD | -41.55 |
| S&P Correlation | -0.04 |

GROWTH OF 1,000 - VAMI

*Diversified Program 22.95 k | 00:00 March 01, 2012*

**PERFORMANCE**

| Year | Jan | Feb | Mar | Apr | May | Jun | Jul | Aug | Sep | Oct | Nov | Dec | YTD | DD |
|---|---|---|---|---|---|---|---|---|---|---|---|---|---|---|
| 2012 | 0.00 | 0.03 | | | | | | | | | | | 0.03 | N/A |
| 2011 | 1.45 | 1.26 | -0.06 | 2.32 | -1.31 | -0.67 | 0.55 | 0.33 | -0.99 | 0.00 | -0.01 | -0.01 | 3.63 | -1.97 |
| 2010 | -0.95 | 0.52 | 1.19 | 1.64 | -3.59 | 0.03 | 0.16 | 0.24 | 3.68 | 2.95 | -0.03 | 1.21 | 6.18 | -3.59 |
| 2009 | 0.55 | 0.13 | -0.42 | 0.19 | 3.13 | -0.43 | 1.29 | 2.59 | 1.69 | -0.33 | 2.38 | -0.21 | 10.45 | -0.43 |
| 2008 | 4.97 | 10.63 | 0.22 | 0.69 | 2.33 | 1.57 | -2.51 | -1.24 | -0.34 | 1.16 | 2.03 | 0.16 | 20.63 | -4.05 |
| 2007 | -2.23 | 1.15 | -1.42 | 0.77 | -0.22 | 2.96 | 3.56 | -5.93 | 8.27 | 4.62 | 5.48 | 4.74 | 23.07 | -5.93 |
| 2006 | 3.80 | -0.26 | -0.77 | 7.74 | 2.35 | -1.07 | -3.02 | -1.96 | 0.25 | -1.49 | 3.37 | -5.52 | 2.68 | -9.19 |
| 2005 | -3.72 | -0.97 | 2.47 | -5.70 | 3.39 | -2.11 | -5.04 | -1.39 | -1.13 | 0.69 | 3.30 | 4.19 | -6.26 | -13.87 |
| 2004 | 1.71 | 5.26 | 2.53 | -5.66 | 0.00 | -3.40 | -1.17 | 0.47 | 2.41 | -0.33 | 5.27 | -0.82 | 2.59 | -12.62 |
| 2003 | 5.25 | 2.41 | -6.92 | 4.66 | 10.47 | -2.46 | 0.52 | 0.69 | 7.22 | 13.07 | -5.30 | 7.26 | 45.75 | -6.92 |
| 2002 | -2.46 | -4.22 | 1.76 | -3.43 | 3.20 | 9.74 | 6.52 | 10.63 | 7.07 | -4.95 | 11.50 | 7.07 | 19.98 | -15.98 |
| 2001 | -1.53 | -9.63 | -1.21 | -1.37 | -0.10 | 3.06 | 4.50 | -1.51 | 1.09 | 10.50 | -6.77 | 3.95 | 9.34 | -6.77 |
| 2000 | -0.42 | 4.24 | 0.73 | -3.51 | 3.87 | 1.56 | 1.06 | 1.56 | -0.49 | -4.61 | 8.14 | 9.06 | 22.45 | -5.25 |
| 1999 | 2.39 | -0.29 | -1.79 | 5.51 | -0.43 | 2.46 | -0.13 | 11.95 | 3.93 | -3.26 | 3.14 | 0.59 | 14.84 | -8.43 |
| 1998 | 1.10 | -2.45 | -1.24 | -4.42 | 0.29 | -3.19 | 0.90 | 27.10 | 7.22 | 1.10 | -3.08 | -1.36 | 20.60 | -10.80 |
| 1997 | 4.12 | 19.73 | 5.48 | -4.25 | -3.57 | 2.65 | 6.90 | 13.32 | 10.85 | -9.60 | -2.43 | 2.64 | 7.09 | -15.33 |
| 1996 | -4.49 | -7.22 | -12.32 | 29.02 | 13.30 | 6.19 | 0.29 | 1.54 | 18.78 | 23.39 | 6.73 | -11.53 | 21.62 | -22.30 |
| 1995 | -15.59 | -3.87 | 19.11 | 3.95 | -7.62 | 2.31 | -19.22 | -10.11 | -3.74 | -2.45 | 4.50 | 12.12 | -24.78 | -35.30 |
| 1994 | -10.76 | -12.57 | 4.32 | -7.73 | 19.42 | 20.58 | 11.50 | -5.41 | 5.58 | 9.23 | 9.41 | 14.61 | 53.27 | -24.90 |
| 1993 | -11.76 | 2.74 | 14.66 | 6.69 | 13.37 | -2.73 | 20.50 | -14.53 | -2.11 | -1.10 | 6.04 | 17.07 | 52.56 | -17.05 |
| 1992 | -19.37 | -1.07 | -4.95 | -3.66 | -7.64 | 4.60 | 3.11 | 12.12 | -12.10 | 10.65 | 17.58 | 5.46 | 9.31 | -25.01 |
| 1991 | -10.96 | -0.64 | 6.00 | -5.70 | -1.52 | 2.20 | -5.81 | -0.51 | -3.98 | -0.60 | -4.13 | 11.33 | -19.54 | -27.73 |
| 1990 | 9.19 | 5.08 | 3.69 | 1.29 | -3.47 | 1.21 | 4.46 | 1.29 | 1.63 | -3.80 | 2.96 | 3.98 | 19.46 | -3.28 |
| 1989 | -4.20 | 0.04 | 10.05 | -9.66 | 27.90 | 6.15 | 2.26 | -7.69 | -0.30 | -3.19 | 7.15 | 3.36 | 29.51 | -10.90 |
| 1988 | | | | | | | | 2.24 | 5.54 | 0.91 | 9.79 | 19.18 | N/A |

PAST PERFORMANCE IS NOT NECESSARILY INDICATIVE OF FUTURE RESULTS. THE RISK OF LOSS IN TRADING COMMODITY FUTURES, OPTIONS, AND FOREIGN EXCHANGE ("FOREX") IS SUBSTANTIAL.

# The Bible of Compounding Money

## Saxon Investment Corporation : Aggressive Diversified Program

| YEAR-TO-DATE | Min. Investment | $2,000k | Inception | Nov 1993 | Assets | $194.7M |
|---|---|---|---|---|---|---|
| **1.67%** ↑ | Mgmt Fee | 0% | Sharpe (RFR=1%) | 0.63 | Worst DD | -65.86 |
| SEP 0.57% | Perf Fee | 25.00% | CAROR | 20.37% | S&P Correlation | -0.06 |

**GROWTH OF 1,000 - VAMI**

* Aggressive Diversified Program 33.36 k | 00:00 October 01, 2012

### MONTHLY PERFORMANCE

| Year | Jan | Feb | Mar | Apr | May | Jun | Jul | Aug | Sep | Oct | Nov | Dec | YTD | DD |
|---|---|---|---|---|---|---|---|---|---|---|---|---|---|---|
| 2012 | 0.00 | 0.06 | -0.07 | -0.38 | -0.61 | 0.00 | 1.55 | 0.55 | 0.57 | | | | 1.67 | -1.06 |
| 2011 | 2.57 | 3.37 | -0.09 | 3.66 | -1.98 | -1.18 | 1.24 | 0.64 | -1.90 | -0.03 | 0.00 | 0.00 | 6.28 | -3.21 |
| 2010 | -1.67 | 0.96 | 1.96 | 2.86 | -5.91 | 0.04 | 0.52 | 0.79 | 6.27 | 5.08 | -1.78 | 2.12 | 11.21 | -5.91 |
| 2009 | 1.08 | 0.25 | -0.75 | 0.36 | 5.55 | -0.56 | 2.18 | 3.66 | 3.02 | -0.51 | 4.03 | -0.34 | 19.24 | -0.75 |
| 2008 | 8.27 | 18.10 | 0.42 | 1.14 | 3.93 | 2.81 | -4.74 | -2.32 | -0.78 | 2.10 | 3.80 | 0.33 | 36.25 | -7.86 |
| 2007 | -4.35 | 2.34 | -2.67 | -1.41 | 0.06 | 5.15 | 6.13 | -10.73 | 15.84 | 8.32 | 9.06 | 7.84 | 38.59 | -10.73 |
| 2006 | 7.79 | 0.67 | -0.54 | 15.27 | 3.79 | -3.20 | -5.15 | -1.54 | 0.68 | -2.86 | 6.94 | -10.15 | 9.92 | -14.87 |
| 2005 | -5.93 | -1.89 | 3.35 | -9.55 | 6.54 | -3.67 | -3.97 | -2.89 | -2.17 | 1.49 | 6.06 | 7.53 | -10.76 | -22.90 |
| 2004 | 3.13 | 6.56 | 4.44 | -10.36 | 0.06 | -6.29 | -5.93 | 0.63 | 4.11 | -0.77 | 10.94 | -1.64 | 4.88 | -20.93 |
| 2003 | 15.21 | 3.87 | -11.59 | 8.85 | 19.12 | -3.69 | 1.43 | 1.20 | 12.04 | 21.16 | -8.70 | 12.34 | 88.82 | -11.59 |
| 2002 | -4.32 | -8.51 | 7.89 | -15.01 | 14.39 | 18.58 | 19.60 | 1.50 | 12.61 | -9.14 | -20.54 | 11.89 | 9.31 | -27.80 |
| 2001 | -3.81 | -1.52 | -2.87 | -3.20 | -0.42 | 4.91 | 8.71 | -2.68 | 1.29 | 19.21 | -11.17 | 8.11 | 14.39 | -11.17 |
| 2000 | -0.26 | 8.01 | 0.66 | -7.50 | 7.09 | 2.50 | 1.67 | 3.34 | -1.24 | -10.39 | 16.48 | 17.55 | 40.18 | -11.50 |
| 1999 | 4.35 | -1.37 | -3.48 | 9.50 | -16.15 | 3.96 | -0.92 | 23.01 | 7.23 | -5.87 | 5.91 | 0.80 | 24.53 | -16.15 |
| 1998 | 1.30 | -4.55 | -3.27 | -7.84 | -0.05 | -8.06 | 0.77 | 47.13 | 12.24 | 2.19 | -5.56 | -2.82 | 26.31 | -20.11 |
| 1997 | 6.83 | 19.29 | 12.09 | -8.24 | -7.10 | 4.23 | 10.49 | -23.15 | 19.32 | -16.04 | -4.89 | 3.56 | 8.56 | -27.96 |
| 1996 | -5.59 | -13.44 | -21.65 | 44.99 | -30.54 | 11.65 | -0.39 | 0.97 | 30.63 | 37.01 | 10.86 | -17.53 | 18.27 | -35.97 |
| 1995 | -25.79 | -6.54 | 38.90 | 7.36 | -13.59 | 3.70 | -34.45 | -19.52 | -6.98 | -4.91 | 6.80 | 19.39 | -46.04 | -58.19 |
| 1994 | -16.98 | -22.70 | 11.59 | -17.90 | 41.14 | 37.85 | 17.52 | -11.67 | 13.99 | 22.30 | 15.43 | 26.96 | 142.60 | -41.21 |
| 1993 | | | | | | | | | | | 9.47 | 27.47 | 39.54 | N/A |

~ 67 ~

## CAMPBELL & COMPANY

Campbell & Company's track record (that I could find) started in 1983. They have a CAROR of 8.84%. The worst peak to valley drawdown has been 29.5%. If you had invested $100,000 with Campbell in 1983, it would be worth $1,269,568.08 today.

Campbell & Company is a pioneer in systematic managed futures and absolute return investment management. Keith Campbell is the principle of Campbell & Company, one of the longest running commodity trading firms and also one of the largest. They transformed their organization for institutions and sovereign wealth funds over the years.

There is a strong focus on research at Campbell & Company. The research efforts are focused to develop new and different approaches to trading, as well as to improve existing strategies. They have six full-time professionals, holding three PhDs spending 100% of their working days to find better ways to make money. Campbell recognizes the markets are always constantly changing and that they need to stay on the cutting edge if we want to remain as an industry leader.

*The Bible of Compounding Money*

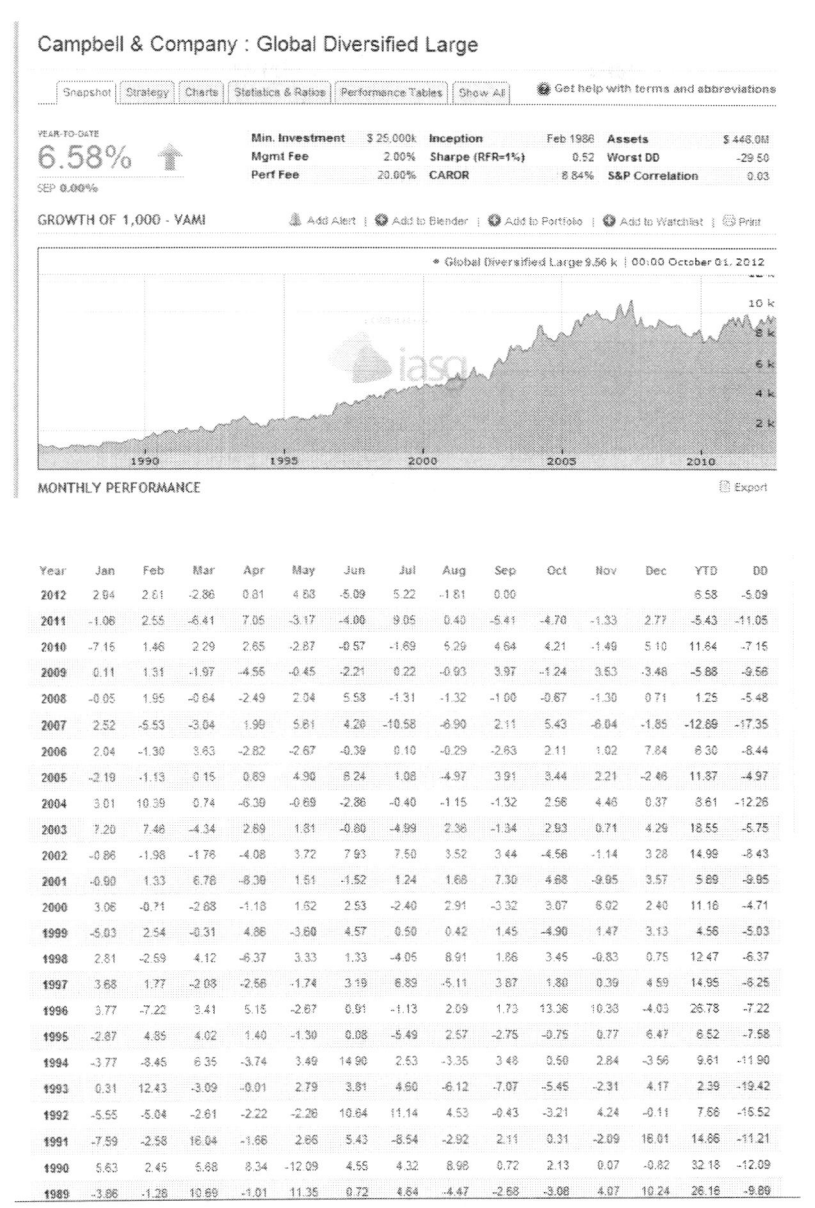

## Campbell & Company : Global Diversified Large

| YEAR-TO-DATE | | | |
|---|---|---|---|
| **6.58%** ↑ | Min. Investment $25,000k | Inception Feb 1988 | Assets $446.0M |
| | Mgmt Fee 2.00% | Sharpe (RFR=1%) 0.52 | Worst DD -29.50 |
| SEP 0.00% | Perf Fee 20.00% | CAROR 8.84% | S&P Correlation 0.03 |

**GROWTH OF 1,000 - VAMI**

*Global Diversified Large 9.56 k | 00:00 October 01, 2012*

**MONTHLY PERFORMANCE**

| Year | Jan | Feb | Mar | Apr | May | Jun | Jul | Aug | Sep | Oct | Nov | Dec | YTD | DD |
|---|---|---|---|---|---|---|---|---|---|---|---|---|---|---|
| 2012 | 2.04 | 2.81 | -2.86 | 0.81 | 4.63 | -5.09 | 5.22 | -1.81 | 0.00 | | | | 6.58 | -5.09 |
| 2011 | -1.06 | 2.55 | -6.41 | 7.05 | -3.17 | -4.00 | 9.05 | 0.40 | -5.41 | -4.70 | -1.33 | 2.77 | -5.43 | -11.05 |
| 2010 | -7.15 | 1.46 | 2.29 | 2.65 | -2.87 | -0.57 | -1.69 | 5.29 | 4.64 | 4.21 | -1.49 | 5.10 | 11.64 | -7.15 |
| 2009 | 0.11 | 1.31 | -1.97 | -4.55 | -0.45 | -2.21 | 0.22 | -0.93 | 3.97 | -1.24 | 3.53 | -3.48 | -5.88 | -9.56 |
| 2008 | -0.05 | 1.95 | -0.64 | -2.49 | 2.04 | 5.58 | -1.31 | -1.32 | -1.00 | -0.67 | -1.30 | 0.71 | 1.25 | -5.48 |
| 2007 | 2.52 | -5.53 | -3.04 | 1.99 | 5.81 | 4.28 | -10.58 | -6.90 | 2.11 | 5.43 | -6.04 | -1.85 | -12.89 | -17.35 |
| 2006 | 2.04 | -1.30 | 3.63 | -2.82 | -2.67 | -0.39 | 0.10 | -0.29 | -2.63 | 2.11 | 1.02 | 7.84 | 6.30 | -8.44 |
| 2005 | -2.19 | -1.13 | 0.15 | 0.89 | 4.90 | 8.24 | 1.08 | -4.97 | 3.91 | 3.44 | 2.21 | -2.46 | 11.37 | -4.97 |
| 2004 | 3.01 | 10.39 | 0.74 | -6.39 | -0.69 | -2.86 | -0.40 | -1.15 | -1.32 | 2.56 | 4.46 | 0.37 | 8.61 | -12.26 |
| 2003 | 7.20 | 7.46 | -4.34 | 2.69 | 1.81 | -0.80 | -4.99 | 2.36 | -1.34 | 2.93 | 0.71 | 4.29 | 18.55 | -5.75 |
| 2002 | -0.86 | -1.98 | -1.76 | -4.08 | 3.72 | 7.93 | 7.50 | 3.52 | 3.44 | -4.56 | -1.14 | 3.28 | 14.99 | -8.43 |
| 2001 | -0.90 | 1.33 | 6.78 | -8.39 | 1.51 | -1.52 | 1.24 | 1.68 | 7.30 | 4.68 | -9.95 | 3.57 | 5.89 | -9.95 |
| 2000 | 3.06 | -0.71 | -2.68 | -1.18 | 1.62 | 2.53 | -2.40 | 2.91 | -3.32 | 3.07 | 6.02 | 2.40 | 11.16 | -4.71 |
| 1999 | -5.03 | 2.54 | -0.31 | 4.86 | -3.60 | 4.57 | 0.50 | 0.42 | 1.45 | -4.90 | 1.47 | 3.13 | 4.56 | -5.03 |
| 1998 | 2.81 | -2.59 | 4.12 | -6.37 | 3.33 | 1.33 | -4.05 | 8.91 | 1.86 | 3.45 | -0.83 | 0.75 | 12.47 | -6.37 |
| 1997 | 3.68 | 1.77 | -2.08 | -2.56 | -1.74 | 3.19 | 6.89 | -5.11 | 3.87 | 1.80 | 0.39 | 4.59 | 14.95 | -6.25 |
| 1996 | 3.77 | -7.22 | 3.41 | 5.15 | -2.67 | 0.91 | -1.13 | 2.09 | 1.73 | 13.36 | 10.33 | -4.03 | 26.78 | -7.22 |
| 1995 | -2.87 | 4.85 | 4.02 | 1.40 | -1.30 | 0.08 | -5.49 | 2.57 | -2.75 | -0.75 | 0.77 | 6.47 | 6.52 | -7.58 |
| 1994 | -3.77 | -8.45 | 6.35 | -3.74 | 3.49 | 14.90 | 2.53 | -3.35 | 3.46 | 0.50 | 2.84 | -3.56 | 9.61 | -11.90 |
| 1993 | 0.31 | 12.43 | -3.09 | -0.01 | 2.79 | 3.81 | 4.60 | -6.12 | -7.07 | -5.45 | -2.31 | 4.17 | 2.39 | -19.42 |
| 1992 | -5.55 | -5.04 | -2.61 | -2.22 | -2.26 | 10.84 | 11.14 | 4.53 | -0.43 | -3.21 | 4.24 | -0.11 | 7.66 | -16.52 |
| 1991 | -7.59 | -2.58 | 16.04 | -1.66 | 2.66 | 5.43 | -8.54 | -2.92 | 2.11 | 0.31 | -2.09 | 16.01 | 14.86 | -11.21 |
| 1990 | 5.63 | 2.45 | 5.68 | 8.34 | -12.09 | 4.55 | 4.32 | 8.98 | 0.72 | 2.13 | 0.07 | -0.82 | 32.18 | -12.09 |
| 1989 | -3.86 | -1.26 | 10.69 | -1.01 | 11.35 | 0.72 | 4.84 | -4.47 | -2.68 | -3.08 | 4.07 | 10.24 | 26.16 | -9.80 |

PAST PERFORMANCE IS NOT NECESSARILY INDICATIVE OF FUTURE RESULTS. THE RISK OF LOSS IN TRADING COMMODITY FUTURES, OPTIONS, AND FOREIGN EXCHANGE ("FOREX") IS SUBSTANTIAL.

*Andy Abraham*

# EMC CAPITAL MANAGEMENT

EMC has been trading since 1985. They have a CAROR of 21.63%. The worst peak to valley draw down has been 45.35%. If you had invested $100,000 with EMC in 1985, it would be worth $35,581,250.09 today.

Most male traders know that women make better traders. What is discussed is that women control their emotions while trading much better than men. There is nothing to prove. No fear of being wrong and it seems easier for women to exit trades that do not work quicker than men. These psychological differences increase returns. There are not a lot of women in the industry and those I can think of offhand are Elizabeth Cheval and Linda Raschke. Both of them are extremely successful and have been trading for decades. I have been an investor of Linda Raschke for a long period of time. I have not invested yet with Elizabeth but she is on my radar screen.

Elizabeth has a B.S. Mathematics degree from Lawrence University. There is a similarity with a math degree among many successful traders but is proved over and over again is that Wharton is not a prerequisite for trading success. Elizabeth started her trading career at the Chicago Board of Trade. She started her career working for Richard Dennis, the famed trader and founder of the turtle program. Ms. Cheval has invested in futures since 1983, when she began investing in financial futures for her own account.

In 1984, she was lucky enough to be chosen for the investment management-training program offered by C&D Commodities. Some traders did much better than others in the turtle program. Elizabeth did fantastic however with volatility. There were three years in a row—1986, 1987 and 1988 that Elizabeth returned 134%, 178% and 124%.

*The Bible of Compounding Money*

In 1990, probably due to the volatilities in the markets she returned an astonishing 187%. As much as she had hit the ball out of the park she experienced deep drawdowns in the range of mid 40%.

The results of the turtle traders varied tremendously even though they all went through the same two-week course. After the turtle program mentor was disbanded in 1988, Elizabeth formed EMC. EMC, which stand for her initials, was incorporated in May 1988.

The EMC trading models invest in over eighty futures markets including stock indices, currencies, financial instruments, metals, agricultural, meats, energies and soft commodities. The concept of being diversified is evident in EMC. Elizabeth is available to trade any of the opportunities that become present in these markets.

Her proprietary systems include ideas of using multi time frames and multi systems. She uses strong risk management.

Her proprietary risk algorithms are based on account equity (core equity), open trade equity, trailing return and drawdown. Additionally EMC utilizes proprietary trade-specific risk controls that are independent of the overall portfolio leverage. Market weight factors, system weight factors and market volatility factors are applied individually to each signal taken at the time of buy or sell.

The goal of most managers is to try to mitigate some of the volatilities of returns. After her big drawdown of 45% she added filters and enhancement to their Classic Program in July of 1996. The goal of these enhancements was to maintain returns consistent with long-term average returns while at the same time trying to reduce the expected drawdown levels and volatility by approximately one half.

This is what smart traders do. After a negative run successful CTAs evaluate what happen and "try" to add filters to mitigate some of these drawdown issues. Her worst drawdown after 1996 was approximately 25%.

*The Bible of Compounding Money*

## EMC Capital Management : Classic

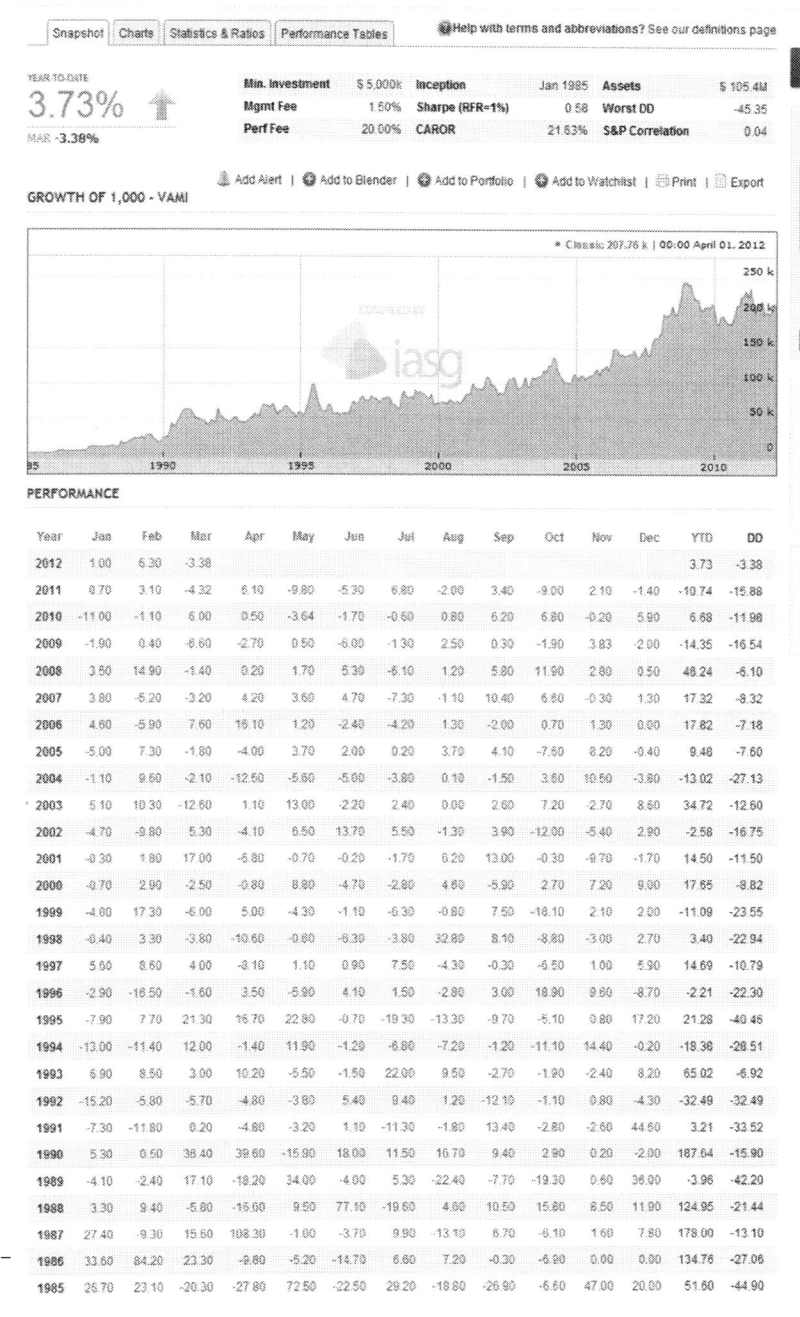

| Snapshot | Charts | Statistics & Ratios | Performance Tables |

Help with terms and abbreviations? See our definitions page

**YEAR-TO-DATE**
**3.73%** ↑
MAR -3.38%

| | | | |
|---|---|---|---|
| Min. Investment | $ 5,000k | Inception | Jan 1985 | Assets | $ 105.4M |
| Mgmt Fee | 1.50% | Sharpe (RFR=1%) | 0.58 | Worst DD | -45.35 |
| Perf Fee | 20.00% | CAROR | 21.63% | S&P Correlation | 0.04 |

Add Alert | Add to Blender | Add to Portfolio | Add to Watchlist | Print | Export

**GROWTH OF 1,000 - VAMI**

* Classic 207.76 k | 00:00 April 01, 2012

### PERFORMANCE

| Year | Jan | Feb | Mar | Apr | May | Jun | Jul | Aug | Sep | Oct | Nov | Dec | YTD | DD |
|---|---|---|---|---|---|---|---|---|---|---|---|---|---|---|
| 2012 | 1.00 | 6.30 | -3.38 | | | | | | | | | | 3.73 | -3.38 |
| 2011 | 0.70 | 3.10 | -4.32 | 6.10 | -9.80 | -5.30 | 6.80 | -2.00 | 3.40 | -9.00 | 2.10 | -1.40 | -10.74 | -15.88 |
| 2010 | -11.00 | -1.10 | 6.00 | 0.50 | -3.64 | -1.70 | -0.60 | 0.80 | 6.20 | 6.80 | -0.20 | 5.90 | 6.68 | -11.96 |
| 2009 | -1.90 | 0.40 | -6.60 | -2.70 | 0.50 | -6.00 | -1.30 | 2.50 | 0.30 | -1.90 | 3.83 | -2.00 | -14.35 | -16.54 |
| 2008 | 3.50 | 14.90 | -1.40 | 0.20 | 1.70 | 5.30 | -6.10 | 1.20 | 5.80 | 11.90 | 2.80 | 0.50 | 48.24 | -6.10 |
| 2007 | 3.80 | -5.20 | -3.20 | 4.20 | 3.60 | 4.70 | -7.30 | -1.10 | 10.40 | 6.60 | -0.30 | 1.30 | 17.32 | -8.32 |
| 2006 | 4.60 | -5.90 | 7.60 | 16.10 | 1.20 | -2.40 | -4.20 | 1.30 | -2.00 | 0.70 | 1.30 | 0.00 | 17.82 | -7.18 |
| 2005 | -5.00 | 7.30 | -1.80 | -4.00 | 3.70 | 2.00 | 0.20 | 3.70 | 4.10 | -7.60 | 8.20 | -0.40 | 9.48 | -7.60 |
| 2004 | -1.10 | 9.60 | -2.10 | -12.50 | -5.60 | -5.00 | -3.80 | 0.10 | -1.50 | 3.60 | 10.50 | -3.80 | -13.02 | -27.13 |
| 2003 | 5.10 | 19.30 | -12.60 | 1.10 | 13.00 | -2.20 | 2.40 | 0.00 | 2.60 | 7.20 | -2.70 | 8.60 | 34.72 | -12.60 |
| 2002 | -4.70 | -9.80 | 5.30 | -4.10 | 6.50 | 13.70 | 5.50 | -1.30 | 3.90 | -12.00 | -5.40 | 2.90 | -2.58 | -16.75 |
| 2001 | -0.30 | 1.80 | 17.00 | -6.80 | -0.70 | -0.20 | -1.70 | 6.20 | 13.00 | -0.30 | -9.70 | -1.70 | 14.50 | -11.50 |
| 2000 | -0.70 | 2.90 | -2.50 | -0.80 | 8.80 | -4.70 | -2.80 | 4.60 | -5.90 | 2.70 | 7.20 | 9.00 | 17.65 | -8.82 |
| 1999 | -4.60 | 17.30 | -6.00 | 5.00 | -4.30 | -1.10 | -6.30 | -0.80 | 7.50 | -18.10 | 2.10 | 2.00 | -11.09 | -23.55 |
| 1998 | -0.40 | 3.30 | -3.80 | -10.60 | -0.80 | -6.30 | -3.80 | 32.80 | 8.10 | -8.80 | -3.00 | 2.70 | 3.40 | -22.94 |
| 1997 | 5.60 | 8.60 | 4.00 | -3.10 | 1.10 | 0.90 | 7.50 | -4.30 | -0.30 | -6.50 | 1.00 | 5.90 | 14.69 | -10.79 |
| 1996 | -2.90 | -16.50 | -1.60 | 3.50 | -5.90 | 4.10 | 1.50 | -2.80 | 3.00 | 18.90 | 9.60 | -8.70 | -2.21 | -22.30 |
| 1995 | -7.90 | 7.70 | 21.30 | 16.70 | 22.80 | -0.70 | -19.30 | -13.30 | -9.70 | -5.10 | 0.80 | 17.20 | 21.28 | -40.46 |
| 1994 | -13.00 | -11.40 | 12.00 | -1.40 | 11.90 | -1.20 | -6.80 | -7.20 | -1.20 | -11.10 | 14.40 | -0.20 | -18.38 | -28.51 |
| 1993 | 6.90 | 8.50 | 3.00 | 10.20 | -5.50 | -1.50 | 22.00 | 9.50 | -2.70 | -1.90 | -2.40 | 8.20 | 65.02 | -6.92 |
| 1992 | -15.20 | -5.80 | -5.70 | -4.80 | -3.80 | 5.40 | 9.40 | 1.20 | -12.10 | -1.10 | 0.80 | -4.30 | -32.49 | -32.49 |
| 1991 | -7.30 | -11.80 | 0.20 | -4.80 | -3.20 | 1.10 | -11.30 | -1.80 | 13.40 | -2.80 | -2.60 | 44.60 | 3.21 | -33.52 |
| 1990 | 5.30 | 0.50 | 38.40 | 39.60 | -15.90 | 18.00 | 11.50 | 16.70 | 9.40 | 2.90 | 0.20 | -2.00 | 187.64 | -15.90 |
| 1989 | -4.10 | -2.40 | 17.10 | -18.20 | 34.00 | -4.00 | 5.30 | -22.40 | -7.70 | -19.30 | 0.60 | 36.00 | -3.96 | -42.20 |
| 1988 | 3.30 | 9.40 | -5.60 | -15.60 | 9.50 | 77.10 | -19.60 | 4.60 | 10.50 | 15.60 | 6.50 | 11.90 | 124.95 | -21.44 |
| 1987 | 27.40 | -9.30 | 15.60 | 108.30 | -1.00 | -3.70 | 9.90 | -13.10 | 6.70 | -6.10 | 1.60 | 7.80 | 178.00 | -13.10 |
| 1986 | 33.60 | 84.20 | 23.30 | -9.80 | -5.20 | -14.70 | 6.60 | 7.20 | -0.30 | -6.90 | 0.00 | 0.00 | 134.76 | -27.06 |
| 1985 | 26.70 | 23.10 | -26.30 | -27.80 | 72.50 | -22.50 | 29.20 | -18.80 | -26.90 | -6.60 | 47.00 | 20.00 | 51.60 | -44.90 |

PAST PERFORMANCE IS NOT NECESSARILY INDICATIVE OF FUTURE RESULTS. THE RISK OF LOSS IN TRADING COMMODITY FUTURES, OPTIONS, AND FOREIGN EXCHANGE ("FOREX") IS SUBSTANTIAL.

# LYNX ASSET MANAGEMENT AB

Lynx has been trading since 2000. They have a CAROR of 13.47%. The worst peak to valley draw down has been 11.59%. If you had invested $100,000 with Lynx in 2000, it would be worth $455,588.40 today.

Lynx is jointly run by Jonas Bengtsson, Svante Bergström, Anders Holst, Jesper Sandin and Martin Sandquis out of Stockholm Sweden. It is hard to find out any information regarding Lynx as their site is password protected. It states on their site only that Lynx Asset Management AB is a quant-driven asset management firm that has a 24h trading operation and invests in futures markets globally, and is managed by Brummer & Partners.

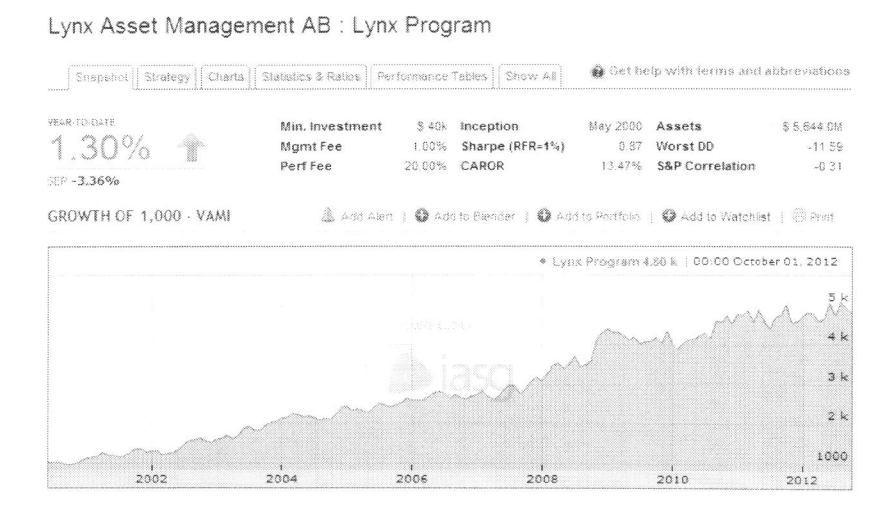

Lynx Asset Management AB : Lynx Program

| | | | | |
|---|---|---|---|---|
| YEAR-TO-DATE | Min. Investment | $ 40k | Inception | May 2000 | Assets | $ 5,644.0M |
| 1.30% | Mgmt Fee | 1.00% | Sharpe (RFR=1%) | 0.87 | Worst DD | -11.59 |
| SEP -3.36% | Perf Fee | 20.00% | CAROR | 13.47% | S&P Correlation | -0.31 |

GROWTH OF 1,000 - VAMI

* Lynx Program 4.80 k | 00:00 October 01, 2012

PAST PERFORMANCE IS NOT NECESSARILY INDICATIVE OF FUTURE RESULTS. THE RISK OF LOSS IN TRADING COMMODITY FUTURES, OPTIONS, AND FOREIGN EXCHANGE ("FOREX") IS SUBSTANTIAL.

*The Bible of Compounding Money*

MONTHLY PERFORMANCE

| Year | Jan | Feb | Mar | Apr | May | Jun | Jul | Aug | Sep | Oct | Nov | Dec | YTD | DD |
|---|---|---|---|---|---|---|---|---|---|---|---|---|---|---|
| 2012 | 1.78 | -0.57 | -4.16 | 2.01 | 7.84 | -6.05 | 6.97 | -2.24 | -3.36 | | | | 1.30 | -6.05 |
| 2011 | -0.60 | 2.39 | -5.76 | 6.56 | -5.90 | -4.10 | 6.83 | 0.95 | 5.41 | -9.12 | 0.91 | 3.06 | -0.90 | -9.76 |
| 2010 | -3.35 | 3.94 | 1.97 | 0.71 | 1.78 | 1.89 | -3.04 | 10.38 | -1.04 | 3.78 | -4.39 | 5.45 | 18.53 | -4.39 |
| 2009 | -1.90 | 0.23 | -2.40 | -2.36 | 1.82 | -4.06 | 1.31 | 0.51 | 2.14 | -3.72 | 7.71 | -7.34 | -8.52 | -8.52 |
| 2008 | 6.19 | 6.02 | 1.57 | -3.83 | 3.45 | 5.16 | -7.20 | 2.01 | 2.71 | 14.90 | 3.86 | 2.48 | 42.26 | -7.20 |
| 2007 | 3.97 | -4.69 | -3.89 | 3.38 | 6.93 | 4.96 | -1.97 | -5.81 | 4.35 | 6.82 | 2.83 | -2.43 | 13.21 | -8.40 |
| 2006 | 0.16 | -0.13 | 3.44 | 3.24 | 1.92 | -2.07 | -4.60 | 3.97 | -3.15 | -1.04 | 2.71 | 1.19 | 5.34 | -6.90 |
| 2005 | -4.18 | 1.61 | -2.10 | -1.20 | 5.60 | 3.58 | -1.35 | -1.60 | 1.53 | 1.96 | 4.48 | -1.44 | 6.59 | -5.83 |
| 2004 | 1.19 | 4.69 | -1.69 | -2.05 | 0.83 | -2.20 | -3.35 | 2.12 | -0.60 | 7.32 | 6.45 | 1.09 | 13.97 | -8.22 |
| 2003 | 2.99 | 3.99 | -4.52 | 4.18 | 10.51 | 3.25 | -5.32 | 0.41 | 6.45 | 4.29 | 1.14 | 3.69 | 34.54 | -5.32 |
| 2002 | 0.40 | -7.30 | 2.70 | 1.60 | 5.65 | 10.75 | 5.27 | 1.48 | 3.35 | -4.56 | -2.85 | 4.73 | 21.82 | -7.30 |
| 2001 | 2.06 | 2.69 | 7.09 | -4.66 | -0.49 | -2.68 | 0.77 | 8.02 | 6.81 | 0.25 | -6.35 | 2.36 | 15.78 | -7.67 |
| 2000 | | | | | 3.35 | -2.25 | 0.88 | -4.29 | -1.34 | 3.09 | 5.69 | 7.54 | 12.76 | -6.88 |

PAST PERFORMANCE IS NOT NECESSARILY INDICATIVE OF FUTURE RESULTS. THE RISK OF LOSS IN TRADING COMMODITY FUTURES, OPTIONS, AND FOREIGN EXCHANGE ("FOREX") IS SUBSTANTIAL.

# WINTON CAPITAL MANAGEMENT

Winton has been trading since 1997. They have a CAROR of 15.09%. The worst peak to valley draw down has been 25.59%. If you had invested $100,000 with Winton in 1997, it would be worth $823,310.87 today.

Winton is one of the largest commodity trading firms. Winton was launched with $1.6 million and as of 2011 it held $22.6 billion in assets under management. Ironically Winton lost approximately 13% of its value in the first month of trading but ended the year up 3.49%. In the following three years WCM returned gains of: 52.18% in 1998, 15.07% in 1999 and 10.44% in 2000.

Winton runs mechanical models developed from scientific research and mathematical analysis. It trades on more than 100 global futures exchanges across a wide range of asset classes.

David Harding is the principle behind Winton. David Winton Harding graduated from the University of Cambridge in 1982 with an honors degree in theoretical physics, but decided he wanted to focus on trading. Quoting Harding with his interesting sense of humor he stated, "I wanted a glamorous job when I left college and I liked all the American investment banks, but they all turned me down. I only applied for one other job; that was the job I had to take. It was with British stockbroker Wood Mackenzie. Within three months of my joining, the London International Futures Exchange opened, which seemed a bit more exciting to me".

Harding formed his own managed futures firm, Adam, Harding and Lueck Ltd., which was acquired by Man Group PLC in 1994. He left Man Group in 1996 and founded Winton Capital Management in 1997. Winton has a staff of over 200 people. More than 100 of the firm's employees are academics doing mathematical research, statistical relationships and trading patterns.

Some investors feel very secure in investing in firms like Winton due to their vast size. As much as their returns have been spectacular it leaves one to question the possibility of the continuance of this.

## The Bible of Compounding Money

### Winton Capital Management : Diversified

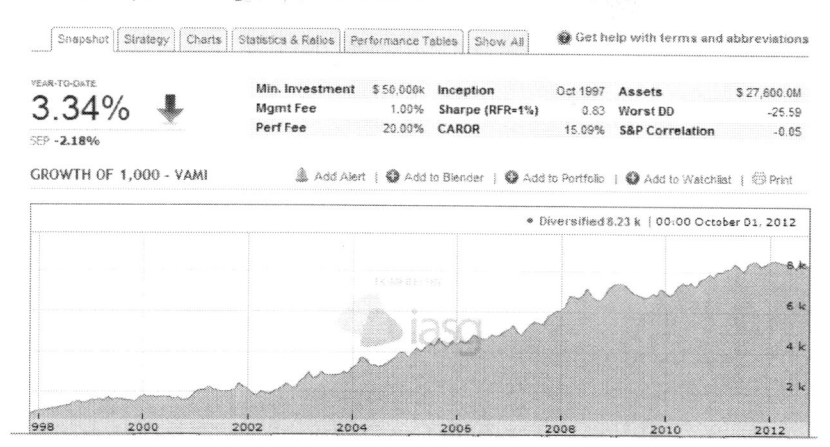

| | | |
|---|---|---|
| Snapshot | Strategy | Charts | Statistics & Ratios | Performance Tables | Show All |

Get help with terms and abbreviations

**YEAR-TO-DATE**
**3.34%** ⬇
SEP **-2.18%**

| | | | | | |
|---|---|---|---|---|---|
| Min. Investment | $ 50,000k | Inception | Oct 1997 | Assets | $ 27,600.0M |
| Mgmt Fee | 1.00% | Sharpe (RFR=1%) | 0.83 | Worst DD | -25.59 |
| Perf Fee | 20.00% | CAROR | 15.09% | S&P Correlation | -0.05 |

**GROWTH OF 1,000 - VAMI**   Add Alert | Add to Blender | Add to Portfolio | Add to Watchlist | Print

*Diversified 8.23 k | 00:00 October 01, 2012*

PAST PERFORMANCE IS NOT NECESSARILY INDICATIVE OF FUTURE RESULTS. THE RISK OF LOSS IN TRADING COMMODITY FUTURES, OPTIONS, AND FOREIGN EXCHANGE ("FOREX") IS SUBSTANTIAL.

### MONTHLY PERFORMANCE                                                                                       Export

| Year | Jan | Feb | Mar | Apr | May | Jun | Jul | Aug | Sep | Oct | Nov | Dec | YTD | DD |
|---|---|---|---|---|---|---|---|---|---|---|---|---|---|---|
| 2012 | 0.63 | -0.83 | -0.68 | 0.12 | -0.22 | -3.17 | 4.41 | -1.29 | -2.18 | | | | -3.34 | -4.72 |
| 2011 | 0.08 | 1.51 | 0.25 | 3.00 | -2.16 | -2.51 | 4.59 | 1.43 | 0.16 | -2.59 | 0.97 | 1.65 | 6.29 | -4.62 |
| 2010 | -2.64 | 2.33 | 4.91 | 1.75 | -1.01 | 1.47 | -2.78 | 4.78 | 0.94 | 2.51 | -2.01 | 3.75 | 14.47 | -2.78 |
| 2009 | 0.99 | -0.21 | -1.64 | -3.01 | -2.03 | -1.26 | -1.52 | 0.32 | 2.85 | -1.59 | 5.12 | -2.45 | -4.64 | -9.31 |
| 2008 | 3.85 | 7.95 | -0.66 | -0.99 | 1.99 | 5.06 | -4.63 | -3.00 | -0.41 | 3.73 | 4.97 | 2.10 | 21.01 | -7.87 |
| 2007 | 3.86 | -5.93 | -3.95 | 6.46 | 5.05 | 1.91 | -1.18 | -0.88 | 6.99 | 2.52 | 2.42 | 0.24 | 17.97 | -9.65 |
| 2006 | 4.20 | -2.58 | 4.01 | 5.66 | -2.94 | -1.17 | -0.47 | 4.54 | -1.10 | 1.48 | 3.24 | 2.14 | 17.84 | -4.53 |
| 2005 | -5.38 | 6.58 | 4.64 | -4.21 | 6.62 | 3.13 | -1.85 | 7.63 | -6.17 | -2.95 | 7.32 | -4.37 | 9.73 | -8.94 |
| 2004 | 2.72 | 11.56 | -0.80 | -8.62 | 0.28 | -2.96 | 1.33 | 3.09 | 5.14 | 4.03 | 6.37 | -0.19 | 22.62 | -11.79 |
| 2003 | 5.95 | 11.95 | -10.80 | 2.45 | 10.19 | -5.20 | -0.68 | 0.62 | 0.28 | 4.72 | -2.48 | 10.27 | 27.76 | -10.80 |
| 2002 | -10.13 | -6.04 | 12.62 | -3.76 | -3.96 | 7.95 | 4.71 | 6.04 | 7.63 | -7.96 | -0.69 | 14.16 | 18.33 | -15.56 |
| 2001 | 4.38 | 0.56 | 7.09 | -5.31 | -2.61 | -2.66 | 0.66 | 0.56 | 4.64 | 13.75 | -7.10 | -5.15 | 7.12 | -11.88 |
| 2000 | -3.96 | 1.72 | -3.28 | 2.06 | -0.26 | -1.27 | -4.58 | 3.23 | -7.76 | 2.09 | 7.33 | 16.81 | 10.43 | -13.72 |
| 1999 | -1.38 | 3.61 | -3.98 | 10.51 | -8.39 | 5.29 | -2.01 | -3.47 | -0.17 | -6.20 | 13.93 | 9.04 | 15.08 | -14.56 |
| 1998 | 1.50 | 3.27 | 7.38 | -1.63 | 8.53 | 2.97 | 1.51 | 10.99 | 4.51 | -5.70 | 1.15 | 9.50 | 52.17 | -5.70 |
| 1997 | | | | | | | | | | -12.97 | 9.96 | 8.14 | 3.49 | -12.97 |

PAST PERFORMANCE IS NOT NECESSARILY INDICATIVE OF FUTURE RESULTS. THE RISK OF LOSS IN TRADING COMMODITY FUTURES, OPTIONS, AND FOREIGN EXCHANGE ("FOREX") IS SUBSTANTIAL.

# COVENANT CAPITAL MANAGEMENT

Covenant has been trading since 1999. Covenant has an original program and the CAROR is 13.82%. The worst peak to valley draw down has been 28.61% in that program. In their aggressive program the CAROR is 22.96% with a drawdown of -20.41%.

If you had invested $100,000 with Covenant in 1999 in their original program, it would be worth $538,073.44 today. If you had invested in the aggressive program which started in 2004, today you would have $522,529.53.

Covenant Capital is a 100% systematic mechanical trading company that looks at a diverse portfolio of the global futures markets. Covenant is managed by Scott Billington as well as Brince Wilford. I have met their marketing people at numerous conferences and they are complete gentlemen.

Alfred Friedberg from Friedberg mercantile group purchased 7½% of the company some years ago. Friedberg has been in the field for decades and is a wonderful stamp of approval.

What shows how competent Covenant's research is and how unique they are is the fact that they are long-biased. When I initially heard this I shied away from them. However after conducting my own research, returns are enhanced and drawdowns diminished when trading from the long side.

*The Bible of Compounding Money*

## Covenant Capital Management of Tennessee LLC : Aggressive Program

| Snapshot | Strategy | Charts | Statistics & Ratios | Performance Tables | Show All |

YEAR-TO-DATE
**10.42%** ↑
SEP 6.25%

| | | | |
|---|---|---|---|
| Min. Investment | $ 3,000k | Inception | Feb 2004 | Assets | $ 104.0M |
| Mgmt Fee | 2.00% | Sharpe (RFR=1%) | 1.05 | Worst DD | -20.41 |
| Perf Fee | 20.00% | CAROR | 22.96% | S&P Correlation | 0.13 |

### GROWTH OF 1,000 - VAMI

* Aggressive Program 6.00 k | 00:00 October 01, 2012

### MONTHLY PERFORMANCE

| Year | Jan | Feb | Mar | Apr | May | Jun | Jul | Aug | Sep | Oct | Nov | Dec | YTD | DD |
|---|---|---|---|---|---|---|---|---|---|---|---|---|---|---|
| 2012 | -1.42 | 2.74 | -2.82 | -4.02 | 2.36 | -5.89 | 11.94 | 2.02 | 6.25 | | | | 10.42 | -10.15 |
| 2011 | -2.05 | 2.40 | -0.89 | 5.51 | -4.88 | -2.52 | 2.20 | 2.08 | -0.54 | -4.47 | 1.14 | 0.88 | -1.64 | -8.09 |
| 2010 | -5.88 | 0.09 | -1.66 | 5.42 | -0.45 | 0.44 | -0.34 | 1.76 | 10.54 | 6.82 | -0.61 | 7.08 | 24.45 | -7.36 |
| 2009 | 3.27 | 1.40 | -5.13 | 2.82 | 9.06 | -3.96 | 1.89 | 10.02 | 3.40 | -6.92 | 12.29 | -2.21 | 26.75 | -6.92 |
| 2008 | 5.26 | 21.53 | -5.01 | 3.92 | 3.83 | 6.38 | -7.46 | -5.42 | 0.80 | 3.40 | 0.49 | -0.24 | 27.55 | -12.48 |
| 2007 | -4.70 | 0.81 | -9.69 | 8.50 | 0.60 | 0.45 | 3.66 | -9.69 | 12.42 | 6.15 | -0.03 | -2.82 | 4.09 | -13.24 |
| 2006 | 8.49 | -6.77 | 0.57 | 0.04 | -8.71 | -0.92 | -1.94 | 0.40 | 0.65 | 3.36 | 1.36 | 4.15 | -0.48 | -16.80 |
| 2005 | -2.77 | 17.12 | 2.19 | 2.85 | 6.19 | 0.97 | 3.84 | 3.72 | 9.36 | -0.78 | 14.15 | 10.12 | 88.52 | -2.77 |
| 2004 | | 1.28 | 6.97 | -5.57 | -3.60 | 3.32 | -5.25 | 4.46 | 4.13 | -1.51 | 23.11 | 10.34 | 40.50 | -10.89 |

PAST PERFORMANCE IS NOT NECESSARILY INDICATIVE OF FUTURE RESULTS. THE RISK OF LOSS IN TRADING COMMODITY FUTURES, OPTIONS, AND FOREIGN EXCHANGE ("FOREX") IS SUBSTANTIAL.

*Andy Abraham*

## Covenant Capital Management of Tennessee LLC : Original Program

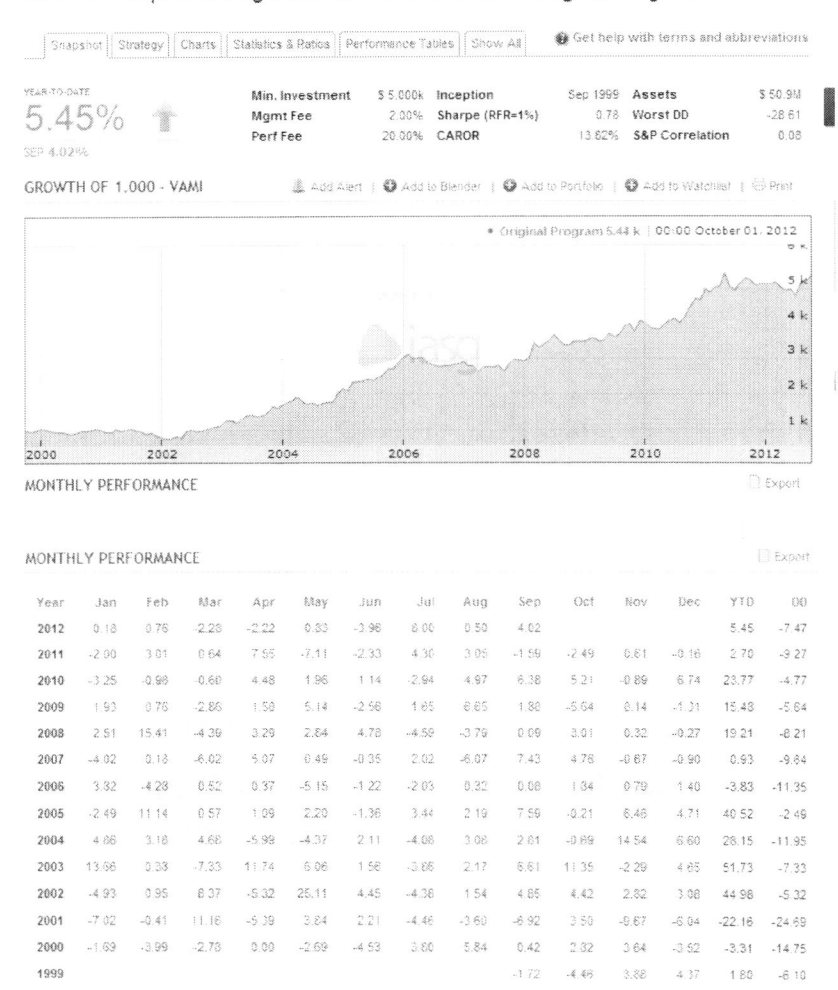

| | | | |
|---|---|---|---|
| **YEAR-TO-DATE** | Min. Investment $5,000k | Inception Sep 1999 | Assets $50.9M |
| **5.45%** ↑ | Mgmt Fee 2.00% | Sharpe (RFR=1%) 0.78 | Worst DD -28.61 |
| SEP 4.02% | Perf Fee 20.00% | CAROR 13.62% | S&P Correlation 0.08 |

**GROWTH OF 1,000 - VAMI**

*Chart: Original Program 5.44 k | 00:00 October 01, 2012, showing growth from 2000 to 2012, reaching ~5k*

### MONTHLY PERFORMANCE

| Year | Jan | Feb | Mar | Apr | May | Jun | Jul | Aug | Sep | Oct | Nov | Dec | YTD | DD |
|---|---|---|---|---|---|---|---|---|---|---|---|---|---|---|
| 2012 | 0.18 | 0.76 | -2.28 | -2.22 | 0.83 | -3.98 | 8.00 | 0.50 | 4.02 | | | | 5.45 | -7.47 |
| 2011 | -2.00 | 3.01 | 0.64 | 7.55 | -7.11 | -2.33 | 4.30 | 3.09 | -1.59 | -2.49 | 0.81 | -0.16 | 2.70 | -9.27 |
| 2010 | -3.25 | -0.98 | -0.60 | 4.48 | 1.96 | 1.14 | -2.94 | 4.97 | 6.38 | 5.21 | -0.89 | 6.74 | 23.77 | -4.77 |
| 2009 | 1.93 | 0.76 | -2.86 | 1.58 | 5.14 | -2.58 | 1.65 | 8.65 | 1.80 | -5.64 | 0.14 | -1.31 | 15.48 | -5.64 |
| 2008 | 2.51 | 15.41 | -4.39 | 3.29 | 2.84 | 4.78 | -4.59 | -3.79 | 0.09 | 3.01 | 0.32 | -0.27 | 19.21 | -8.21 |
| 2007 | -4.02 | 0.18 | -6.02 | 5.07 | 0.49 | -0.35 | 2.02 | -6.07 | 7.43 | 4.78 | -0.67 | -0.90 | 0.93 | -9.64 |
| 2006 | 3.32 | -4.28 | 0.52 | 8.37 | -5.15 | -1.22 | -2.03 | 0.32 | 0.08 | 1.34 | 0.79 | 1.40 | -3.83 | -11.35 |
| 2005 | -2.49 | 11.14 | 0.57 | 1.09 | 2.20 | -1.36 | 3.44 | 2.19 | 7.59 | -0.21 | 6.46 | 4.71 | 40.52 | -2.49 |
| 2004 | 4.06 | 3.18 | 4.68 | -5.99 | -4.37 | 2.11 | -4.08 | 3.08 | 2.61 | -0.69 | 14.54 | 6.60 | 26.15 | -11.95 |
| 2003 | 13.66 | 0.33 | -7.33 | 11.74 | 6.06 | 1.58 | -3.86 | 2.17 | 6.61 | 11.35 | -2.29 | 4.85 | 51.73 | -7.33 |
| 2002 | -4.93 | 0.95 | 8.37 | -5.32 | 25.11 | 4.45 | -4.38 | 1.54 | 4.85 | 4.42 | 2.82 | 3.08 | 44.98 | -5.32 |
| 2001 | -7.02 | -0.41 | 11.16 | -5.39 | 3.84 | 2.21 | -4.46 | -3.60 | -6.92 | 3.50 | -9.67 | -6.04 | -22.16 | -24.69 |
| 2000 | -1.69 | -3.99 | -2.78 | 0.00 | -2.69 | -4.53 | 3.80 | 5.84 | 0.42 | 2.32 | 3.64 | -3.52 | -3.31 | -14.75 |
| 1999 | | | | | | | | | -1.72 | -4.46 | 3.88 | 4.37 | 1.80 | -6.10 |

PAST PERFORMANCE IS NOT NECESSARILY INDICATIVE OF FUTURE RESULTS. THE RISK OF LOSS IN TRADING COMMODITY FUTURES, OPTIONS, AND FOREIGN EXCHANGE ("FOREX") IS SUBSTANTIAL.

*The Bible of Compounding Money*

# BLACKWATER CAPITAL MANAGEMENT

Blackwater has been trading since 2005. Their program has a CAROR of 11.6%. The worst peak to valley draw down has been 25.18%. If you had invested $100,000 with Blackwater in 2005, it would be worth $215,600.30 today.

I have included Blackwater due to the pedigree and experience of the perspective managers, even though they are slightly short of my 10 year rule. Their fund is almost 8 years old.

Blackwater Capital Management is managed by Jeff Austin and Andy Silowitz. The two partners met at Eagle and jointly worked on system development. In conjunction of gaining their pedigree while at Eagle they honed their skills of trading. They decided to go out on their own and co-founded Blackwater Capital Management in 2005. The pedigree or learning curve was passed from mentor to student.

Eagle Trading's principle is Menachem Sternberg. Sternberg was the head trader for the Bruce Kovner's fund Caxton. Bruce Kovner was featured in the Market Wizards book by Jack Schwager. This is a common thread with successful traders.

The system that is run by Blackwater is a medium to long-term pattern recognition program that trades 45 markets with strict profit targets. The model uses price and volatility patterns as well as some breakout elements. As in many other commodity trading advisors they use multiple models. After launching the program in 2005 they added a second model that is longer term. Quoting Jeff, "It is two models and two signals. The second model is based on the same structure; the patterns that we are looking for are a bit bigger. Once we hit these profit objectives we are switching to a proprietary momentum indicator that tells us when we view the markets as stalling. If the markets are screaming we will stay with the trade until we see any kind of weakness."

What is ironic to me is that they do not use trailing stops. They have profit targets and utilize wide stops.

Both managers have had long careers in the industry. Jeff started his career working on the floor of the Chicago Mercantile Exchange in 1994, taking care of the CTA business for Dean Witter. Andy traded spot forex and forex options. Jeff left the floor and gained further experience at Rotella Capital, a large commodity trading advisor. After that he started working at Eagle Trading Systems in Princeton, N.J.

**Blackwater Capital Management : Global Program**

YEAR TO DATE: **14.08%** ↓
SEP -2.94%

| | | |
|---|---|---|
| Min. Investment | $5,000k | |
| Mgmt Fee | 2.00% | |
| Perf Fee | 20.00% | |

| | | |
|---|---|---|
| Inception | Jul 2005 | |
| Sharpe (RFR=1%) | 0.64 | |
| CAROR | 11.80% | |

| | | |
|---|---|---|
| Assets | $480.0M | |
| Worst DD | -25.18 | |
| S&P Correlation | -0.11 | |

GROWTH OF 1,000 - VAMI

**MONTHLY PERFORMANCE**

| Year | Jan | Feb | Mar | Apr | May | Jun | Jul | Aug | Sep | Oct | Nov | Dec | YTD | DD |
|------|-----|-----|-----|-----|-----|-----|-----|-----|-----|-----|-----|-----|-----|-----|
| 2012 | -3.16 | 2.63 | -5.12 | -0.91 | 4.54 | -12.41 | 5.96 | -2.36 | -2.94 | | | | -14.06 | -14.46 |
| 2011 | 2.27 | 1.57 | -1.05 | 8.06 | -5.48 | -4.47 | 7.29 | -2.73 | 10.29 | -10.12 | -3.57 | 0.92 | 1.02 | -13.33 |
| 2010 | -5.75 | 0.60 | 5.66 | -3.87 | -1.65 | 1.49 | -4.85 | 0.04 | 9.73 | 1.17 | -4.37 | 12.02 | 8.82 | -6.70 |
| 2009 | -0.67 | -1.40 | -0.06 | 2.26 | 15.12 | -1.23 | 5.18 | 0.74 | 3.74 | -2.29 | 5.46 | -2.21 | 15.99 | -9.95 |
| 2008 | 9.29 | 10.98 | 2.95 | 0.71 | 2.14 | 3.57 | -5.73 | 1.02 | 8.23 | 10.77 | 1.42 | 1.02 | 55.61 | -5.73 |
| 2007 | 1.43 | 0.33 | 2.14 | 3.82 | 3.06 | 8.67 | 0.25 | -9.41 | 3.48 | 7.17 | -1.34 | -0.29 | 23.55 | -9.41 |
| 2006 | -2.58 | 0.05 | -0.97 | 11.60 | 0.04 | 1.35 | -3.51 | -0.60 | 1.03 | 2.63 | 1.35 | 3.85 | 14.32 | -4.09 |
| 2005 | | | | | | | 0.56 | 3.93 | -1.53 | -1.73 | -0.47 | -8.64 | -7.96 | -12.05 |

PAST PERFORMANCE IS NOT NECESSARILY INDICATIVE OF FUTURE RESULTS. THE RISK OF LOSS IN TRADING COMMODITY FUTURES, OPTIONS, AND FOREIGN EXCHANGE ("FOREX") IS SUBSTANTIAL.

*The Bible of Compounding Money*

## DRURY CAPITAL

Drury has been trading since 1997. They have a CAROR of 11.45%. They have experienced a rough two year period which has lowered their CAROR. The worst peak to valley draw down has been 32.97%. If you had invested $100,000 with Drury in 1997, it would be worth $508,394.79 today.

Bernard Drury is the principle of Drury Capital. Drury Capital was founded in Illinois in 1992 to trade initially a fundamentally oriented grain trading program. Bernard worked and focused on the grain markets from 1978 before shifting his focus to mechanical and algorithmic system development.

While earning his M.B.A. from the University of Chicago, Bernard became interested in quantitative, systematic approaches to the futures markets. He was fascinated with the benefits that systematic trading could offer. This was a huge difference coming from a discretionary trading background. A computerized system offered consistency as well as diversification of different synergized models. This was the beginning for him to develop and refine his own trend-following system.

Bernard gained further trading experience at Louis Dreyfus Corporation, Commodities Corporation and Goldman Sachs Princeton. His extensive research and development, along with his grain trading skills have served as a foundation for his trading career.

In 1994, he joined Commodities Corporation in Princeton, New Jersey, where he further developed his systematic trend-following trading system, operating as an independent entity within the firm. Through system testing Bernard became a firm believer that systemic ruled based approach to trading could give greater potential than discretionary trading in a single sector. His systematic approach was thoroughly tested, d researched and applied robustly to a broadly diversifie portfolio. He began trading client funds in the Drury Diversified Trend-Following Program in May of 1997.

Bernard's Diversified Trend-Following Program's trading methodology approach is built on elements of trend following and diversification. The thoroughness of research and precision in execution was paramount to his model. The trading system has evolved over time to include additional systems and markets. Initially it only traded 30 markets and was only one system. By May of 2008 he increased the number of markets to 70 and included 3 other systems, making a total of 4 distinct systems.

These enhancements on the methodology have reduced expected volatility from 25% to 18%. As far as risk per trade, there are a large number of small trades; the risk allocation to any given trade is very small. This is a common theme amongst successful trend followers.

The model is broadly diversified across 6 sectors, which are equally weighted approximately. He maintains an exposure to 50% commodities and 50% financials. The portfolio emphasizes diversification by trading metals, agricultural products, foreign exchange, stock index futures, energy products, financial instruments and softs such as cocoa and coffee. The speed of trading is slower than that of longer-term trend followers. As with most successful trend followers, the risk management system emphasizes the protection of equity. His unique methods of risk and money management result in different entry and exit points from other trend followers. His average hold period is 4 months and when trades are working this can be up to 8 months. He, like most other trend followers, exits losing trades quickly. Over a 5 year time period even with all of the inherent drawdowns he has been profitable. His models do suffer as would most trend followers when there is a long period of broad non-directional high volatility price behavior.

*The Bible of Compounding Money*

Drury's minimum for managed accounts is $10,000,000. In addition to the managed accounts he maintains a fund in which an investor can gain access with a minimum of $100,000. He is currently managing approximately $366 million dollars. He went through his worst drawdown in 2004 through 2006. He declined from his peak was -32.52%.

Drury Capital : Diversified Trend-Following Program

| | | | | | | | |
|---|---|---|---|---|---|---|---|
| Min. Investment | $ 5,000k | Inception | May 1997 | Assets | $ 366.1M |
| Mgmt Fee | 2.00% | Sharpe (RFR=1%) | 0.58 | Worst DD | -32.52 |
| Perf Fee | 20.00% | CAROR | 11.45% | S&P Correlation | -0.21 |

YEAR-TO-DATE: **1.91%**
SEP -3.41%

GROWTH OF 1,000 - VAMI

MONTHLY PERFORMANCE

| Year | Jan | Feb | Mar | Apr | May | Jun | Jul | Aug | Sep | Oct | Nov | Dec | YTD | DD |
|---|---|---|---|---|---|---|---|---|---|---|---|---|---|---|
| 2012 | 0.98 | 4.23 | 2.87 | -0.25 | -0.20 | -7.50 | 3.17 | -1.27 | -3.41 | | | | -1.91 | -9.40 |
| 2011 | 3.49 | 6.21 | -7.05 | 3.73 | -9.48 | -7.00 | 0.52 | -8.34 | 8.00 | -8.96 | 1.38 | 2.30 | -16.16 | -26.45 |
| 2010 | -6.25 | -1.95 | 6.12 | 0.38 | -7.87 | 0.18 | -4.88 | 2.66 | 4.19 | 4.12 | -4.19 | 9.06 | 0.65 | -13.51 |
| 2009 | -1.82 | 2.10 | -3.64 | -2.72 | 1.32 | -0.23 | 6.57 | 2.67 | 1.54 | -3.53 | 6.48 | 0.09 | 9.04 | -6.26 |
| 2008 | 6.78 | 11.17 | -3.45 | -5.44 | 7.44 | 6.63 | -9.45 | 1.92 | 16.95 | 23.37 | 6.56 | 5.15 | 75.65 | -13.43 |
| 2007 | 3.33 | -3.51 | 0.98 | 3.21 | 3.39 | 7.79 | -5.60 | -6.31 | 2.93 | -0.87 | 3.56 | -3.29 | 5.05 | -10.81 |
| 2006 | -0.51 | -0.69 | 0.37 | 2.38 | -2.15 | -1.28 | -6.44 | -1.22 | 0.91 | -4.47 | -6.34 | 3.38 | -15.40 | -19.40 |
| 2005 | -2.34 | -4.57 | 0.27 | -5.56 | -4.02 | -2.42 | -0.65 | 1.83 | 1.15 | 0.95 | 7.85 | -2.78 | -10.47 | -17.68 |
| 2004 | 2.45 | 11.09 | 2.33 | -6.97 | -6.06 | -1.21 | -0.45 | -5.85 | 7.78 | -1.13 | 7.20 | -0.36 | 7.27 | -19.08 |
| 2003 | 7.76 | 6.94 | -6.32 | -4.10 | 9.42 | -6.35 | -4.41 | -0.87 | 4.17 | 13.80 | -1.03 | 6.64 | 25.77 | -12.77 |
| 2002 | 0.52 | -1.32 | -2.05 | -3.68 | -5.13 | 11.82 | 4.82 | 3.75 | 4.35 | -9.42 | -5.97 | 10.19 | 5.55 | -14.83 |
| 2001 | -6.20 | 4.95 | 15.46 | -4.19 | 2.41 | 4.97 | -3.66 | 2.03 | 6.23 | 3.82 | -8.34 | 4.82 | 20.62 | -9.34 |
| 2000 | -5.58 | 0.35 | -1.59 | 11.91 | 1.14 | -4.41 | 1.49 | 4.92 | -1.70 | 3.26 | 6.33 | -0.12 | 15.80 | -8.76 |
| 1999 | 0.06 | 6.05 | -2.82 | 4.46 | -5.56 | -0.36 | -4.43 | 8.54 | -3.59 | -1.24 | 5.20 | 4.83 | 10.46 | -10.07 |
| 1998 | 7.84 | 6.11 | 6.60 | -5.48 | 7.78 | 2.20 | -1.38 | 19.34 | -5.22 | -2.74 | 4.25 | 2.46 | 47.21 | -7.82 |
| 1997 | | | | | -4.57 | 14.98 | 12.49 | -2.12 | -2.08 | -9.35 | 17.34 | 3.64 | 30.42 | -13.12 |

PAST PERFORMANCE IS NOT NECESSARILY INDICATIVE OF FUTURE RESULTS. THE RISK OF LOSS IN TRADING COMMODITY FUTURES, OPTIONS, AND FOREIGN EXCHANGE ("FOREX") IS SUBSTANTIAL.

## CHADWICK INVESTMENT GROUP

One might want to consider Chadwick for a watch list. They have a CAROR of 17.19%. The worst peak to valley draw down has been 24.75%. If you had invested $100,000 with Chadwick in 2007, it would be worth $259,025.98 today.

Chadwick Investment Group Inc. was formed by Justin Vandergrift in 2003. Justin's CTA is still small, approximately $11 million dollars, however his firm grasp of trend following it would be easy to believe he could be an upcoming player in the commodity trading advisor world. He has the proverbial characteristics of a successful trend follower, passionate, hungry and driven. Justin has contributed to the books *Trend Following* and *The Complete Turtle Trader* written by Michael Covel. As well he was featured in Michael Covel's latest book *The Little Book of Trading*.

Justin Vandergrift got his start at Futures Truth. I would assume his mentor at Futures Truth was John Hill Senior. John has been in the industry for decades. He has researched and developed thousands of trading systems utilizing a multitude of indicators. He has utilized his applied engineering and mathematical background to trading technology. John is well known in the industry due to his magazine that ranks 200 different 100% mechanical publicly offered commodity trading systems.

With the name Futures Truth, he dispels the false Holy Grail claims of systems and gives an unbiased truthful approach to systematic trading. He has written several books on trading techniques and mechanical system trading. I spoke to Justin approximately two years ago and do not recall exactly what he specifically did for Futures Truth.

I found Justin to be extremely knowledgeable about mechanical trading systems and his focus on risk was impressive. He used the statement that future profitability is built on today's risk management. All of his trading decisions start with risk management, not charting patterns or technical indicators. This is a point I have tried to express throughout this book. During my conversation with Justin he brought up the point that one of his original investors, a doctor, buys into his drawdowns. This was similar to my trading mentality. The doctor has been able to compound money at a greater rate by adding to his allocation during drawdowns.

I recently invested with Justin. He was having a 22% drawdown at the time and thought it was as good as any time to invest with him. I am surely not buying in at the bottom nor do I have any plans to exit. I hope to invest with him over many years and compound money. I know that it could be a bumpy road as all trend followers experience drawdowns.

As in many other successful trend followers, Justin's system looks for trading opportunities in 40+ global markets in the following market sectors: Currencies, Energies, Grains, US based Interest Rates, International Interest Rates, Meats, Global Soft Commodities, and Global Stock Indexes. He uses a quantitative trading system based on a statistical trading model created from research on historical price movements. He uses a money management system to limit the amount of exposure taken in one market. Trade duration can last from a few days to five months or more.

Justin has the ability to hit the ball out of the park. In 2008 he returned 82.60% for himself and his investors. His compound rate of return is approximately 19%. These returns are not without drawdowns obviously. His worst peak to valley drawdown lasted for 16 months from December 2008 till April 2010. During this period he experienced a drawdown of -24.75%. I would assume over time this will be exceeded as the worst drawdown is always ahead of you.

*Andy Abraham*

## Chadwick Investment Group : Global Trend Following

| | | | |
|---|---|---|---|
| Min. Investment $250k | Inception Jun 2007 | Assets | $11.0M |
| Mgmt Fee 2.00% | Sharpe (RFR=1%) 0.68 | Worst DD | -24.75 |
| Perf Fee 20.00% | CAROR 17.19% | S&P Correlation | -0.26 |

YEAR-TO-DATE: **2.77%** ↑  SEP 0.57%

GROWTH OF 1,000 - VAMI

*Global Trend Following 2.33 k | 00:00 October 01, 2012*

### MONTHLY PERFORMANCE

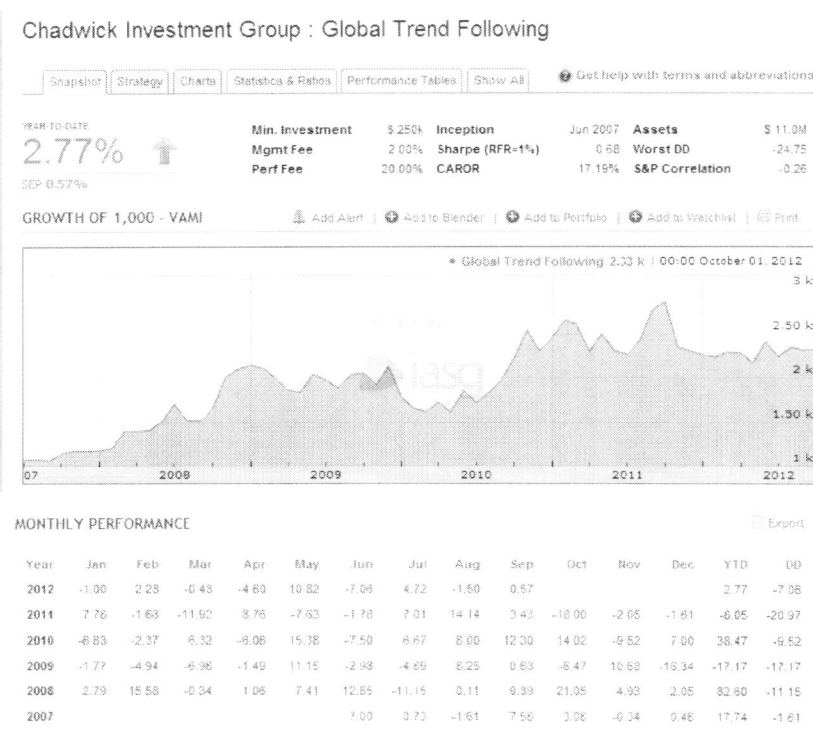

| Year | Jan | Feb | Mar | Apr | May | Jun | Jul | Aug | Sep | Oct | Nov | Dec | YTD | DD |
|---|---|---|---|---|---|---|---|---|---|---|---|---|---|---|
| 2012 | -1.00 | 2.28 | -0.43 | -4.60 | 10.82 | -7.06 | 4.72 | -1.50 | 0.57 | | | | 2.77 | -7.08 |
| 2011 | 7.76 | -1.63 | -11.93 | 8.76 | -7.63 | -1.78 | 7.01 | 14.14 | 3.43 | -18.09 | -2.05 | -1.61 | -8.05 | -20.97 |
| 2010 | -6.83 | -2.37 | 6.32 | -8.06 | 15.38 | -7.50 | 6.67 | 8.09 | 12.30 | 14.02 | -9.52 | 7.00 | 38.47 | -9.52 |
| 2009 | -1.77 | -4.94 | -6.98 | -1.49 | 11.15 | -2.93 | -4.89 | 8.25 | 0.83 | -6.47 | 10.63 | -16.34 | -17.17 | -17.17 |
| 2008 | 2.79 | 15.58 | -0.34 | 1.06 | 7.41 | 12.65 | -11.15 | 0.11 | 9.39 | 21.05 | 4.93 | 2.05 | 82.60 | -11.15 |
| 2007 | | | | | | 7.00 | 0.73 | -1.61 | 7.58 | 3.08 | -0.34 | 0.48 | 17.74 | -1.61 |

PAST PERFORMANCE IS NOT NECESSARILY INDICATIVE OF FUTURE RESULTS. THE RISK OF LOSS IN TRADING COMMODITY FUTURES, OPTIONS, AND FOREIGN EXCHANGE ("FOREX") IS SUBSTANTIAL.

Have a long term outlook or as I call it, a lifetime strategy. I strongly suggest managed futures as they are a hedge against inflation and can provide you positive returns in all types of market environments. Allocate to the great money managers of our time that have a CAROR over 15% for at least 10 years. Bear in mind some managers will have this proverbial 15% CAROR but due to a period of time this CAROR can be lowered. You need to look at their contemporaries to see how they did in the same period. There are periods of times that any strategy will struggle.

Be selective. You have to search them out. They do not advertise nor are they readily known to the vast majority of the investing community. As well, once you identify them, in order to create a margin of safety you need to do the uncomfortable by allocating to them when they are going through a drawdown. This is far from a guarantee, as we are dealing in the unknown and the only certainty is uncertainty.

Putting aside my preferred avenue of investing with commodity trading advisors there are stock market money managers that have proven themselves over time. My only negative is that they look at just one market, the stock market. However at times they have a place in your portfolio but use common sense. If measurements tell you that stocks are low and we have started to come out of a bear market, you can emphasize high-potential managers. If stocks are high, you can emphasize cautious, unleveraged stock managers, but I would be wary.

# CHAPTER 3 SUMMATION

At first glance many feel that in today's environment it is impossible to achieve 15% compounded rates of returns over long periods of time. This chapter proves with various examples that world class money managers exist and have compounded in the range of 15% on average over long periods of time.

## CHAPTER 4

# Inflation

Inflation has been called a wealth destroyer. The extreme version of inflation is hyperinflation. Hyperinflation is when inflation goes parabolic and currencies get destroyed. Too few understand just how disruptive hyperinflation can be. If past experience is any barometer of the future, it would be a nightmare. Imagine prices at the food store and gas pump not just going up a few cents at a time, but doubling in a matter of months, weeks, or even days. This is what has occurred in the past and throughout history.

There are some American economists and market experts that think many of the ingredients for hyperinflation are brewing in America. "We're certainly at a flashing yellow alert," stated Art Cashin, Director of Floor Operations at UBS Financial Services.

There have been years of nonstop U.S. government borrowing, bailouts, wars and wasted spending. The situation escalated after the 2008 financial crisis, with the U.S. Federal Reserve's policies of "quantitative easing" and creating even more money. We have had QE1, QE2 and QE3. No one rings a bell before hyperinflation hits. It can sneak up in that it often appears at first to be only higher-than-normal conventional inflation.

History has shown us repeated examples. In our recent history we have witnessed both the German Weimar period and Zimbabwe, and today we are witnessing the effects of inflation and hyperinflation in Iran. Repeatedly it has been proven that that government cannot be trusted to manage money.

Quoting Thomas Jefferson:

**"A government big enough to give you everything you need, is a government big enough to take away everything that you have...."**

## WEIMAR PERIOD IN GERMANY

When World War I broke out on July 31, 1914, the Reich Bank, the German Central Bank at the time, suspended to redeem its notes in exchange for gold. When a country's currency is not redeemable in gold, its value depends entirely on the judgment and the integrity of the politicians. After the Reich Bank decided against redeeming notes in gold there was no legal limit as to how many notes it could print. In order to placate the masses of Germany, the government did not impose heavy taxes during World War I to pay for the war. Instead it borrowed huge amounts of money which they thought were to be paid by the Allies after Germany had won the war. The monetary system of Germany was completely manipulated by the Reich Bank. Borrowing was discounted and monetized by the Reich Bank (sound familiar to what is happening in the US?). The printing press began their rapid roll. It was not just Germany in 1914, all the participants of World War I experienced inflation. However the German government and the German Reich Bank mismanaged the economy totally.

After the war there was a period of stability in Germany. However by 1923 inflation started once again. The Allies imposed harsh reparation payments on Germany. These harsh reparations or forced payments caused the German Mark to depreciate against foreign currencies. To make matters worse, Germany's new democratic socialist leaders promised their citizens increased wages, reduced hours, an expanded educational system, and all new social benefits in order to be re- elected. In order to pay for all of these social services, the government kept issuing new money. The currency in circulation increased by 50% and the floating debt of the Reich Bank increased by 100%; this was just another straw that broke the proverbial camel's back.

Inflation picked up in intensity. Unbelievably prices started to increase at feverish levels. In some cases prices doubled in a few hours. Hoarding of goods became prevalent. People wanted goods or food instead of cash. Putting things into perspective; in 1914, before World War I, a loaf of bread in Germany cost the equivalent of 13 cents. Two years later it was 19 cents, and by 1919, after the war, that same loaf was 26 cents—doubling the prewar price in five years. One year later a German loaf of bread cost $1.20. By mid-1922, it was $3.50. Just six months later, a loaf cost $700, and by the spring of 1923 it was $1,200. As of September, it cost $2 million to buy a loaf of bread. One month later, it cost $670 million, and the month after that—$3 billion. The vast majority of the German people found that their life's savings would not buy even a loaf of bread. They became destitute almost overnight.

From mid-1922 to November 1923 hyperinflation raged out of control. Wrongly, the Reich Bank officials believed that the basic trouble was the depreciation of the Mark in terms of foreign currencies. In late 1922 they tried to support the Mark by purchasing it in the foreign exchange markets. However, since they continued printing new currency at a feverish rate, the attempt failed. They merely succeeded in buying worthless marks in return for valuable gold and foreign exchange. This exacerbated the problem even further.

By late 1923, 300 paper mills were working around the clock and 150 printing companies had 2000 presses around the clock turning out currency. By mid-1923 workers were being paid as often as three times a day. Their spouses would meet them, take the money and rush to the shops to exchange it for goods. Food riots broke out. Parties of workers marched into the countryside to dig up vegetables and to loot the farms. Businesses started to close down and unemployment suddenly soared. The economy began to collapse. The middle-class people who depended on any sort of fixed income found themselves penniless. In order just to survive the middle class sold their furniture, clothing, jewelry and works of art. Millions of middle class Germans were ruined by the hyperinflation. Some of the German citizens turned to Hitler and some turned to the Communists to help them survive.

We all know the rest of the story. World War II ensued from the turmoil of the inflation and hyperinflation. In retrospect, the inflation was caused by the government issuing a flood of new money, causing prices to rise. What is somewhat ironic was that not all were impacted. Many big business leaders accepted the inflation with great joy. The inflation made it cheaper for them to pay back their creditors and wiped out their debts. (Sound familiar with the extreme US Deficit being run?) Some clever businessman speculated on various hard currencies on the foreign exchange markets. They bought US dollars and gold. As well they purchased stocks that had been decimated. This was a time they prospered. They had a plan, however they were only the very few.

## ZIMBABWE'S BOUT WITH HYPERINFLATION

Zimbabwe is another example of massive inflation and hyperinflation in our recent past. The cause of this massive inflation has several roots. Starting in early 1990s President Robert Mugabe instituted land reforms intended to redistribute land from white landowners to black farmers to correct the social injustices of colonialism. Prior to this period, Zimbabwe was economically sound and was renowned for its strong agricultural sector. Tobacco was widely grown and was a cash crop which brought in hard currency into Zimbabwe.

Due to the reforms and harsh treatment, many whites were forced to leave Zimbabwe. The white farms were confiscated and turned over to cronies and friends of Mugabe. In place of the experienced farmers Mugabe put local farmers who had no experience or training in running production on large enterprise farms. The agricultural sector imploded as did the flow of hard currencies into Zimbabwe.

During the year's 1999–2009, the country experienced a sharp drop in food production and the economy tumbled. Food shortages ensued as well as hard currencies stopped flowing into Zimbabwe. Widespread poverty and violence further undermined confidence in the future of the country as well as the currency. To counter this, Mugabe ran the printing presses. This only made the problems worse.

In 2007, the government declared inflation illegal. By June 2008 the annual rate of price growth was 11.2 million percent. The worst of the inflation occurred in 2008, which caused the Zimbabwe government to abandon its own currency. In its place Zimbabwe used a combination of foreign currencies, mostly US dollars. Over the decade Zimbabwe still has not recovered and is just another example of government mismanagement.

Zimbabwean inflation rates since independence (official up to Jul. 2008, estimates thereafter)

| Date | Rate | Date | Rate | Date | Rate | Date | Rate | Date | Rate | Date | Rate |
|------|------|------|------|------|------|------|------|------|------|------|------|
| 1980 | 7% | 1986 | 15% | 1992 | 40% | 1998 | 48% | 2004 | 132.75% | 2008 Sep | 3,840,000,000,000,000,000% |
| 1981 | 14% | 1987 | 10% | 1993 | 20% | 1999 | 56.9% | 2005 | 585.84% | 2008 Mid-Nov. | 89,700,000,000,000,000,000% |
| 1982 | 15% | 1988 | 8% | 1994 | 25% | 2000 | 55.22% | 2006 | 1,281.11% | | |
| 1983 | 19% | 1989 | 14% | 1995 | 28% | 2001 | 112.1% | 2007 | 66,212.3% | | |
| 1984 | 10% | 1990 | 17% | 1996 | 16% | 2002 | 198.93% | 2008 Jul. | 231,150,888.87% | | |
| 1985 | 10% | 1991 | 48% | 1997 | 20% | 2003 | 598.75% | 2008 Aug. | 471,000,000,000% | | |

# TODAY'S EXAMPLE OF HYPERINFLATION WITH IRAN

Iran's bout with hyperinflation is happening as I am writing this book. Instead of military acts, the US has placed economic sanctions against Iran in order to stop them from developing nuclear weapons. A multitude of sanctions have caused the Iranian rial to collapse. The collapse of the rial is having the exact results the US sought. There have been protests and riots in the streets throughout Iran. The rial has risen from about 10,000 rials to the U.S. dollar to more than 35,000 on the street while the official exchange rate quoted by the Iranian government falsely stands at 12,600 rials. At the current rate of inflation, the value of a savings account is now barely 40% of what it was *one month ago*. On a monthly basis currently inflation is running at a rate of approximately 69%. Prior to the US sanctions the inflation rate was .69%. Detailing this further the current situation;

    1. Prices are doubling approximately every 39 days

    2. Some goods such as meat and chicken are doubling quicker

3. The daily rate of inflation is 1.78%. The US yearly rate of inflation is 1.69%

The Iranian government has censored currency exchange websites such as Mesghal.com and Mazanex.com. These sites have had rates blanked out for the rial's value against other nations' currencies as an attempt to stop the deluge of the rial.

The government has responded by cracking down on demonstrations and shuttering Tehran's foreign exchange black market. The depreciation of the rial continues however. It is highly believed from the depreciation and hyperinflation, political ramifications will occur. This was actually the goal of the US government. In all actuality, the US sanctions are waging a war of attrition against the Iranian people, not the regime. There are estimates that inflation has reached nearly 70 percent currently (October 2012). Iran's middle class and more so the poor, cannot keep up with the rising costs of food and fuel. Chicken and meat have become luxury items.

As history has shown, if Iran prints more money to finance expenditures, inflation will only rise faster. It seems the only alternative is if Iran will accede to Western demands to have the sanctions lifted. If Iran remains obstinate it is highly likely there will be civil unrest. What is more important to the average Iranian—food on the table or nuclear weapons?

*Again we can see how governments can cause inflation and hyperinflation.*

# EXPLANATION OF INFLATION

Inflation can be divided into two types: **Price Inflation** and **Monetary Inflation**, the first type (about prices) is when there is a rise in the general level of prices of goods and services over a period of time, the second type (monetary) is when there is a rise in the quantity of money in an economy. Both types are many times interrelated, and both have negative effects on the economy and individuals.

Regarding price inflation, there is a sustained increase in the general level of prices for goods and services. It is measured as an annual percentage increase. As inflation rises, every dollar (or whatever currency you use) buys a smaller percentage of a good or service. What this means is your money becomes worth less and less as inflation rises. The diminishing value of money leads to hoarding. People will try to get rid of cash before it is devalued, by hoarding food and other commodities, creating shortages of the hoarded objects. It is advisable to keep an eye on M2, a measure of the nation's money supply, particularly how much money is in circulation. The government reports this number every week. A sudden spike could signal the start of hyperinflation.

With inflation, the price of any given good is likely to increase over time; therefore both consumers and businesses may choose to make purchases sooner than later. This effect tends to keep an economy active in the short term by encouraging spending and borrowing and in the long term by encouraging investments. But inflation can also reduce incentives to save, so the effect on gross capital formation in the long run is ambiguous.

As time progresses however, prices increase and people tend to spend less. The domino effect is that there is a decrease in consumption which directly affects the economy. Obviously a decrease in consumption is bad for business. This can lead to recessions as well as currency depreciations.

*The Bible of Compounding Money*

The domino continues because of the price increase and a country is less competitive.

It is not always a one-way street. If inflation is expected, salaries increase to adjust. The problem arises if the inflation is unexpected it can be easily a wealth destroyer! Inflation redistributes income from people on fixed incomes to people on variable incomes or has investments that benefit from inflation. This redistribution is from poorer people to richer people. The reality is that the people with fixed incomes are stuck with added costs and actually get buried in additional costs. These people become poorer. Most people are on salaries and have fixed incomes. These people become the victims of inflation. People with variable incomes are relatively richer and have the potential to offset inflation via their investments such as real estate, stocks or commodity investments.

Inflation has effects not just on the personal level but on national levels. Inflation erodes international competitiveness. Exports can cost more abroad. This can cause a decrease in demand for exports. That in turn can lead to a decrease in demand for the currency and to a devaluation of the currency. When inflation erodes international competitiveness, most governments make controlling inflation the central pillar of their economic policy.

Most have not experienced inflation in their lives. The "accepted" rate of inflation is 2-3% per year. Hyperinflation is a completely different story and we need to always believe anything is possible. As discussed in the previous paragraphs, there are historical cases when this has led to the breakdown of a country's monetary system. The most notable example in the last 100 years was not Zimbabwe, but rather Germany. The hyperinflation which occurred in Germany in 1923 witnessed price increases of 2,500% in one month! This can easily explain why in 2008 there was a shortage of gold coins and bullion in Germany. The grandchildren learned the lesson of their grandparents.

Inflation occurs when the purchasing power of the dollar shrinks to the degree that the nominal supply of dollars grows faster than the real demand to hold dollars. An accepted mathematical approach is to analyze the connection between the money supply ($M$) and the general price level ($P$) uses an accounting identity called the "equation of exchange": $MV = Py$

Our purchasing parity is greatly diminished during periods of inflation or what our currency can buy. Inflation is an extremely important issue to consider. The danger of inflation is greater to the extent that the *actual* inflation rate differs from the *anticipated* inflation rate. When the inflation rate is *incorrectly* anticipated, financial trades are off balanced. When the inflation rate turns out to be higher than anticipated, a borrower gets to repay in less valuable dollars, at the expense of the lender who gets less back in purchasing power than expected. If the inflation rate turns out to be lower than anticipated, the lender gains at the expense of the borrower (assuming the borrower is able to make the greater real payment).

During inflationary periods over time, clearly the cost of goods and services increase. The flipside of this is the value of a dollar is going to fall because a person won't be able to purchase as much with that dollar as he/she previously could. While the annual rate of inflation has fluctuated greatly over the last half century it has ranged from nearly zero inflation to 23% inflation. What is interesting is that in recent years, Japan has experienced negative inflation, or "deflation," of around 1 percent per year, as measured by the Japanese CPI.

When economies are truly based on gold and silver the overall experience of inflation over the centuries historically was close to zero.. However with paper currencies, the story is much different, including the US dollar. In 1971 the U.S. government cut the U.S. dollar's gold link. This cut ended the US FED's commitment to redeem dollars for gold at a fixed rate for foreign central banks. Now the US dollar is a paper currency, the same as any other paper currency just based on "confidence".

The term "Fiat" money comes to light. When our money was backed by gold and silver, people couldn't just sit in some fancy building in Washington and push a button to create new money. They would have to engage in some type of activity with another party that already had some gold in their possession and earn the money. Now we have the FED who plays God with our economy. Fiat money is a dangerous addiction. With the current financial system there exists the temptation to push the easy money button. We saw the effects of the easy money button during the US housing crisis. Hundreds of thousands lost their homes and the social fabric of the US was unseated.

The quick knee-jerk reaction that could be foolish is to liquidate our paper currencies and simply buy gold as storage of value. Well, this is near sighted, as gold was reaching $2000 an ounce recently only to fall to the mid $1550 level. Even the US dollar, which so many loathed, did not fall that much. Bottom line—there is no silver bullet. There is no magic to investing. It is TOUGH! What we have at our disposal however as long as there is not currency control laws, is that we can easily shift into other currencies or need be gold.

What I find most interesting is that during the Great Depression it was illegal to own gold. Many considered it the great gold robbery. During the Great Depression Roosevelt instituted the "New Deal". In 1933, when Roosevelt became president, the United States had the largest gold reserves of any nation in the world. Roosevelt announced on March 8, 1933, a few days after taking office, that the gold standard was safe. However three days later, he issued an executive order forbidding gold payments by banks. The ban on bank gold payments created widespread uncertainty about the Roosevelt administration's intentions and people started hoarding gold. On April 5, 1933, Roosevelt commanded all citizens to surrender their gold to the government. No citizen was permitted to own more than $100 in gold coins, except for rare coins with special value for collectors. In reality this caused further panic. Shockingly the order stayed on the books until 1974.

Roosevelt banned citizens from owning gold in 1933 and forced people to rely on the unbanked promises of politicians for the value of their currency; the dollar has lost about 93 percent of its purchasing power since his presidency. Roosevelt's gold seizure was based on the principle that in order for government to save the people, it must be permitted to breach all the promises it made to the people. Yes, there was trying times in the Great Depression but was confiscation of gold the answer?

The refusal to convert paper dollars into gold meant that the government was "free" to flood the country with paper money and sabotage the currency's value. The stability of the value of currency is one of the clearest measures of a government's trustworthiness. Before Roosevelt took office, Americans clearly recognized the moral implications of inflation. Vice President Calvin Coolidge had bluntly declared in 1922: "Inflation is repudiation." Inflation is a tax whereby the government prints extra money to finance its deficit spending. The value of money is largely determined by the ratio of money to goods; if the quantity of money increases faster than the increase in the amount of goods, the result is an increase in the ratio of money to goods and an increase in prices. Thus, the government's printing presses devalue people's paychecks and effectively allow the government to default on the value of its debt.

## *My simple question to you is, "What is different now in 2012?"*

The Bernanke printing presses are running at full tilt. No one can predict precisely when, or even if, a period of hyperinflation might strike. As I have described in previous paragraphs, the consequences would be so devastating, it necessitates being prudent and aware of the current situation.

Hyperinflation in America would create havoc in the markets. The reality is that our investments must overcome rates of inflation. If not, our purchasing parity falls. There are those that believe they are protected by stocks or real estate, however they are deluding themselves. Bonds would become toxic, stocks could plummet and real estate does not put bread on the table. Precious metals like gold and silver would soar, as would commodities like oil, sugar and wheat. Foreign currencies would also skyrocket against the dollar. In times like this liquidity is even more important.

Managed futures offer not just potential protection but potential profits in a case of hyperinflation or extreme inflation. In regard to managed futures, you can easily shift your assets in contracts into a large group of currencies or even gold. Managed future contracts are highly regulated and there are exchanges such as the CME and the CBOT in the United States as well as there are exchanges located in London, Tokyo, Malaysia and other capitals in Europe. You can purchase a contract for a specific amount and you do not have counter party risk. This is much different when a bank sells you a forward contract. For every buyer there is a seller on the futures exchanges. More so you have the right to take possession of any contract.

For example if you purchased a contract for Gold, you can actually take possession of the physical gold at expiration. The same applies if you want corn or wheat or even Swiss Francs. The other alternative is to invest in commodity trading advisors who trade commodities or currencies. Many of the commodity trading advisors out there trade algorithmically. It is not a complete black box. These systems are based on trends and have risk controls. Not all commodity trading advisors are the same nor do they maintain the same risk profiles.

If prices of a commodity rise due to inflation and if you are long in the contract you benefit. However you must have a complete trading plan with all contingencies thought out. We will discuss in further sections how to invest with these types of money managers. However in times of inflation, as we witnessed in 2007-2008 with the prices of wheat and crude oil, tremendous profits were generated. The same can be said with what occurred in the period of the 1980s. In the 1980s some unique commodity trading advisors made their clients over 1,000% on their investments.

*Instead of being wiped out by inflation, commodity trading proved to be wealth hedge!*

### *An Asset Class You Probably Did not Think About*

Throughout the years I have had friends and family tell me they are conservative investors. These same friends and family tell me they only buy blue chip stocks. They know that since 1994 I have been trading a basket of commodities as well as investing with commodity trading advisers. In their minds they feel this is gambling and they are being conservative. They believe that they are true investors and will compound their money over long periods of time. Many in this group include fundamental investors. They read 10Ks

*The Bible of Compounding Money*

and 10Qs and try to decipher accounting statements. They tell me they only go for blue chips and put them away in a drawer to compound money.

A colleague of mine told me was putting his entire 401K into Hewlett Packard. This was back in 2004 and he gave me every reason why this stock was so wonderful and how much money he would make. Well 10 years later, this great stock he paid approximately $20.00 for is now trading at $12.44. So much for managing risk!

*Chart Created in Thomson Reuters MetaStock.
All rights reserved. Past Performance is not necessarily indicative of future performance.*

My friends and family have seen me make money over the years trading commodities but simply refuse. This refusal has neglected their financial horizons. However I want to be extremely clear—investing in commodities is volatile and not for everyone. There are always drawdowns and sometimes very steep drawdowns. There are always losses. Losses can never be avoided.

For these same investors it is ok for them to go through a 50% drawdown (they think). However in my own trading in commodities, I have not had a 50% drawdown yet (even though I know my biggest drawdown is ahead of me). Even "Blue Chip stocks" like IBM experienced 50% drops. To these so called investors this was OK. I wonder how many held on during a 50% drop?

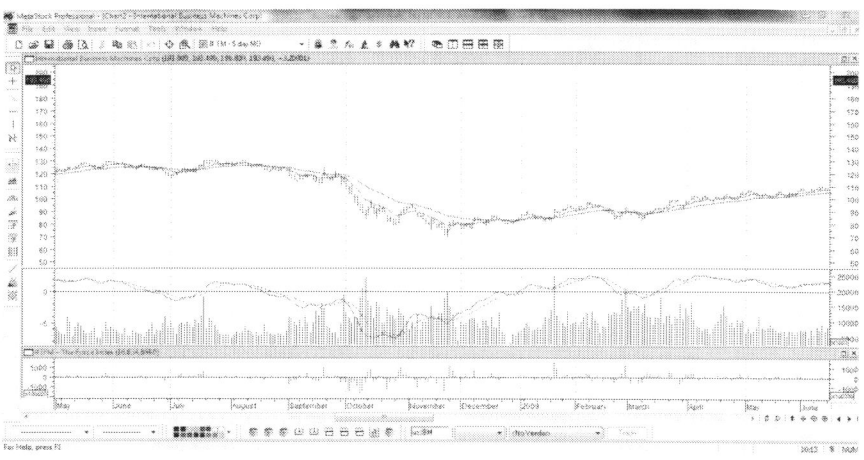

PAST PERFORMANCE IS NOT NECESSARILY INDICATIVE OF FUTURE RESULTS. THE RISK OF LOSS IN TRADING COMMODITY FUTURES, OPTIONS, AND FOREIGN EXCHANGE ("FOREX") IS SUBSTANTIAL.

I believe anything can happen. I really do not believe anything is truly safe. Commodity trading is not safe. Rather we have to attempt to manage the risks. Even leaving cash in a bank is not safe due to potential inflation.

## CHASING DIVIDENDS

I recently had a phone call from a friend who was all excited about Pitney Bowes and its dividend. He loves to "try" to buy cheap and sell high. He explained to me how they were changing their business model and that he "studied" their latest financial reports. He was so excited about a 13% dividend he did not take into account that this stock has been in a downtrend forever.

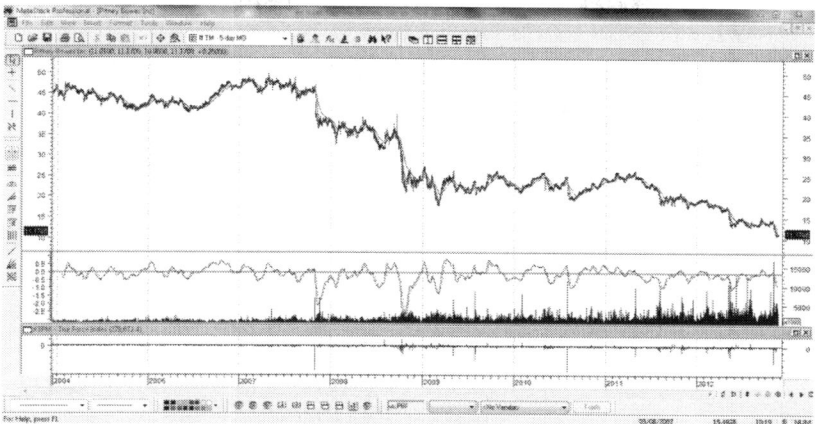

Chart Created in Thomson Reuters MetaStock. All rights reserved. Past Performance is not necessarily indicative of future performance

My friends and family do not have a trading plan. They do not know how much of a stock to buy or sell nor do they know when to exit with either a profit or a loss. They listen to their advisers and refuse to be open. They consider managed futures to be volatile and only for the faint of heart.

There are many professional investors and family offices who shun the sector as thinking this sector is reserved for gunslingers and gamblers. Contrary to this misconception, some of the world class traders who focus on managed futures are more *risk aware* than their fundamental counterparties. It is a generalization and not true for all managers or commodity trading advisors in the managed futures arena. What these investors also have not taken into account is if there will be a strong period of inflation. One of the only asset classes, in my opinion to produce profits could be commodities. In 2007 and 2008 when virtually every asset class was imploding, commodity traders had double digit positive returns.

In my trading and the managers in which I have invested with;

*Andy Abraham*

## *The World Class Commodity traders that I have invested with are not big risk takers!!!!!!!!*

Prudent commodity trading advisors measure risk at every juncture risk. This does not mean in the slightest that they do not have drawdowns or long periods in which they do not make money. There are no ways to avoid losing trades.

### *Risk is measured on the trade level, on the sector level as well as the portfolio level.*

To put things in the proper context, before I put on a trade, depending on which trading program I am trading, I will only risk 50 basis points of my account size on a trade in my Formula 72 L model. In my Formula 72 M I risk only 75 basis points of my account size on a trade and in my Formula 72 H I am risking 1.25% of my account size. Clarifying this, in my Formula 72 L a unit is $300,000. I am willing to risk on average $1500 on a trade. In my Formula 72 M a unit is $300,000. I am willing to risk on average $2250 on a trade. Lastly on my in my Formula 72 H a unit is $150,000. I am willing to risk on average $1875 on a trade.

After the trade level I look at my sector level and do not want to have a heavy correlation in any sector. More so on my portfolio level I look to cap that at a certain threshold in order to "attempt" to mitigate some drawdowns. Think about mutual fund managers or even many hedge funds. Do they analyze risk in the same context? I have not found many of them to do so. The most successful money managers whom I consider world class are more risk adverse than the vast majority of money managers (and even Warren Buffett). They attempt to keep their losses small. They know there will always be losses but the key to successful investing is to "try" to keep these losses small.

## THE BIG PICTURE

There is a much larger reason that you need to become aware of managed futures as an asset class and that is the ***"threat of inflation".*** I have included in this book a complete chapter on inflation and the potential for wealth devastation caused by inflation. Not too many people are currently worried about inflation because right now inflation is low and poses no immediate threat. But inflation is the most significant future danger to the dollar, interest rates and most importantly the US government debt (bubble).

The Fed and many of the world's central banks have been printing money at an unprecedented pace. Inflation is caused by an increase in the nation's money supply. The real cause of inflation is increasing the money supply beyond what is needed to keep up with economic growth. The Fed has printed money and increased the money supply in order to attempt to solve the country's economic woes. All the Fed really has done, in my opinion, is postpone the inevitable. This printing of money is analogous to a ballistic missile that has already been launched.

In the last several years, the Fed has massively increased the U.S. money supply beyond what is needed to keep up with economic growth in an attempt to stimulate the economy. We have had one bailout after the next. We had QE1, QE2 and possibly a QE3. This massive increase will stimulate the economy, and especially asset prices, such as the stock market, in the short term, but longer term it could create much higher inflation. We have seen a bull market in stocks since March of 2009.

Once inflation hits and interest rates rise, the stock market, the real estate market, private debt markets, and even discretionary spending will be hit hard. Rising inflation causes interest rates to rise, which makes money more expensive to borrow. When money is more expensive to borrow, less lending occurs. When less lending occurs, less buying occurs, and when less buying occurs, the demand for assets such as real estate, stocks, consumer purchases and all dollar denominated assets falls. Higher interest rates will worsen the already falling real estate bubble. Higher interest rates translate into more expensive mortgages, which will discourage home buyers and prevent home values from rising. The dominos will keep on falling as home inventories will rise and home prices will fall further. It becomes a self-fulfilling prophecy. People buy less as products cost more and interest on the credit card debt increases. Demand falls and asset values plunge. It becomes a vicious circle and wealth is destroyed.

*Why would you consider investing in real estate?*

In January 2006 I sold my personal residence. I thought we were in an un-sustainable real estate bubble. Couples were fighting over our house. We tripled our money on the house. While we were on a family ski trip to Deer Valley, Utah, the phone did not stop ringing. Granted we had a great house on a small cul-de-sac which was formerly owned by a famous NFL quarterback, but to me as a professional trader, it was a bubble.

*For the same reasons I felt so uncomfortable with the housing market, I am uncomfortable with the extreme low interest rates and the printing of money by central banks around the world.*

*I cannot help but believe we will have massive inflation.*

## MARTY ZWEIG'S THOUGHTS

Have you heard the quote "Don't fight the Fed."? This phrase was coined by Marty Zweig when he was a professor at Baruch College and Iona University. Marty Zweig later went on to become a famous hedge fund manager.

According to Zweig's theory, when interest rates are going down, stocks will go up, and when interest rates are going up stocks will go down. More so, one of Zweig's major pieces of advice was never to hold stocks—even of the best companies—in a bear market, since even they could disappoint. So why would you only consider being invested in the stock market?

We are in uncharted waters due to all the cheap money floating around the world. We have seen a recent Dot com bubble, a housing bubble and now Government printing of money as if it was toilet paper. *This time maybe it is different, however I extremely doubt it.* We have had rising inflation before, and we've had rising interest rates before, and although it wasn't great for the economy, nothing too terrible happened. However the back drop was not the same.

Currently we still have a high unemployment rate and a tremendous amount of debt. This debt ranges from personal debt, corporate debt to government debt. Debt has to be serviced or paid back. When interest rates rise this cost gets even greater.

High inflation and high interest rates will make asset values across the board plummet. Higher interest rates will diminish business' desire to borrow money. Businesses will not expand or hire more employees. There will be greater unemployment which will further impact the already weak economy further. As businesses do not grow, their stock prices fall. It all becomes a vicious cycle. Rising interest rates will cause bond values to fall, businesses to do poorly, stock prices to drop, and home prices to decline even further. The dominos keep on falling.

Most of the Federal Government's debt is short term. This debt has to roll over and the new refinanced debt is subject to higher and higher interest rates, which could get very expensive very quickly. We are currently at $16 trillion dollars of debt. The servicing of this debt is immense. The massive government budget deficit is ever increasing.

## MY INVESTMENT SOLUTION

So how does one position themselves in an inflationary environment? I strongly believe you can try to fight the distinct possibility or you can ride inflation to protect your wealth. In an inflationary environment, prices of commodities will rise. We saw this inflation in the 1980s and even though we were in a terrible recession, the stock market was terrible, interest rates were at all-time highs and yet the commodity markets boomed. During this period some unique world class commodity trading advisors increased their money almost 10 times. However every period is different and there are no guarantees that the same situation will be evident. I find it almost impossible that there will not be any inflation. My bet is with commodity traders and futures trading.

In 1998 we saw what debt did to the Asian tiger economies. These countries experienced debt deflation which brought on inflation. ***Why should this current period be different?*** Let's say I am wrong and the world will be wonderful. I still feel the greatest potential is in investing in commodities. Look at this way. China, Brazil, India and even Russia's economies have been growing tremendously and an emerging middle class has arisen. This new middle class wants the good life. This means a change in diet and an increase in desire of material items. There are limited resources in the world; because of this there will be an increase in prices of commodities. As Jim Rogers, the famous commodity bull has stated so often, have you ever met a farmer or a miner? I have not nor do I know anyone who wants to get into farming. So simple math is possibly that we have an increasing world population who wants a better life and we have the same or less production, ***prices should increase***.

Either way we can have inflation from Central Banks printing of money or simply growth in the world economy; it is very clear to me commodity prices are headed up either of which way we look. For this reason I focus on commodity trading.

Many commodity trading advisors are trend followers. Trend followers trade without opinions and follow the trends in the markets when they become apparent. Trend followers who understand risk have every possible outcome pre-thought out and taken into account. Contrarily where was the risk management on behalf of the investors who allocated to long term capital or some of the internet darlings such as Worldcom, Netflix or even Enron?

All managed futures money managers cannot be painted by the same brush. There are commodity trading advisors that trade the following strategies:

1. Arbitrage
2. Momentum
3. Counter trend

4. Fundamental
5. Various Option strategies
6. Pattern recognition
7. Seasonality
8. Cycles
9. Trend Following

*Why are Managed Futures a Viable Alternative?*

**CTA's (commodity trading advisors)** are highly regulated. Commodity trading advisors offer both managed segregated accounts as well as funds. Both vehicles are subject to comprehensive documentation and performance records that need to be filed with the NFA (National Futures Association). It is preferable to invest via managed accounts as these offer complete transparency and liquidity. Investment transparency is a major issue and my personal preference. However this does not mitigate risk or uncertainty. Anything can and will happen. Both individuals and institutions are becoming more interested in the managed futures space. Growth of CTA's (commodity trading advisors) over the past 10 years has exponentially increased from relative obscurity in the late '80's to over $260 Billion today... a quadrupling since 2002 alone– and there are solid reasons for it.

*Potential to Profit regardless of Bull Market, Bear Market,*
*Inflation or Deflation*

## CHAPTER 4 SUMMATION

Inflation is a wealth destroyer. It has destroyed countries and economies over the years. Paul Singer's warnings need to be taken into account. A financial plan in which inflation is held in check needs to be present in everyone's portfolio. No one rings a bell when inflation starts. A prudent approach is an allocation to commodity trading which is a hedge against inflation.

## CHAPTER 5

# Trend Followers Lead the Pack

The vast majority of the traders of managed futures are trend followers. These traders operate from a technical standpoint without any opinions. They do not look at fundamentals, rather the vast majorities of commodity trading advisor look solely at price. These technical traders and trend followers have a complete plan. All potential eventualities have been thought out. They know exactly what to buy or sell. They know exactly how much to buy or sell as well as they know exactly when to exit with a profit or a loss.

Traders who use this approach use various current market price calculations, moving averages and channel breakouts to determine the general direction of the market and to generate trade signals. From these signals trend followers place their bets. These trend followers were not the victims as in 1987, 2000 or 2008. Some of these trend followers made the most of amount of money during their careers during the worst stock market conditions. They feel all market activity is represented in the prices.

Managed futures are not an esoteric concept. The commodity markets and futures markets are involved in all aspects of our lives on a daily basis. Each of one these markets experiences bull and bear markets.

Here are some examples that reflect this:

- We have coffee and orange juice in the morning

- We use sugar in our baked products

- We all love a good piece of chocolate (cocoa)

- We eat bread made from wheat

- We heat our homes with heating oil

- We put gasoline in the cars we drive

- We buy clothes made of cotton

- We enjoy a fine steak dinner (cattle)

- We invest in the stock and bond markets

- We buy gold and silver jewelry

- We travel abroad and convert our US Dollars into foreign currencies, such as the Euro or British pound

- We borrow money from banks and pay various interest rates (the cost of money)

*The Bible of Compounding Money*

These traders have a common trait in trend following, however there are differences. Even though trend followers are categorized together they use different techniques and time frames to identify trends. Many mistakenly consider all trend followers to be synonymous; however they are not always correlated to one another.

Tom Basso, in the book *Trade Your Way to Financial Freedom* sums up what trend following really is

> *Let's break down the term Trend Following into its components. The first part is "trend". Every trader needs a trend to make money. If you think about it, no matter what the technique, if there is not a trend after you buy, then you will not be able to sell at higher prices..."Following" is the next part of the term. We use this word because trend followers always wait for the trend to shift first, then "follow" it.*

The concepts utilized by Richard Donchian are the basis. Donchian is considered by many to be the father of trend following. Donchian was a fundamental investor during the Great Depression until he lost everything while investing in the Stock Market during the period. However by the 1940s he learned from his mistakes and started the concept of trend following. He would base his trades on a simple technical concept. He would buy breakouts and look to stay with a trade as long as it was moving in the direction he placed his trade. Donchian continued trend following for almost 53 years thereafter until his death in his 90's. Donchian's trend following strategy worked in the past and will likely continue to be successful in the future. It does not matter—bear market, bull market, inflation or deflation—there are potentials for profit. It is not easy as there will always be losing periods and ugly drawdowns.

Trend following which is a version of technical trading was further made famous by a wager between two successful traders in the 1980s. Richard Dennis made a bet with his colleague William Eckhardt that trend trading can be taught. Richard Dennis was a guru trader, who compounded an initial investment of several thousand dollars into a fortune estimated at $200 million. This wager led to a group of traders called turtles. The turtles and their offspring were very successful. There are traders that made the Forbes Richest List by trend following and technical trading.

## JAMES SIMONS

James Simons is more than just a technical trader. Simmons is a PHD and looks at the markets from a mathematical approach. In 1968, he was appointed chairman of the math department at the Stony Brook University. In 1978, he left academia to run an investment fund that traded in commodities and financial instruments on a discretionary basis. Simons founded Renaissance Technologies Corporation in 1982.

As a hedge fund manager, Simons' exploits market inefficiencies using complex computer-based mathematical models. These models are based on analyzing as much data as can be gathered, then looking for non-random movements to forecast future price movement. This is a world of difference than fundamental traders. In his fund he is managing over $30 Billion dollars. Throughout the years he has outperformed countless managers.

## BRUCE KOVNER

Bruce Kovner is also on the Forbes list is a trend follower. He recently stepped down from his fund Caxton. He ran Caxton a $10 billion hedge fund, **for almost three decades** during which he traded everything from soybeans to

Japanese yen futures and returned twice as much as the Standard & Poor's 500 Index. Comparably, Kovner's Caxton Global Investment fund returned an average of 21 percent a year since inception, compared with an average gain of 11 percent including dividends by the Standard & Poor's 500 Index.

## PAUL TUDOR JONES

Paul Tudor Jones is a well-known name in the trading world as well as he is on the Forbes list. He cut his teeth in the cotton markets. He was mentored by Eli Tullis a famous cotton broker. In 1980 he opened his firm **The Tudor Group**, which is involved in the global equity, venture capital, debt, currency, and commodity markets. In 1987 he predicted the stock market crash and tripled his money for himself and his fortunate clients.

## D.E. SHAW

D.E. Shaw is another Forbes alumnus. His company manages hedge funds that make extensive use of quantitative methods and proprietary computational technology to manage its investments. He started the fund in 1988 and has assets under management of approximately $28 billion dollars.

## CHAPTER 5 SUMMATION

Managed futures as a strategy have various approaches. Trend following is making oneself available to profit without any preconceived notions or opinions. Some of the world's greatest investors have made the Forbes list by utilizing trend following strategies.

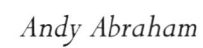

## CHAPTER 6

# Why Invest in Managed Futures?

The benefits of managed futures in a diversified portfolio have the following attributes:

1. Opportunity for reduced portfolio volatility risk
2. Potential for enhanced portfolio returns
3. Low to negative correlations to traditional markets (stocks and bonds).
4. Opportunity to participate in hundreds of markets worldwide
5. Opportunities in all market environments from inflation, deflation and bull and bear markets.

Adding managed futures to a traditional portfolio can improve the efficiency of an investor's overall asset allocation and help to realize the benefits of diversification. This is substantiated by an extensive body of academic research, including the landmark study by Dr. John Lintner of Harvard University, in which he concluded that, "The combined portfolios of stocks (or stocks and bonds) after including judicious investments...in leveraged managed futures accounts show substantially less risk at every possible level of expected return than portfolios of stocks (or stocks and bonds) alone."

Mentioned in number 3 above, the low correlation was exemplified recently in the last decade of trading. It's that lack of correlation that makes it such a great tool to bring into anyone's investment portfolio from a diversification standpoint. If you look at years like 2000, 2001, 2002, and 2008, which were very challenging years for equities markets, managed futures tended to perform very well in those markets. Actually in 2007 and 2008 some commodity trading advisors generated 20% these years back-to-back. The fact that commodity trading advisors can be both long and short with equal ease gives them advantages over many long only managers. They just need the markets to move in a direction in order to profit. It means that in a negative market environment, they can go short in the market. They can be short against stock indices. So I think that unique diversification means it really fits in almost any portfolio.

## MANAGED FUTURE REGULATION

Commodity trading advisors must be registered with a national regulatory body. CTA's trading futures in the U.S. are regulated by the Commodity Futures Trading Commission (CFTC) and the National Futures Association (NFA). In conjunction of being registered the National Futures Association conducts random audits to assure compliance and integrity. The other great advantage of managed futures is the elimination of counter party risk. Commodity trading advisors trade on regulated exchanges also under governmental regulation. A disclosure document has to be submitted to the NFA before a commodity trading advisor and look to raise assets.

A disclosure document is a description of the CTA's trading program and procedures that apply to accounts under the CTA's control. CTA's are required to provide sufficient disclosure to the investor. The document which is submitted to the NFA and CFTC and describes the fees, trading program, procedures for entry and exit, past performance and rules for the overall trading program. Each disclosure document is different, so ensure you read fully the CTA's disclosure document before investing. You must sign off on the commodity trading advisor's disclosure document. The disclosure document (or D-Doc) includes an agreement whereby the client authorizes the CTA to direct trading in the client's commodity account.

## THE GOAL OF ABSOLUTE RETURNS

It is the goal, however it is challenging. As mentioned there is a low correlation to the stock and bond markets and this gives you the chance to build absolute returns. This ability to post "absolute returns," paired with low correlation makes investing in a managed futures vehicle a perfect candidate for portfolio diversification. With the concept of absolute returns is the concept of bear market protection. Commodity trading advisors have made money for their clients in some of the worst bear markets such as in 2008. The idea of going short is an edge that many other investment products do not offer.

# NOTIONAL FUNDING

A characteristic unique to managed futures accounts is the ability to use notional funding to trade. Because a futures trade requires only posting margin or a bond with the exchange equal to roughly the amount of money that position could lose in a day, there is often a large difference between a CTA's required minimum investment amount and the amount which technically needs to be in the account to cover the performance bonds, or margin. This opens up the possibility of being able to deposit $50,000 to trade as $100,000, for example. One caveat however is that the commodity trading advisor will charge you fees on the notional balance ($100K in our example), and those will be a much higher percentage of your actual balance ($50K in our example). The norm in the industry is a 2% management fee and 20% incentive fee.

# TAX BENEFITS

Managed futures accounts are taxed based on their value at the end of the year. This is good news for investors, as futures gains or losses are treated as 60% long term capital gains and 40% short term capital gains, NO MATTER the holding period. For example, an investor who holds a futures position for just a few minutes, or hours, can book 60% of the profits on that trade as long term gains—even though the trade was anything but long term. What a fantastic legal tax loophole!

There is also no trade by trade accounting in futures, no wash sale rules, and losses can be carried back three years on futures based investments.

# BE A PATIENT INVESTOR IN MANAGED FUTURES

By reading this book you will understand that investing in managed futures is a commitment. It is not a get rich quick or retirement in a box strategy. In order to truly succeed in investing in managed futures one needs to be committed to being invested for long periods of time. There can easily be periods ranging of 3 years and even possibly greater that no profits are generated. Then out of the blue 50% returns or even greater manifest themselves. This is just one of the reasons it is so difficult for investors in managed futures to stay focused.

Many investors who invest even with world class money managers lose money. What these investors do is buying when these world class money managers have a run up in equity. Psychologically this is much easier than buying a drawdown which gives somewhat of a margin of safety. What invariably happens many times is that these investors become frustrated after they thought that they would make money and actually nothing happens or they experience a drawdown. The following charts show this exactly.

## Abraham Trading Company

Abraham Trading Group, whom I consider world class, had a very good 2007 and 2008 while most of the world was experiencing terrible drawdowns. Abraham Trading group has a CAROR of 18.12% since 1988. Their assets under management went from $130 million dollars in late 2007 to $631 million dollars by mid-2011. In 2007 they generated 21.80% with an intra-year drawdown of -6.23%. In 2008 they generated 28.80% with only a 4.19% intra year drawdown.

| Year | | | | | | | | | | | | | |
|---|---|---|---|---|---|---|---|---|---|---|---|---|---|
| 2008 | 6.44 | 6.57 | -0.21 | 0.34 | -0.94 | 2.04 | -4.19 | 0.08 | 5.55 | 4.73 | 2.01 | 3.76 | 28.80 | -4.19 |
| 2007 | 1.08 | -4.00 | -2.32 | 6.50 | 4.96 | 3.66 | -2.54 | -3.73 | 5.20 | 4.32 | 1.16 | 6.47 | 21.80 | -6.23 |

PAST PERFORMANCE IS NOT NECESSARILY INDICATIVE OF FUTURE RESULTS. THE RISK OF LOSS IN TRADING COMMODITY FUTURES, OPTIONS, AND FOREIGN EXCHANGE ("FOREX") IS SUBSTANTIAL.

Source: Chart with permission from Iasg.com

However from 2009 to now the end of 2012 Abraham Trading Group has not made any money for their investors.

*Three years of nothing!*

*Would you still be invested?*

*What have you done for me lately?*

Remember they have an average compounded rate of return of 18%. In order to compound money over long periods, one needs the fortitude to get through the inevitable drawdowns. One thing I can promise you, you will always have drawdowns and past performance is not necessarily indicative of future performance. At least the positive is that they did not experience a steep drawdown. Assets under management have started to slip from $631 million to currently October 2012 to $448 million dollars.

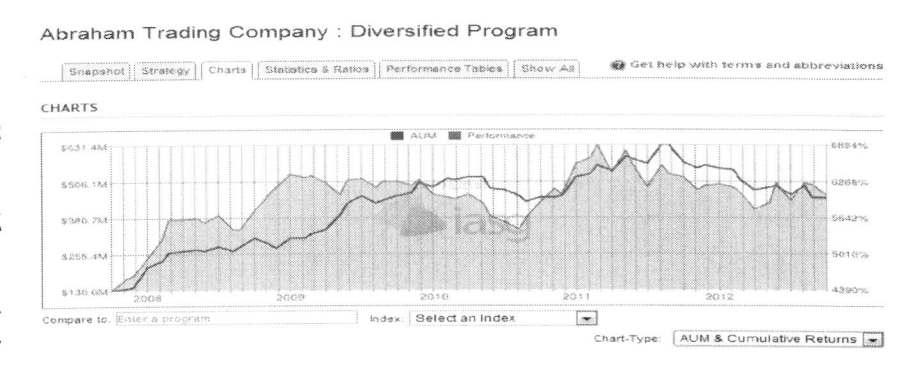

Source: Chart with permission from Iasg.com

This is a common theme.

*The Bible of Compounding Money*

## INVESTORS CHASING RETURNS

Drury Capital's Diversified Trend-Following Program started at the right time in 1997. They had an amazing return for years running. Who would not want to invest with them?

| 2003 | 7.76 | 6.94 | -6.32 | -4.10 | 9.42 | -6.35 | -4.41 | -0.87 | 4.17 | 13.80 | -1.03 | 6.64 | 25.77 | -12.77 |
|---|---|---|---|---|---|---|---|---|---|---|---|---|---|---|
| 2002 | 0.52 | -1.32 | -2.05 | -3.68 | -5.13 | 11.62 | 4.82 | 3.75 | 4.35 | -9.42 | -5.97 | 10.19 | 5.55 | -14.83 |
| 2001 | -6.20 | 4.95 | 15.48 | -4.19 | 2.41 | 4.97 | -3.66 | 2.03 | 6.23 | 3.82 | -9.34 | 4.82 | 20.62 | -9.34 |
| 2000 | -5.58 | 0.35 | -1.59 | 11.91 | 1.14 | -4.41 | 1.49 | 4.92 | -1.70 | 3.26 | 6.33 | -0.12 | 15.80 | -6.76 |
| 1999 | 0.06 | -6.05 | -2.62 | 4.46 | -5.56 | -0.36 | -4.43 | 8.54 | -3.59 | -1.24 | 5.28 | 4.30 | 10.46 | -10.07 |
| 1998 | 7.84 | 6.11 | 6.60 | -5.46 | 7.78 | 2.20 | -1.38 | 19.34 | -5.22 | -2.74 | 4.25 | 2.46 | 47.21 | -7.82 |
| 1997 |  |  |  |  | -4.57 | 14.98 | 12.49 | -2.12 | -2.08 | -9.35 | 17.34 | 3.64 | 30.42 | -13.12 |

PAST PERFORMANCE IS NOT NECESSARILY INDICATIVE OF FUTURE RESULTS. THE RISK OF LOSS IN TRADING COMMODITY FUTURES, OPTIONS, AND FOREIGN EXCHANGE ("FOREX") IS SUBSTANTIAL.

Bernard Drury, the principle of Drury Capital, started with approximately $2 million dollars in 1997. Due to his great returns he raised several hundred millions of dollars very quickly. Drury made 30.42% in 1997. In 1998 he made 47.21%. In 1999 he made 10.46%. In 2000 he made 15.80%. In 2001 he made 20.62%. In 2002 he made 5.55% and in 2003 he made 25.77%. How easy it was. It seemed the success could never end.

However 2005 and 2006 were very difficult markets. Drury experienced back to back drawdown years. Assets under management fell very quickly. In 2005 Drury had a drawdown of -10.47% with an intra-year drawdown of -17.88%. In 2006 Drury had a drawdown of -15.40% with an even worse intra- year drawdown of -19.40%. Putting it all into perspective however, since 1997, Drury has returned a CAROR of 11.47%. I dare you to compare this to the stock market on not just on the basis of returns but on basis of drawdowns.

| 2006 | -0.51 | -0.69 | 0.37 | 2.38 | -2.15 | -1.28 | -6.44 | -1.22 | 0.91 | -4.47 | -6.34 | 3.38 | -15.40 | -19.40 |
| 2005 | -2.34 | -4.57 | 0.27 | -5.58 | -4.02 | -2.42 | -0.85 | 1.83 | 1.15 | 0.95 | 7.85 | -2.78 | -10.47 | -17.88 |

PAST PERFORMANCE IS NOT NECESSARILY INDICATIVE OF FUTURE RESULTS. THE RISK OF LOSS IN TRADING COMMODITY FUTURES, OPTIONS, AND FOREIGN EXCHANGE ("FOREX") IS SUBSTANTIAL.

In 2007 and 2008 Drury recouped his losses and he hit the ball out of the park. Assets under management increased once again. In 2008 Drury Diversified returned 75.65%. After assets under management fell dramatically in 2005 and 2006 however in 2008 AUM went from approximately $100 million dollars to a high of $410 million before starting to decrease once again due to 2011 and 2012 performance (-16.16% and so far in 2012 -1.91%).

## MONTHLY PERFORMANCE

| Year | Jan | Feb | Mar | Apr | May | Jun | Jul | Aug | Sep | Oct | Nov | Dec | YTD | DD |
|------|-----|-----|-----|-----|-----|-----|-----|-----|-----|-----|-----|-----|-----|-----|
| 2012 | 0.98 | 4.23 | 2.87 | -0.25 | -0.20 | -7.50 | 3.17 | -1.27 | -3.41 | | | | -1.91 | -9.40 |
| 2011 | 3.49 | 6.21 | -7.05 | 3.78 | -9.48 | -7.00 | 0.52 | -8.34 | 8.00 | -8.98 | 1.38 | 2.30 | -16.16 | -26.45 |
| 2010 | -6.25 | -1.35 | 6.12 | 0.38 | -7.87 | 0.18 | -4.88 | 2.66 | 4.19 | 4.12 | -4.19 | 9.06 | 0.65 | -13.51 |
| 2009 | -1.82 | 2.10 | -3.64 | -2.72 | 1.82 | -0.23 | 6.97 | 2.67 | 1.94 | -3.53 | 6.48 | 0.09 | 9.04 | -6.26 |
| 2008 | 6.78 | 11.17 | -8.45 | -5.44 | 7.44 | 6.63 | -9.45 | 1.92 | 16.95 | 23.37 | 6.56 | 5.15 | 75.65 | -13.43 |

PAST PERFORMANCE IS NOT NECESSARILY INDICATIVE OF FUTURE RESULTS. THE RISK OF LOSS IN TRADING COMMODITY FUTURES, OPTIONS, AND FOREIGN EXCHANGE ("FOREX") IS SUBSTANTIAL.

Source: Chart with permission from Iasg.com

*The Bible of Compounding Money*

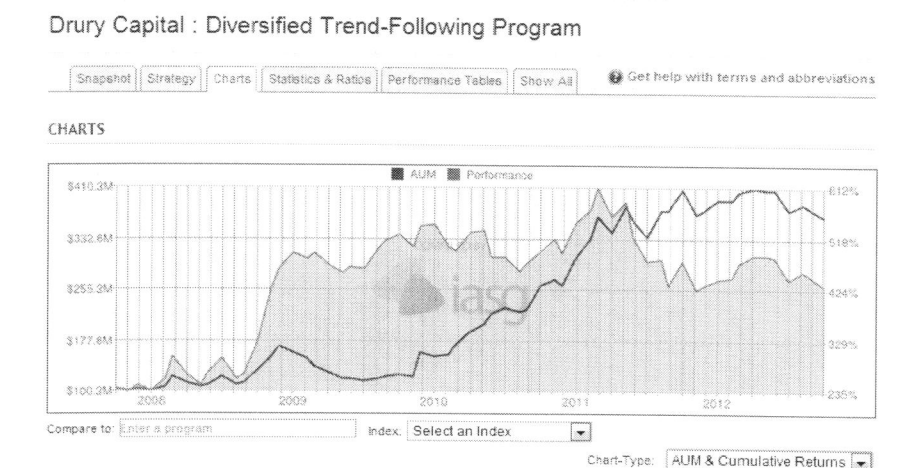

Drury Capital : Diversified Trend-Following Program

Clarke Capital runs several programs. One program in particular called Global Basic. This program I consider world class but needs to approached in the proper context. From its start in 1996 it has a CAROR of 22.13%. Very impressive, however it has steep drawdowns. His worst drawdown so far has been - 46.51%. What I have done personally with my family's investment with Global Basic is buy the steep drawdowns and then scale out upon recovery. It is not perfect but it smooths the equity curve. You will notice in the next chart how assets climbed and fell depending on performance.

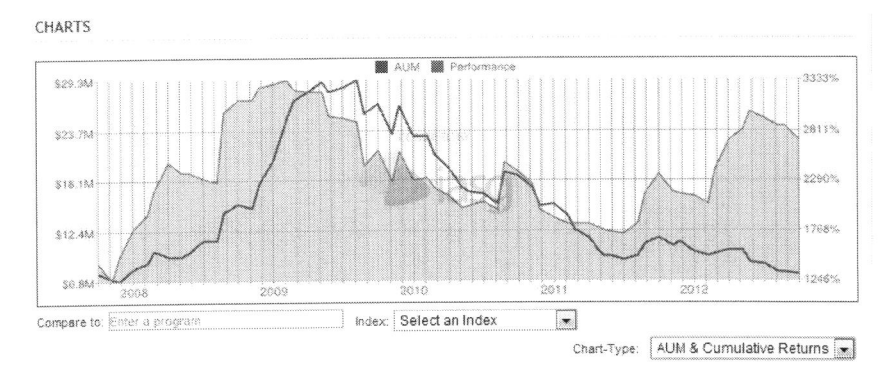

Before you even consider actually investing with any world class money manager you need to temper your expectations and realize that ***anything can happen***. The only certainty is uncertainty. Realize that even with world class money managers there will be long and ugly drawdowns and long periods when profits are elusive. Realize that you need to be patient and have a long term time frame to compound money and create wealth. I strongly suggest utilizing the *potential* of a margin of safety.

I look to buy drawdowns of world class money managers who meet my objectives of a 15% compounded rate of returns over at least 10 years that offer liquid and transparency in strategies that I completely understand. Buying drawdowns is doing the uncomfortable. Most investors favor investing when money managers have a positive run and that they are managing a great deal of money. My real world experiences over the last 18 years differ and have proven themselves.

## SUCCESSFUL MONEY MANAGERS ARE PASSIONATE

*The Bible of Compounding Money*

My neighbor's son has soccer net in their backyard. It seems he is playing more 24 hours a day; this boy practices getting the ball into the goal. I am up at 5am for my trading and he is kicking that ball. I go to sleep and he is still kicking the ball into the goal. He is passionate. He knows he will succeed. I would bet he practices 120 hours from all angles of the yard. Is it fair to assume that because of all his practicing he is better than most 17 year olds who play soccer and only practice 10 hours a week? There are a lot of great soccer players out there, but there is practice and passion. Do you think 1 out of 10 is as good as this boy?

1 out of 100?

1 out of 1000?

Do you believe that someone who practices more deserves to be a better professional? What do you think? Does the guy who does the most or tries the most achieve the ultimate best results? In every profession or sports there are wannabees and r bees. Many of the wannabees want the title, prestige and money but they do not put in the work. There are money managers who want to make millions but they are not willing to put in the work. Even though they say they are money managers they are not passionate. Passionate means putting in the thousands of hours.

## PLAYING BY THE RULES

Investment success is contingent on how we think. It is not easy nor will it ever be. Investing is like sports.

You need to play by the RULES!

You need to have rules!

If you don't follow the rules – You will not win!

What always gets me is when potential investors ask me how last month or last year was? That has absolutely no bearing. You want to invest with world class money managers and you do not want to compromise.

- Like soccer…hours of back and forth but the game is won on a few quick scores.
- Like football… hours of gains and losses and a touchdown wins the game in the 4th quarter.
- Like baseball, innings of boredom followed by a few key runs.
- What do you expect to happen when they go to a soccer game?
- Do you expect to see scoring every minute?

## MAKE SURE THE SAME PEOPLE ARE MANAGING THE MONEY

Some money managers have built almost all the great records. If the team moves, the record moves. An example for me personally was Monroe Trout from Markets Wizards fame. I invested in a feeder fund of theirs in 1994. It was more luck than knowledge. I forget exactly, either in 2005 or 2006, Monroe Trout retired. I invested $200,000 in 1994 and compounded the funds to approximately $1,400,000. When he retired I thought to take my chips off the table. One of his lieutenants was running the organization however my comfort level was gone.

An organization could have a successful method which transcends the people in it. As I say all the time…the only certainty is uncertainty. Most money managers are not lone wolves. They usually have a core group of decision makers. When one or two people leave the company sometimes even a lone genius does not compensate. It is hard to decide whether the original team today is substantially the same as the one that built the record and capable of respective returns in the future.

## FOLLOWING THE HERD

You do not want to follow the herd. One of the tenants of my investing mantra is look for managers who have been around at least 10 years. They have seen various cycles. In most cases these managers simply observe the markets without opinions. Contrarily most people are optimistic at market tops. It is easy to be part of the herd. It is hard to be a lone wolf. Beware the experts especially. Here are some quotations from experts in 1929, before and during the great depression.

**September 1929**
"There is no cause to worry. The high tide of prosperity will continue." — Andrew W. Mellon, Secretary of the Treasury.

**October 14, 1929**
"Secretary Lamont and officials of the Commerce Department today denied rumors that a severe depression in business and industrial activity was impending, which had been based on a mistaken interpretation of a review of industrial and credit conditions issued earlier in the day by the Federal Reserve Board." — New York Times

**December 5, 1929**
"The Government's business is in sound condition." — Andrew W. Mellon, Secretary of the Treasury

## December 28, 1929

"Maintenance of a general high level of business in the United States during December was reviewed today by Robert P. Lamont, Secretary of Commerce, as an indication that American industry had reached a point where a break in New York stock prices does not necessarily mean a national depression." — Associated Press dispatch.

## January 13, 1930

"Reports to the Department of Commerce indicate that business is in a satisfactory condition, Secretary Lamont said today." – News item.

## January 21, 1930

"Definite signs that business and industry have turned the corner from the temporary period of emergency that followed deflation of the speculative market were seen today by President Hoover. The President said the reports to the Cabinet showed the tide of employment had changed in the right direction." – News dispatch from Washington.

## January 24, 1930

"Trade recovery now complete President told. Business survey conference reports industry has progressed by own power. No Stimulants Needed! Progress in all lines by the early spring forecast." – New York Herald Tribune.

## March 8, 1930

"President Hoover predicted today that the worst effect of the crash upon unemployment will have been passed during the next sixty days." – Washington Dispatch.

### May 1, 1930
"While the crash only took place six months ago, I am convinced we have now passed the worst and with continued unity of effort we shall rapidly recover. There is one certainty of the future of a people of the resources, intelligence and character of the people of the United States – that is, prosperity." – President Hoover

### June 29, 1930
"The worst is over without a doubt." – James J. Davis, Secretary of Labor.

### August 29, 1930
"American labor may now look to the future with confidence." – James J. Davis, Secretary of Labor.

### September 12, 1930
"We have hit bottom and are on the upswing." – James J. Davis, Secretary of Labor.

### October 16, 1930
"Looking to the future I see in the further acceleration of science continuous jobs for our workers. Science will cure unemployment." – Charles M. Schwab.

### October 20, 1930
"President Hoover today designated Robert W. Lamont, Secretary of Commerce, as chairman of the President's special committee on unemployment." – Washington dispatch.

### October 21, 1930
"President Hoover has summoned Colonel Arthur

Woods to help place 2,500,000 persons back to work this winter." – Washington Dispatch

**November 1930**
"I see no reason why 1931 should not be an extremely good year." – Alfred P. Sloan, Jr., General Motors Co.

**January 20, 1931**
"The country is not in good condition." – Calvin Coolidge.

**June 9, 1931**
"The depression has ended." – Dr. Julius Klein, Assistant Secretary of Commerce.

# LOOKING FOR PASSION

I have been investing since 1994 and I learned there are money managers that are really PHDs. These real PHDs are passionate, hungry and driven. They love what they do. Then there are those money managers who only want to charge management. They are not passionate or they do not understand the principles of winning. You want to invest with real PHDs that love the work they do.

One of my mentors was a dentist whom I consider a true PHD (completely different from the PHDs from long term capital that blew up to the tune of billions). The dentist put in all the work. He has the passion and knows the principle of winning. He started in 1979 before there were computers and built hand charts of numerous commodity markets. He did not go to Harvard or Yale but trading is his passion. He was far from perfect. He had countless losing trades and long periods of time when he did not make money. He only traded his own account but these are the characteristics of money managers you and I want to invest in.

## Sometimes professionals make difficult things look easy- but they are not!

Many times people think they can do that but in reality it is a much different story. My next door neighbor makes it look simple, getting the ball into the net. Not really sure if I could. However he makes it look so simple. Investing with world class money managers is not easy as it should be expected.

World class money managers inspire varying degrees of confidence. We want to believe in them as long as they keep on making us money. However when they run into an invariable drawdown we question them. Compare Jon Paulson who jumped so dramatically due to his correct call of subprime who is now struggling versus Warren Buffett with his 50 year record, albeit many questioned Buffett and still do today.

Some money managers work in a disciplined style which you can understand and count on; others use an eclectic or ad hoc approach as Paulson. Some can describe exactly what they do; others are less articulate, or have indescribable methods. Sadly investors just chase these returns without understanding them. Compare this to Buffett who has a fifty year record and is still very much in charge. His style is disciplined and easily understood. I would find it hard if someone could explain to me Paulson's exact strategy.

# CHAPTER 6 SUMMATION

The benefits of managed futures in a diversified portfolio have the following attributes:

1. Opportunity for reduced portfolio volatility risk

2. Potential for enhanced portfolio returns

3. Low to negative correlations to traditional markets (stocks and bonds).

4. Opportunity to participate in hundreds of markets worldwide

5. Opportunities in all market environments from inflation, deflation and bull and bear markets.

# CHAPTER 7
# World Class Trading Program

In my 18 years of studying and investing in the markets, I have come across a number of principles that have worked over time. I had a great experience with a firm that operated in Florida. This was a small boutique firm that specialized in mechanical commodity trading systems. My friends in Florida saw it all. My friends knew there was a huge difference between theory and what works in the real world. My friends in Florida would start with some basic questions such as, what markets does your system trade? If they heard things like lumber, rough rice, propane, orange juice, and other thin markets, they knew right away, there was no sense wasting time with that program.

The back tested results might look good, but this system would never work in the real world. My friends might ask, "What amount of slippage and commission have you factored in?" If the answer was $25 or $50 dollars per trade, they knew there was no need to waste time with that system either. That system was flawed and designed to disappoint in the real world. As a result of what the guys in Florida specialized in, they heard thousands of stories, met hundreds of system developers and programmers, and they got to manage and experience first-hand what **worked in the real world over long periods of time**. They also got to see what did not work.

You gain confidence that you can win when you work with professionals who have had significant success over the years and have identified principles that have repeatedly lead to success. I was blessed to be a client of this firm in Florida for a number of years. The principle became one of my mentors. This firm was recently sold. A spectacular programmer has helped me enhance the programs that I use in my money management firm on the same principles that delivered the world class returns of this boutique firm.

## HOW EASY IT REALLY *WASN'T*

When you look at first glance, it is deceptively simple however when you focus on the chart in greater detail, the reality emerges. Looking simply at a compounded rate of return is deceptive.

*The Bible of Compounding Money*

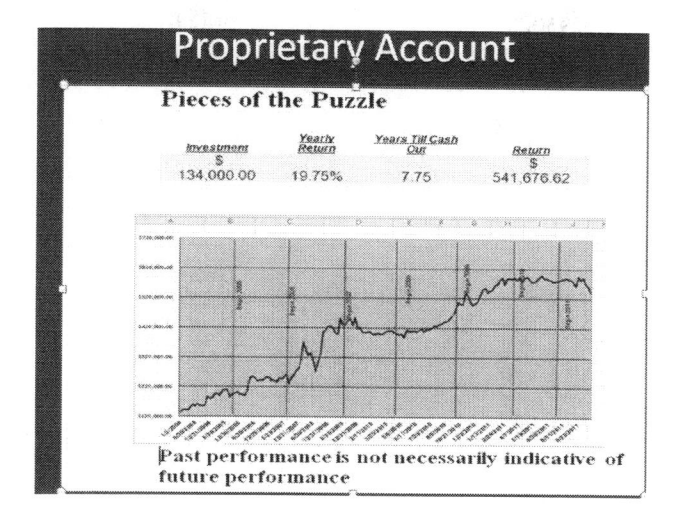

**Proprietary Account**

**Pieces of the Puzzle**

| Investment $ | Yearly Return | Years Till Cash Out | Return $ |
|---|---|---|---|
| 134,000.00 | 19.75% | 7.75 | 541,676.62 |

Past performance is not necessarily indicative of future performance

    You would think that anyone would want this to be their account; after all, the returns are world class. But I can say it is very possible, that if this was your account, most of you would be long gone. If is highly possible that many of you dropped out after the first 7 months of sideways movement. If that didn't get you, the next 10 months of sideways movement could have knocked more of you out of the game.

*Andy Abraham*

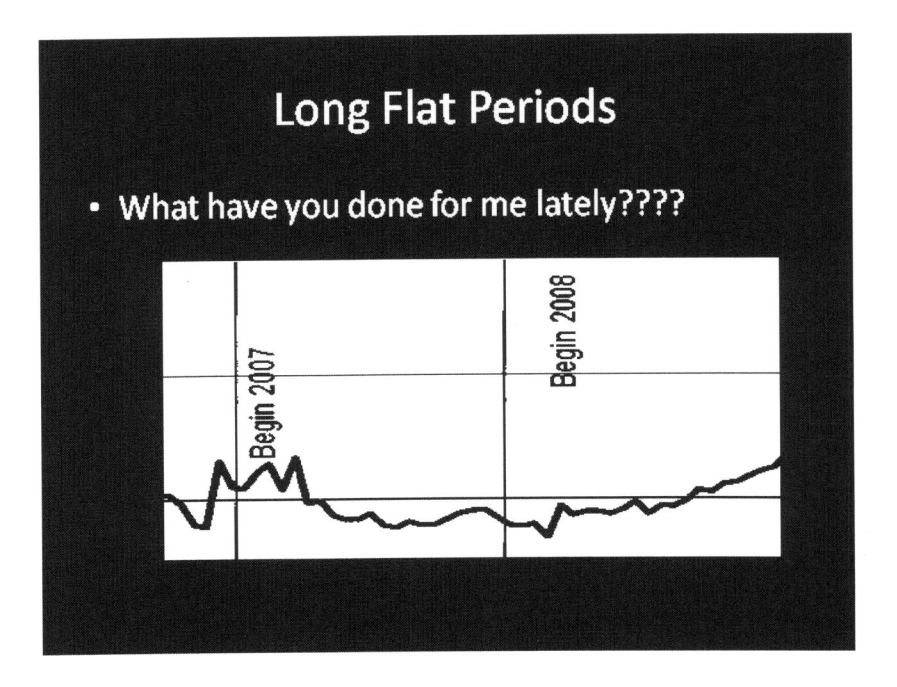

**Long Flat Periods**

- What have you done for me lately????

*[Chart showing Begin 2007 and Begin 2008]*

If I asked for a show of hands...How many of you would have been around after a 30% + price drawdown? How would you feel having your account going from $370,000 to $270,000?

Would you say to yourself at this point and maybe rightly so?

*This system is broken.*

*This system stinks.*

*The money manager does not know what he is doing?*

*GET ME OUT OF HERE!!!!*

*The Bible of Compounding Money*

### Steep and Ugly Draw Downs

- Account went from $370,000 to $270,000

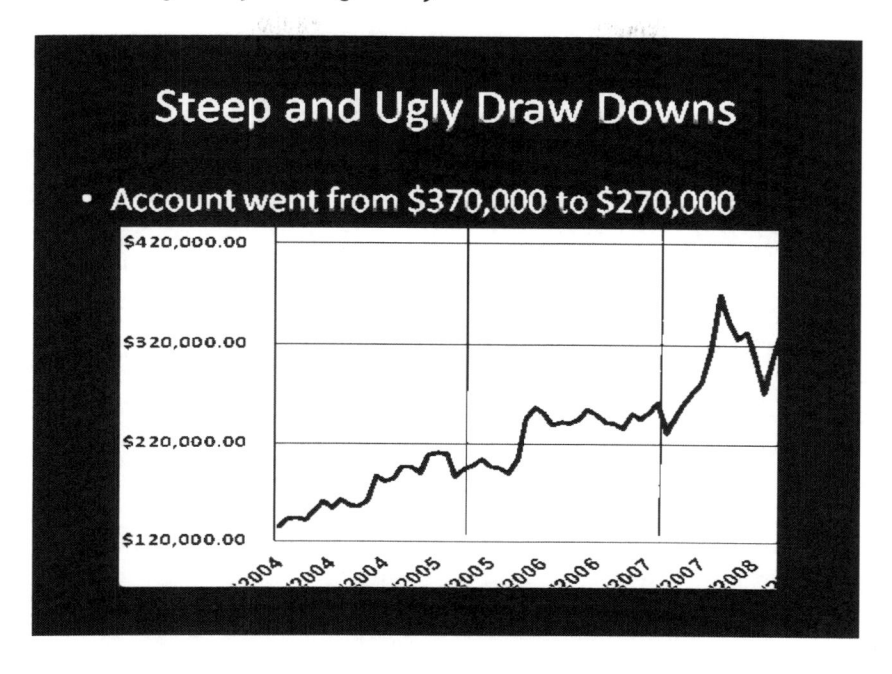

Look at this section. This is why it is difficult for investors to compound money. No one really has explained to potential investors the real pain you must go through. My goal is not to sugar coat anything rather prepare you for the realities of trading in order that you can compound money over long periods of time. In the real world, you don't get a nice smooth bell curve. You don't go to new highs every month unless you invest with Madoff. In fact there is no guarantee that you will ever go to a new high. And with many money managers or poorly designed programs, you won't.

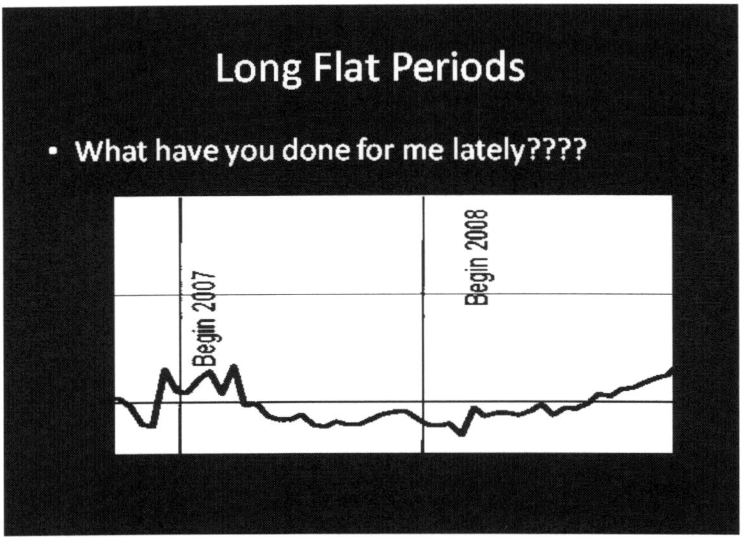
Long Flat Periods
• What have you done for me lately????
Begin 2007
Begin 2008

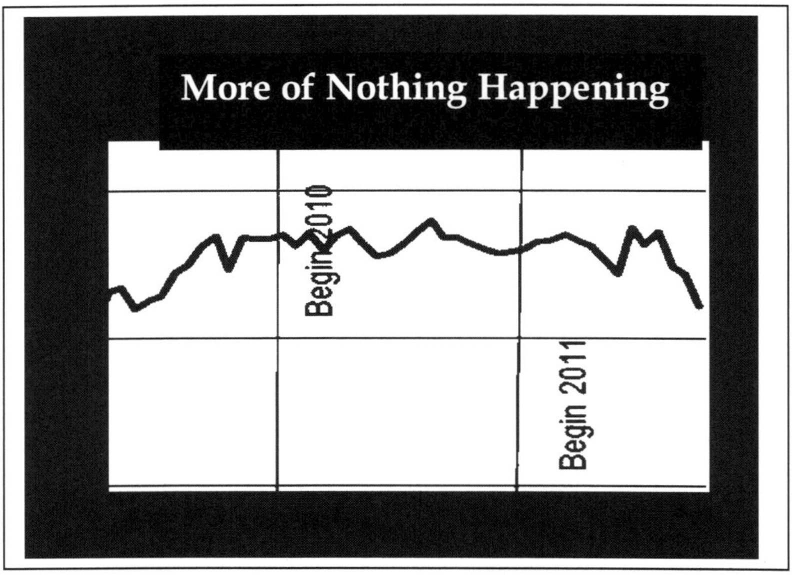
More of Nothing Happening
Begin 2010
Begin 2011

It is really unbelievably difficult to get investors to sit and to take no action during inevitable drawdowns and long periods of elusive profits like the above. When you look at these examples of sideways flat periods and steep price drawdowns, I have to tell you, that to achieve world class returns; you would have been in drawdown and sideways activity over 70% of time (In this case the 7 ¾ years that the program ran). Compare this to Warren Buffett that everyone would have thought would have been so easy to invest in and did not even think of the several 50% drawdowns.

Here's the thing....even if you have a world class program, it just isn't easy to hang in there.

You want to win? Then start with some world class money managers; but that isn't nearly enough. Have the program explained to you in detail so that you know what types of price and equity drawdowns you are likely to experience. Develop the mental fortitude to get through the drawdowns. And then surround yourself with professionals that are putting their money up in these same programs and who have been through these experiences before. Winning isn't easy. But surrounding yourself with professionals who know how to help you in the tough times is very rewarding.

In my prior book with Wiley Books *The Bible of Trend Following: How Professional Traders Compound Money and Manage the Risk*, David Druz from Tactical summed it quoting:

*"I spent a lot of time learning things the hard way, a lot of trial and error, a lot of hard knocks. Trading is still a lot of hard knocks. Drawdowns can go on seemingly forever. You can have days, weeks, even months on end without much in the way of profits. It can feel like you are a punching bag or a movie double who takes all the hits. But that's the nature of the game, of the business. Even after you've learned how to do it, you still take your hits. To succeed you just need to stand up every time you get knocked down. You need to have the confidence that standing up is the right thing to do. You need to know when to stand back up and how. And just by*

*standing up again and again and staying standing as long as you can before you get hit again, well, you can actually make more money than you lose over the long run in trend trading."*

Very few people succeed in this process. The learning curve is too steep and the correct psychology is too hard to implement. If you have any *attachment* to making money, and who doesn't, it is very tough to trade correctly.

There are a lot of people out there who somehow think they can outperform the market, but there are fewer of them who can actually do it. Even if you have the success in finding these world class managers, it is not easy. The vast majority of investors would have found it very difficult to stay invested in the managed account above. Moreover, it's harder and harder for the rest of us to find these successful unique money managers. The reason is, many of the guys who do very well stay small." That's because they concentrate on trading, not marketing. In the upcoming sections you will see highlighted money managers that have had 20% CARORs yet they are only managing one hundred or possibly two hundred million dollars. Compare this to substandard mutual funds that have accomplished less than single digits over the last 10 years and are managing billions of dollars..

## PROPER PSYCHOLOGY OF INVESTING IN WORLD CLASS MANAGERS

You have completed all of your due diligences both quantitative and qualitative. You possibly have done the uncomfortable and bought the drawdown of whom you feel is a world class money manager. This world class money manager has a liquid and transparent strategy that you understand. He or she has at least a 10 year real time track

*The Bible of Compounding Money*

record with a compounded annual rate of return on average of 15% or greater. You basically are ready to go. You have full expectation for success.

However after you invest, nothing happens. Actually nothing really has to happen. You get frustrated. You think to yourself you possibly made a mistake. There's much more to investing with world class money managers than just having a selection strategy. Only time, knowledge, experience, realistic expectation and guidance can assist you.

There are countless examples of investors who selected world class money managers and at best did not make money. The flip side of this is they lost money with world class money managers. What some of these investors did was bought the run-ups of these money managers and did not have the stomach to sit through the though drawdowns.

**Investors are their biggest enemy because of their emotions such as Fear and Greed!**

In order to develop the right mindset, you need to know what to expect when investing. Many investors mistakenly believe that investing with world class money managers will result in a consistently rising account balance, like having an ATM in their office. But you already know that losses are a part of our business as investors.

There will be some months and even years when your investments exceed your expectations, but more likely there will be periods when your trading results are far worse than you expected.

Following are two examples from the same money manager William Eckhardt.

The first one is a great period with the consecutive gains.

….and clearly there is always balance the consecutive losses.

## Consecutive Gains

| Run-up | Length (Mos.) | Start | End |
|---|---|---|---|
| 84.15 | 3 | 9/1/1996 | 11/1/1996 |
| 81.55 | 4 | 2/1/1995 | 5/1/1995 |
| 72.13 | 5 | 4/1/1993 | 8/1/1993 |
| 70.92 | 7 | 1/1/1997 | 7/1/1997 |
| 65.34 | 4 | 6/1/1992 | 9/1/1992 |
| 59.49 | 3 | 11/1/1995 | 1/1/1996 |

PAST PERFORMANCE IS NOT NECESSARILY INDICATIVE OF FUTURE RESULTS. THE RISK OF LOSS IN TRADING COMMODITY FUTURES, OPTIONS, AND FOREIGN EXCHANGE ("FOREX") IS SUBSTANTIAL.

## Consecutive Losses

| Run-up | Length (Mos.) | Start | End |
|---|---|---|---|
| -38.33 | 3 | 1/1/1992 | 3/1/1992 |
| -34.00 | 5 | 6/1/1995 | 10/1/1995 |
| -28.85 | 1 | 1/1/1994 | 1/1/1994 |
| -28.42 | 4 | 5/1/1996 | 8/1/1996 |
| -18.08 | 2 | 12/1/1994 | 1/1/1995 |
| -17.61 | 1 | 10/1/1994 | 10/1/1994 |

PAST PERFORMANCE IS NOT NECESSARILY INDICATIVE OF FUTURE RESULTS. THE RISK OF LOSS IN TRADING COMMODITY FUTURES, OPTIONS, AND FOREIGN EXCHANGE ("FOREX") IS SUBSTANTIAL.

It's paramount that you maintain a long-term perspective. I call my investing as well as my own trading a marathon. Too many investors focus on short-term results and lose their perspective. Money is made over long periods of time. I am asked all the time, "How did you do last month or last year with your trading?" I answer that it really does not matter as my time frame is the rest of my lifetime and want to compound money. The reality is, any month or even year is meaningless as long as I do not have losses. If I had a great month or year does that mean I will have a great month or year following? Probably not! I am at the mercy of the markets and the skill of the money managers. If markets do not trend I doubt I will make any money. I know markets do not have to do anything. There will be periods of contraction and expansion. This is the nature of the markets.

Investors that do not have the proper understanding and expectations will have issues after experiencing a losing period. Many times investor give up at the first drawdown and start looking for what they think is the next guru. This becomes a vicious cycle as every money manager will have losses (except Madoff). You have to accept the fact there will be losses and that we are dealing with uncertainty. If you jump around looking for the newest and greatest guru you are destined to lose money. It becomes a vicious cycle.

My goal for you is that you become objective and have patience and discipline with world class money managers, even when they go through their inevitable drawdowns. This is where the vast majority fail. What comes to my mind, why isn't everyone rich? All they had to do was invest with Warren Buffett and sit through his 50% drawdowns. Money is made by sitting, not by jumping.

It's important to focus on the big picture:

*Your money will be made over a long series of time.*

*No single trade of any manager means anything.*

*No month or any year of any manager means anything.*

My goal is to get you into the mindset of successful investing and what is entailed in order to succeed. Learning the proper attitudes and mindset are critical for successful. It is always easy to quit at the first instance of a drawdown. However there is nothing perfect in this world. There is neither a magic manager nor magic system. When I allocate to what I believe is a world class money manager, all that I can expect is that something will happen. There are only four possibilities:

- Big losses
- Small losses
- Big profits
- Small profits

These are the only possibilities. Before I allocate I look at the money manager's worst draw down. I am fully aware that his worst drawdown is ahead of them and not behind them. In order to give myself somewhat of a margin of safety I look to buy the drawdowns. This is far from perfect as we are dealing in uncertainty. It does give me a slight margin of safety. I am fully aware that this drawdown can get worse and that even the manager might close.

There are no perfects. That is why I only invest 1-5% of our family's money in any one money manager, world class or not. I have accepted the uncertainty and inherent risks. The only way I know to succeed is to accept the risk and temper my expectations. Thinking in this context will put you in the proper mindset.

# CHAPTER 7 SUMMATION

Even investing with world class money managers and trading concepts there will always be losses and drawdowns. An educated client who understands the methodology and the inevitability of drawdowns and extended periods of drawdowns has the better chance of compounding money over time.

It's important to focus on the big picture:

*Your money will be made over a long series of time.*
*No single trade of any manager means anything.*
*No month or any year of any manager means anything.*

## CHAPTER 8

# Common Investor Mistakes

One of the most typical mistakes that investor's make is that they chase returns. They look at the "best money manager" who had a good run in a particular category and blindly invest with him/her. They do not understand the strategy or the risks. They simply look at returns quantitatively and neglect any and all due diligence.

One would assume institutional or professional investors should be of a higher level of experience than others. It is assumable many professional investors went to Ivy League schools. This Ivy League education should make them better investors than others. However this is not the case many times. I am not trying to make a generalization but I have seen some of these issues over and over. I want to point them out so other institutional and professional investors do not make these same mistakes.

I have had countless conversations over the years with institutional investors, allocators as well as money managers themselves. To my dismay I am shocked how many simply run with the pack or herd or buy the proverbial highs of a money manager thinking it is now "safe" to invest. (Note the section of institutional investors of Bernie Madoff in prior section)

Too many institutional investors and professional investors have forgotten or did not pay attention while in school the golden rule of compounding wealth or as I call it "The Holy Grail".

## THE HOLY GRAIL IS REASONABLE RETURNS + TIME + COMPOUNDING = ENORMOUS WEALTH OVER TIME.

This is really the ultimate goal.

The goal is what the investment looks like in 10 years or 15 years or even 20 years. Too many institutional investors look for the new hot Hedge fund or commodity trading adviser. The reality is that the vast majority of new Hedge funds or commodity trading advisers have longevity of less than 5 years. Pension funds and family offices need to compound money in order to pay out way in the future pensions as well as perpetuate family wealth.

Look at the simple example with 15%;

*The Bible of Compounding Money*

| | | |
|---|---|---|
| Current Principal: | $ | 100,000.00 |
| Annual Addition: | $ | 0 |
| Years to grow: | | 10 |
| Interest Rate: | | 15 % |
| Compound interest | 1 | time(s) annually |
| Make additions at ● start ○ end of each compounding period | | |
| **Calculate** | | |
| **Results** | | |
| Future Value: | $ | 404,555.77 |

I am sure the first question will be, "How can you guarantee me 15% return in any investment?" Truthfully no one can. However on average over many decades there have been some top tier commodity trading advisers who have averaged over 15%. The same can be said for top tier hedge funds. Money managers that generate these returns are rare. However you want to maximize your money. You should only want to invest with superior managers that both create these returns and at the same time manage the risks.

*Underscoring the common mistake that the vast majority of investors make, I am asked by both so-called professional allocators and simple investors, how was last month or last year?*

I find this question almost ridiculous. Does it mean if I have a great run one year or one particular month I am a genius and they should invest monies with me? Contrarily if I have a bad run due to inevitably choppy or non-directional markets I am no longer a "genius". Investors that think in terms of how was last month or last year will never get to the point of compounding money to extreme wealth. Their time horizon is too short.

Successful investing needs to be a lifetime strategy in which compounding and time has a chance to work. On another tangent, very few actually really want to dig deep and understand exactly how mine or any other money manager trading methodology works.

I have had similar conversations with other colleagues who manage money. One manager jokingly told me that he had an investor come in to his fund after two years of consecutive 30% returns. He was not overly interested in understanding the actual trading methodology. He was simply chasing returns. As Murphy's Law would have it, after 24 months of spectacular returns the money manager encountered a drawdown. In commodity trading it is not unrealistic to have a draw down right after your biggest runs up. After being up in the 60% range, the manager gave back 10%. He experienced several months of lack luster returns and was down 10%. This unfortunate return chaser thought he was secure and to his shock he was down 10%. He bought the highs and then panicked. He sold out his position, took his loss only to see the manager recover shortly thereafter.

There are other institutional and professional investors that believe that size of the fund correlates with safety. However many times the vast size of funds can be their undoing and can impact their returns. Winton is managing over $22.6 Billion dollars. It seems just due to his immense size institutional investors feel secure. Winton was launched by Adam Harding with $1.6 million and as of 2011 it held $22.6 billion in assets under management. Ironically Winton encountered a 13% draw down in the first month of its existence however ended the year up 3.49%. In the following three years Winton did very well and returned profits to their investors; 52.18% in 1998, 15.07% in 1999 and 10.44% in 2000.

*The Bible of Compounding Money*

Winton marketed themselves to Japanese investors. Winton was on a roll, however by late 2001, they endured a four-month period of drawdowns following the September 11th attacks. They, like other successful commodity trading advisers, understand risk recovered the drawdown and from the company's inception through the mid-2000s, its annual rate of return was approximately 19%. Using the concept of the rule of 72, every 3 ½ years, investors' money double. However as demonstrated in the below chart the annual rate of return has fallen to 15.65%. As well a notable mention is that Winton even experienced a peak to valley drawdown of 25.59%.

Winton is a world class money manager yet was not able to avoid a drawdown of this magnitude. A forgotten issue is that Winton cannot easily enter and exit all markets. Their focus must be the most liquid due to their immense size. For example the interest rate markets, stock indexes and currencies are able to be traded with large size and have witnessed big moves. The reality is that at times these most liquid markets are quiet.

The question arises how could a manager with large assets deploy in times of quiet markets? Clearly he stands the possibility of underperforming a smaller manager. Not that I am privy to the trades that some of the large commodity trading advisers however as example, cotton in 2010 had an amazing run. Since cotton is not one of the most liquid commodities I would doubt this trade would have been a possibility for a large size commodity trading adviser. Cotton went parabolic from 40 ranges all the way to virtually 220. This was a massive move. Smaller commodity trading adviser managers like me were able to participate and profit from this move. Actually due to taking a piece out of this move in 2010 I was able to generate 34% net in one of my programs.

~ 159 ~

My point is that large managers, regardless if they trade stocks or commodities, are not as nimble as smaller mangers when they are first starting out. This does not negate large managers' experience or propensity to generate positive returns for their investors. It does negate the markets that they can participate in though.

What I have done over the years is look to invest with a money manager who has been around for a period of at least 10 years, and buy their inevitable drawdowns as long as I understand how they manage the risks. I do not simply follow the crowd or buy a manager after a good run as I truly believe anything can happen. I feel if I simply buy a manger that is not in a drawdown I increase my risk and potential drawdown with that manager. I look to play defense and more defenses. As nothing is perfect there are times with managers whom I would like to invest with and have not had an opportunity.

In the following examples, I recently allocated to Tactical, a Hawaii based commodity trading adviser who has been in the field since the 1980s. After a terrific year in 2010 of 69% returns, Tactical had a drawdown of in the 30% range. I invested in his program in January and the drawdown extended now to the current drawdown of 36.51%. Only liars catch bottoms. Time will tell if my investment was prudent.

This was not an all or nothing investment. I invested a small percentage of my net worth. I do not allocate to any money manager more than 5% of my family's assets to any idea. This concept attempts to avoid huge volatility in my portfolio.

Saxon is a money management firm that the vast majority in the investment world has not heard about. As per the website of Saxon, Howard Seidler, is a graduate of the

Massachusetts Institute of Technology (MIT) with degrees in Chemical Engineering and Management Science, is the president and sole trader for Saxon. Mr. Seidler has professionally managed futures accounts for over 26 years.

What is fascinating is Saxon's trading record. Seidler was one of the original Turtle Traders (a group of traders that were taught per a bet between William Eckhardt and Richard Dennis). Siedler's compounded rate of return since 1993 is 20.5%. In the beginning of his career his returns were rather volatile with drawdowns reaching 60%. However over the last decade the volatility has diminished. He has lowered volatility dramatically.

Howard exemplifies the proof that all trend followers or CTAs are not the same. Overly the last several years in which most CTAs struggled Saxon was able to sidestep the negative periods and even make money. In 2011 and in 2009 most CTA trend followers struggled.

My key goal is: identify the top money managers that have been around for a minimum of 10 years that are aware of risk and as long as there is not a strategy shift stay with them for decades and compound money. These top money managers are very rare.

The reason I want to see at least a 10 year record is that these managers have been exposed to various market cycles and not only survived but had top tier returns. It is a great deal of work identifying and preforming the proper due diligence. In later chapters I will discuss this in much greater detail.

# CHAPTER 8 SUMMATION

Many investors underperform even successful world class money managers by not understanding what they will have to go through in order to achieve success over long periods of time. Too many investors focus on the short term. Wealth is only created over time and with much patience.

The Bible of Compounding Money

## CHAPTER 9
# Money Manager Blow Ups

**Since Late 2006 At Least**

# 117

**Major Funds at 71 Outfits Have Imploded!!!**

**Billions of Dollars Have Been Vaporized!**

*Andy Abraham*

# NO SUCH THING AS GENIUS

The only thing we are dealing with in life and in investing is uncertainty. The only certainty is uncertainty. Every time we leave our house we do not really know if we will return. There are car accidents or unexpected events that we could never have imagined. The same holds true for our investments. There is absolutely no guarantee with any money manager. Many are deluded that the bigger the money manager, the safer he is.

Investment history has proven this to be a major fallacy. Another delusion is based on investment success and intelligence. Long term capital encompasses this concept. Roger Lowenstein wrote the book *When Genius Failed* in 2000, which detailed the story of long term capital.

John Meriwether, a famously successful Wall Street trader, put together a team of PHD genius in 1998. He gathered together his former disciples and a handful of super economists from academia and built Long Term Capital. The money flowed into the geniuses. At Long-Term, Meriwether and his geniuses believed that their computer models could negate risk, and allow them to profit with near mathematical certainty. Those investors who blindly threw their money at Long term were benefitted initially. It seemed the geniuses in Greenwich couldn't lose.

**A short** four years later, when a default in Russia set off a global storm that Long-Term's models hadn't anticipated, its supposedly safe portfolios imploded. In five weeks, the geniuses went from being mega-rich to discredited failures. With the firm about to go under, its staggering $100 billion balance sheet threatened to drag down markets around the world.

At the eleventh hour, fearing that the financial system of the world was in peril, the Federal Reserve Bank hastily summoned Wall Street's leading banks to underwrite a bailout. Ironically as the geniuses lost money, some of the world class trend followers profited. These trend followers were not noble prize winners or geniuses. They understood risk. Understanding risk keeps you compounding money.

## ATTICUS $20 BILLION DOLLAR IMPLOSION

Atticus was an event driven hedge fund run by Tim Barakett and his partner David Slager. At the peak Atticus had $20 billion dollars of money under management. When it became clear, after steep losses, Barakett and Slager decided to close and assets had fallen to $3.5 billion dollars. Atticus was ranked #2 on a list of the top 10 asset losers of hedge funds.

The Atticus Global strategy was launched in December 1996 and had compounded investor's capital at over 19% net annually since inception. However, Atticus's two main hedge funds were hit with losses of between 25 percent and 32 percent during the last bear market.

What irritated investors more than the losses was a side pocket setup by Barakett. Barakett set up the side-pocket fund for Atticus' investment in Deutsche Boerse. Investors were livid. So much for liquidity! The investors did not they have the ability to redeem. That caused one fund-of-funds investor to warn others he didn't think Barakett could turn his lagging fund around. From this point the dominos just kept on falling.

## WHAT IS REALLY SAFE?

You would think the name Safe Capital would mean your money was safe. **Wrong!** Austin Capital Management Ltd had a fund called Safe Harbor Fund. Safe Harbor fund, with all of their institutional genius, invested with Bernie Madoff. KeyCorp bought Austin Capital Management in 2006. The hedge fund firm had about $900 million of assets under management at the time. Putting things into perspective, KeyCorp is one of the nation's largest bank-based financial services companies, with assets of approximately $87 billion. I am a simple commodity trading advisor and investor and I could not understand how Bernie Madoff did not have losing months. Due to this fact, I did not feel comfortable investing with him. I had my opportunity; I grew up in South Florida and was connected. The story just did not make any sense. No one is perfect. Not to have losing months. My friends and colleagues called me a "Shmuck" for not investing with Madoff.

I was told I was paranoid and just did not get it. Well, the fact is they got it. They lost their money. You would have thought one of the largest financial services companies in the US would have realized that no one is perfect. I have never met any trader or investor who did not have losses. Safe capital was not safe. Common sense could have been used in this instance. Key Corp and Austin "Safe Harbor" lost at least $186 million to the notorious Ponzi scheme.

## MORTGAGE HEDGE FUND BLOWUP!

Hedge fund implosions are just because of the subprime or 2008 bear market. When I started in 1994 I remember the implosion of David Askin. David Askin was a mortgage trader who had invested in mortgage securities.

On the promise of liquidity high and leverage low, "risk neutral" investment strategies sounded great for investors chasing returns. Askin had approximately $630 million dollars in three funds: Granite Partners, Granite Corporation, and Quartz Hedge Fund. In 1994, interest rates spiked.

Clearly when interest rates rise, prepayments come down and the value of Askin's fund imploded. Askin's funds with $600 million in assets filed for bankruptcy. Investors lost everything, and the collapse generated a string of lawsuits.

## FRAUDSTERS AND SCAMMERS

Before you invest, you must complete a full due diligence. You do not want to simply chase numbers. There are always frauds and scams. You cannot just count on the regulators. One of the safer concepts is to have a managed account. When you have a managed account the money manager only has power of attorney to complete buys or sells.

*He can never touch your money.*

Frauds never stop. Donald O'Neill ran a hedge fund that specialized in trading forex. Shockingly he ended up having institutional clients who did not do adequate due diligence. He embezzled the money he was supposedly managing and went on junkets to Las Vegas and even had the audacity to purchase a multimillion dollar house.

O'Neill faked account statements from his brokerage firms and finally the regulators caught up with him.

## MARKET WIZARDS ARE NOT IMMUNE

Even market wizards are not immune. In one of the stock market *Wizard's* books by Jack Schwager there was a chapter on Michael Lauer. The SEC must not have read Jack Schwager's book *Market Wizards*.

Quoting the SEC web site;
*On July 10, 2003, the SEC obtained a temporary restraining order and asset freeze against a number of defendants involved in a billion dollar hedge fund fraud. The defendants included two hedge fund advisors and the principal that controlled these entities, Michael Lauer. The SEC also named in the civil action a number of hedge funds as relief defendants. The SEC's complaint alleged that from at least March 2000 to the time the SEC filed its complaint, the defendants engaged in a scheme to over-inflate the performances and net asset values of three hedge funds. Lauer took advantage of the thin market for these stocks to claim higher values for them than was reasonable, and both Lancer's auditor and bank went along with it. That allowed the fund to report great gains to customers rather than the losses that were occurring when a more reasonable market valuation was used. When the SEC opened its investigation, investors ran for the gates, which forced the fund to sell its illiquid penny stocks at penny prices. Lauer blamed the losses on the SEC, but the SEC did not agree. Instead, it shut down the fund and held Lauer in contempt of court.*

## PONZI SCHEME FROM THE BAYOUS

Ponzi schemes have been around for almost 100 years. Ponzi schemes were named after Charles Ponzi and his fraud in the 1920's. Ponzi was a businessman and con artist in the U.S. and Canada. Charles Ponzi promised clients a 50% profit within 45 days, or 100% profit within 90 days. This was through a supposed arbitrage of postal reply coupons. In reality, Ponzi was paying early investors using the investments of later investors. Nothing ever really changes. Investors are greedy and Ponzi schemes flourish throughout the ages.

Bayou Group LLC was a hedge fund founded by Samuel Israel. I have to admit I looked at Bayou due to a quantitative search on returns. The quantitative were very interesting. I was working with a fund of funds and called Bayou. I wanted more information. I called several times and they did not return my phone calls. All I could think was, if I wanted to give them money and they did not have the courtesy to return my phone call how would they react when I wanted my money back?

I passed without further pursuing. I can say I was lucky that I missed a bullet. However proper due diligence would have raised a red flag. This is why it is so important to complete a full qualitative due diligence. One major red flag was the fact that Sam Israel's brokerage firm, Bayou Securities, executed all the hedge fund's trades. Bayou ended up stealing close to $450 million dollars.

## LEVERAGE IS DEADLY

Not every implosion is fraud. Amaranth Advisors was one of the largest known trading losses and hedge fund collapses in history. Amaranth was managed by Nicholas Maounis with $9 billion in assets under management and collapsed in September 2006 after losing approximately $5 billion on natural gas futures.

Amaranth started in the convertible arbitrage sector, however due to the success of energy trader Brian Hunter more assets were given to him. Hunter had tremendous success in 2005 in his trading due to hurricane Katrina and his bullish bets on natural gas. Success begot success however Hunter traded too large and could not exit his positions. Hunter repeatedly used borrowed money to double-down on his bets.

Amaranth was squeezed until it imploded. Once again supposed institutional investors were decimated. They simply chased returns without understanding the risks they were taking on. Chasing returns is a common theme of investment failure.

Please address this nice long list before you think to chase returns in strategies you might not fully understand or do not offer liquidity or transparency. Actually this is just a small part from the Hedge Fund grave yard. I could fill a book with more names.

Satellite Asset Management

Parkcentral Global Hub

Weavering Capital - Macro Fixed Income Fund

Highland Capital Management

Ascot Partners LP

Gabriel Capital LP

Bernard L. Madoff Investment Securities

Okumus Capital

ING Diversified Yield, Regular Income, etc.

Centaurus Alpha Fund

BlueBay Emerging Market Total Return Fund

Trident European Fund (JO Hambro)

Tontine Partners

Lancelot Investment Management

Epic Limited Partnership

*The Bible of Compounding Money*

Gordian Knot - Sigma Finance, Ltd.

Modulus Europe (Powe Capital)

Ospraie Fund

Dalton Melchior Japan Fund

Windmill Management (SageCrest funds)

Turnberry Capital Management

Absolute Capital Management

Lydia Capital

RREEF REFlex Fund

Endeavour Capital

Old Lane Partners (Citigroup)

Rumson Capital

Russell Investments (Alternative Strategies Funds)

Cornerstone Quantitative Investment Group

GoldLink Capital

North American Equity Opportunities (Goldman Sachs)

Pentagon Capital Management

Absolute Capital Group

Drake Management - Global Opportunities

ASAT Finance (Citigroup)

MAT Finance (Citigroup)

Blue River Asset Management

Carlyle Capital Corporation

Tequesta Mortgage Fund

Focus Capital

Peloton ABS Master Fund, Multi-Strategy Fund

Falcon Strategies (Citigroup)

CSO Partners (Citigroup)

Sailfish Capital Partners

Polar Capital - Lotus, Tech. Absolute Funds

Standard Chartered - Whistlejacket SIV

Deephaven Event Fund

Rhinebridge Plc (IKB)

Niederhoffer Matador Fund

Cooper Hill Partners

Pirate Capital (Activist Funds)

Synapse High Grade ABS Fund

Cheyne Finance LLC (Cheyne Capital Management)

Geronimo Multi-Strategy, Sector Opportunity, and Option & Income

Basis Capital Fund Management, Ltd. - Basis Yield Alpha

Solent Capital Partners LLP, Mainsail II

Sentinel Management Group

Sachsen LB: Ormond Quay conduit fund

Parvest Dynamic ABS, BNP Paribas ABS Euribor and BNP Paribas ABS Eonia (BNP      Paribas)

Union Investment Asset Management Holding AG

Oddo: Cash Titrisation; Cash Arbitrages; and Court Terme Dynamique

Sowood Capital Management

Galena Street Fund

United Capital Markets Holdings Inc.: Horizon Funds

Caliber Global Investment

Lake Shore Asset Management

Ritchie Capital Management

Bear Stearns High Grade Credit Funds

Dillon Read Capital Management (UBS)

*Proper due diligence is paramount with diversification*

*This is just one of the reasons I wrote this book!*

# IT IS EASY TO FORGET THE PAST

It is human nature to forget the past. However for those who forget the lessons of the past will make the same mistakes. It is much better to learn from others mistakes as opposed to your own.

Not looking that far back, in 2008 it seemed the financial system was imploding. The lessons learned have been forgotten by all too many. Institutions that existed hundreds of years blew up. Governments and central banks around the world rushed to attempt to save the financial system. As of this writing it seems that the "Day of Reckoning" has only been postponed. I am neither a bear nor a bull. However using common logic I do not understand how trillions of bad loans on books of the world can just go away and the world would be beautiful once again.

The question was asked

### *How did we get into this situation?*

The definition of fear was forgotten as was the words "Cheap Money". Banks were not just lending to zombie borrowers. Borrowers who had no source of income were virtually being paid to close on houses. Borrowers walked away from closing tables with money in their pockets. What happened to the good 'ole days that you had to prove your income and put down a large down payment?

Hedge funds dwarfed themselves into lenders for emerging markets. Hedge funds became a source of capital for banks in Kazakhstan to Russia as well as to dairy farms in the Ukraine. They were drawn to the elixir of high interest rates & currency appreciation. The herd of Hedge funds grew this trade and became self-sustaining. Who needed due diligence? This time it was different. It is *always* different until something blows up.

However nothing is ever different as was when Julian Robertson borrowed Yen to buy US Treasuries. Many other hedge funds did the same trade until it blew up. What the banks and hedge funds did not take into account was liquidity. They could not get out of their positions when the proverbial "shit hit the fan". There was no counterparty. They were frozen!

The failure of Lehman Brothers signified the end of the modern investment bank model. Lehman and its contemporaries borrowed countless billions in the short term money markets which in turn they purchased assets that were hard to liquidate. I have to chuckle as at one point in my

*The Bible of Compounding Money*

investment career an investor informed me, he was not interested in my trading because I did not work for Lehman or Bear Stearns. I am still trading and compounding and they're toast.

Once the crisis hit, short term lending froze up. After Lehman the next domino was Merrill Lynch. A year prior Merrill shares were trading at approximately $90 a share. However with failure of the Lehman Brothers and Bear Stearns, Bank of America gobbled up Merrill at $29 a share which they were happy to get.

With the implosion of Lehman, Bear Stearns and Merrill, it was openly assumed that Goldman Sachs and Morgan Stanley were next. The deadly elixir of high debt, high leverage and the absence of short term financing left them extremely exposed.

On CNBC quotes were posted on Goldman and Morgan Stanly that many traders considered a death countdown.

Next on the chopping block was the ever so powerful AIG. AIG wrote credit default swaps on the possibility of bonds or even mortgages failing. The US government came in and bailed out AIG with a shocking $85 billion dollar "loan". The rumor mill flew.

It was speculated that Morgan was somehow exposed to AIG. With this speculation, Morgan's stock fell approximately 40%. Hedge funds and high net worth investors clamored to get all of their assets out of Morgan Stanley and Goldman Sachs. These investors did not fully have a complete and thought out plan. Hedge funds were facing margin calls and imploding.

Citadel, one of the most famous hedge funds was rumored to be blowing up. During the deluge Citadel was down 55%. The losses at Citadel were estimated to be $9 billion dollars. To put this into context, this was double the losses of Long Term Capital. More than 1,500 hedge funds blew up.

> *"What happened in September 2008 was a kind of bank run. Creditors lost confidence in the ability of investment banks to redeem short-term loans, leading to a precipitous decline in lending in the repurchase agreements (repo) market."* --Robert E. Lucas, Jr., Nancy L. Stokey, visiting scholars, Federal Reserve Bank of Minneapolis, May 2011.

## THE CULPRIT, LEVERAGE AND LIQUIDITY

Blue Chip Hedge funds had extreme losses.

Harbinger capital lost $1 billion when Lehman brothers cratered. Chris Hohn of the Children's Investment fund was down 42%.

Long Term Capital original founders, John Meriwether and Myron Scholes, who had opened another fund, were on the floor once again.

Investors scrambled to exit hedge funds however many managers placed redemption restrictions. Even Paul Tudor Jones locked in investors by suspending quarterly redemptions and "gating" their money.

*So much for liquidity!*

The point of this section is to exemplify several points. Even the so called Hedge Fund gurus many thought were blue chip can lose money.

More importantly are the questions that must be asked:

Who is my counter party?

What is the stability of my counterparty?

Do you give me full transparency?

Do you give me full liquidity?

Remembering these aspects will prevent a great deal of problems and potential losses in the future.

*You must believe that anything can happen and will happen.*

# FRAUD IS IMPOSSIBLE TO FIGHT

I closed the last paragraph that anything can happen. What happened to MF Global not many expected? On Halloween 2011, MF Global, one of the world's largest commodity trading firms for hundreds of years went bankrupt. With the bankruptcy the sworn statement of the futures industry that segregated accounts were safe, went to ashes. Client's segregated accounts were pilfered in order to make margin calls for MF Global to JP Morgan. Quoting Wikipedia, On October 31, 2011, MF Global executives admitted that transfer of $700 million from customer accounts to the broker-dealer and a loan of $175 million in customer funds to MF Global's U.K. subsidiary to cover (or mask) liquidity shortfalls at the company occurred on October 28, 2011. MF could not repay these monies with its own funds.

Improper co-mingling, or mixing, of company and client funds took place for days before the illicit transfer and loans—and perhaps many other days earlier in the year.

According the New York Times, "MF Global dipped again and again into customer funds to meet the demands", perhaps as beginning as early as August 2011. As per the trustee James W Giddens who liquidated the company after its collapse, the losses incurred by customers of MF Global stood at $1.6 billion because of the debacle as of April 2012.

The vast majority of these funds have not been returned to customers; I was one of those clients. I had 14 accounts since 1994 all segregated, dating back to the days when MF Global purchased EDF Man. What is most shocking is that emails appeared that Jon Corzine (JC personally ordered the movement of client segregated funds). The fact is that Corzine was a major supplier of campaign contributions to the Obama campaign. Joe Biden once called Jon Corzine the smartest man on Wall Street.

*The smartest man on Wall Street to gamble over $6 billion dollars, use client segregated funds to make margin calls yet walk away not prosecuted.*

It is nice to have friends in high places.

# THE WORLD'S SAFEST PLACE TO DEPOSIT YOUR MONEY

My wife always has called me obsessive compulsive paranoid. I thank her for this lovely comment. What saved me from the MF Global fraud was that I left a large amount of my trading accounts at Treasury Direct (The Federal Reserve Bank of the United States). Before the MF Global bankruptcy I was spooked by what was happening and closed 4 accounts and wired out the proceeds. I did not want to complicate my trading record for my commodity trading advisory and for my accountant so I thought to wait till the end of the month. I transferred my positions to another FCM

## The Bible of Compounding Money

however the cash which was supposed to been wired out the Thursday before Oct 31 2011 never happened.

Monday morning the news broke and EVERYTHING was frozen. I considered myself lucky. I dodged a lethal bullet. However I was still struck. I still had a large amount of cash stuck at MF Global. Worse were the countless traders and commodity trading advisors who had open positions. They could not liquidate them. I know of one commodity trading advisor who had three people calling on speed dialers around the clock to close their positions. He had unlimited risk with open positions. I know of other traders who flew to Chicago to unwind their open positions, however to no avail.

*The lesson that I learned as well as my colleagues have learned is to have multiple accounts at multiple futures clearing firms and leave only margin required plus a small amount of liquidity.*

We can try to do be diligent. I have setup Google news alerts on all of my brokers. Possibly out of paranoia I closed my accounts at one FCM even though they were wonderful to me because their stock was hovering around a 52 week low and I got spooked. After MF Global we learned that really nothing was safe. Imagine if your bank made bad loans and went into your bank account and took your money. This is exactly what happened at MF Global.

What is ironic is that if someone robs a bank with a gun, they go to jail for an extended vacation. However if you're a good friend of President Obama and pilfer client segregated accounts you do not go to jail, rather you spend your summer in the Hamptons for vacation.

*The biggest question for many: where were the regulators and why isn't Jon Corzine in jail?*

## MF GLOBAL PART 2

The issue of the absence of regulators became evident in another fraud PFG (Peregrine). The PFG fraud was only eight months after MF Global's fraud. Russell Wasendorf ,the CEO of Peregrine falsified information in filings and overstated the company's bank deposits, leaving a shortfall that currently, and has previously since 2010, exceeded $200 million. In a suicide note, Wasendorf admitted, *"Through a scheme of using false bank statements I have been able to embezzle millions of dollars from customer accounts at Peregrine Financial Group, Inc., twenty years ago and have gone undetected until now."*

## WHERE WERE THE REGULATORS?

MF Global really has only been a warning. The financial markets are far from being fixed. As spun wrongly in the news, the financial crisis was not caused by homeowners extending themselves. It was caused by giant financial institutions borrowing too much money, much of it from each other on the repurchase (repo) markets. The problem was based on the Repo market. MF Global and all their colleagues were allowed to repo client funds overnight (REG 1.23 & REG 1.29).

*"Without some repo reform, we are at risk for another panic."* --Gary B. Gorton, Professor of Management and Finance, Yale School of Management, November 16, 2010.

*Repo has a flaw: It is vulnerable to panic, that is, 'depositors' may 'withdraw' their money at any time, forcing the system into massive deleveraging. We saw this over and over again with demand deposits in all of U.S. history prior to deposit insurance. This problem has not been addressed by the Dodd-Frank legislation. So, it could happen again. The next shock could be a sovereign default, a crash of some important market -- who knows what it might be?"* --Gary B. Gorton, *Professor of Management and Finance, Yale School of Management, August 14, 2010.*

As I strongly believe, the only **Certainty is Uncertainty;** the only thing we can rely on as investors is diversity among our investments, I allocate 1-5% of available capital to any money manager and always know where the cash is sitting in any investment. You also want to make sure there is diversification among your cash in any investment.

There are those that argue against this diversification. However we are not just looking for return on capital we are at some point looking for the return of capital.

## CHAPTER 9 SUMMATION

There will always be money managers that implode for various reasons. This implosion ranges from fraud to leverage. The golden rule is never allocating more than 5% of your trading capital to any one idea.

*Andy Abraham*

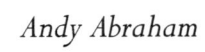

## CHAPTER 10

# Doing the Uncomfortable: Buying the Drawdown

One strategy I have used for years to enhance the margin of safety is buying the drawdowns of world class money managers that *understand risk*. Most people can't do this. It is uncomfortable. They have more comfort when a money manager is doing well. They think this lowers their risk or more so they might think they do not have any risk. I do not look for comfort. I look to "try" to increase my margin of safety. However I am well aware we are dealing with uncertainty and the drawdowns can worsen (as exemplified in the following paragraphs). There are no perfects when we invest. Anything can and will happen. Even buying the drawdowns of established world class money managers does not ensure us of anything. Drawdowns can worsen and even world class managers can close up shop.

There are always two sides of a coin. The negative of this strategy of buying drawdowns is that one can miss long periods of time when world class money managers can compound money. In order to "attempt" to compensate for this I have in cases invested a small amount just to get started with a prospective manager that I feel *understands risk.*

As any trade or investment is 50/50 the concept of scaling in is a way to get started with a manager. Again there is no perfect. It does not exist. There have been times scaling into a money manager who has not experienced a recent drawdown has worked as well as other times I have bought the recent highs of that money manager only to enter a steep draw down. Scaling in can give the potential of upside as well as one would have only made a relative allocation and would be saving the powder for the future. This opens all of types of potentials.

Contrarily there have been managers who have had substantial drawdowns and not recovered. Nothing is perfect. More so you must accept the risk when you invest. Most do not. Not accepting the inherent risk leads to unfilled expectations and disappointment.

It should not be any surprise to you that some money managers have closed due to business reasons or have just lost the desire to continue after a steep or lengthy drawdown. Managers close due to operational issues not just trading issues. It is really a fine line when we invest and a potential of margin of safety. This margin of safety is only an attempt and be should be thought about before potential returns. The big benefit of this margin of safety is to "TRY" to mitigate the inherent drawdown's going.

*I cannot say it enough....We are dealing with uncertainty.*

Once you truly accept this fact, you will not feel you missed out or feel badly when things do not work out. I suggest allocating between 1% to 5% of your investable assets in any idea or even possibly less and diversify. This is how I have personally invested my family's money over the last 18 years. Even with my own firm's trading, I do not invest all of our money, even though I believe I have a world class strategy.

There are those who say investing in this manner is over diversifying and possibly they are correct. One can over diversify but when you are diversifying with world class managers who trade diversified strategies and who have succeeded over decades, you put the possibility of success on your side. I cannot stress those words enough—**"The Possibility"**.

### What Does the Smart Money Do?

Over the years I have had countless conversations with which I consider world class money managers and ask them who are their most successful investors and what they do right?

*The common theme amongst successful investors is having a long term focus, riding out the drawdowns as well as using drawdowns as entry points to invest.*

The conversation usually shifts to what the majority of investors do. The vast majority of investors become only interested in a manager based on a quantitative approach when a manager has a good run. Simply put, they are chasing returns. When managers have a good run, the money flows in. Conversely when the manager hits a drawdown these type of investors run for the exits.

Invariably it is very difficult for these investors to successfully compound money over the years. They are looking for the so-called easy approach to investing. Investing is very difficult and we are always dealing with uncertainty. For those that want certainty, investing is not one of those fields.

I use the word world class money manager; I have specific rules for identifying as well as the proper due diligence. **To be intentionally repetitious**, I consider a world class money manager, one that has been around for a minimum of 10 years and has a compounded rate of return over these 10 years of at least 15% on average, who gives me liquidity and transparency and *understands risk*. Not too much to ask for right?

I have watch list for these managers. I do not just simply buy them and dive right in. I might scale in to a small degree at times, depending on my liquidity, but the vast majority of the time I wait for the inevitable drawdown. In order to succeed long term investors must accept the uncertainty and more importantly the inherent risks in trading and investing. I diversify among them as I am aware that anyone of them can have a major issue or blowup.

## ONLY LIARS CATCH BOTTOMS OR TOPS OF ANYTHING

There have been times I have invested in a drawdown of a manager in which I consider world class and who *understand risk* only to experience greater drawdowns. Do not think for one second that you will catch the bottom. Only liars at cocktail parties are that smart. In most cases months or maybe even years might go by until you start seeing profits. You must have the patience to stick it out. This is truly a game of patience, discipline and the only certainty is uncertainty.

John Henry, a trend following guru presents us an interesting contrary example. At his peak John Henry was managing in excess of $2.5 billion dollars. He was in partnership with Dean Witter. Dean Witter suggested to their clients that due to possible inflation it was prudent to invest a minimum of 5% of their net worth with their approved managed futures manager John Henry.

JWH was founded in 1982 and took off. The pedigree could not be better. JWH became one of the founding fathers of managed futures and the systematic trend following approach. JWH traded the worlds markets and historically had generated returns non-correlated to those of equity and fixed income investments. The firm managed assets for retail, institutional and private investors from around the world.

However as of the date of the writing of this book November 2012, John W. Henry & Company: Global Analytics Program has been struggling. They endured their worst drawdown of approximately 38% with duration of 17 months. Assets under management fell from in excess of $2 billion dollars to a paltry $91 million. JWH would swing for the fences (with no pun intended since that John Henry owns the Florida Marlins and the Boston Red Sox).

With JWH swinging for the fences did he put more focus on baseball? Was his passion and hunger diminished? One of the points I always look for is the proverbial PHD. I want managers that I invest in to be passionate, hungry and driven. Without these characteristics, continued performance could be doubtful.

John Henry was always volatile. Actually too volatile for my comfort level!

JWH seemed to me more concerned with generating high returns as opposed to managing the risks. John Henry had a fantastic run up in 2007-2008 +79.88% in 7 months between 9/1/2007 and 3/1/2008. However with that type of volatility one would expect drawdowns as volatile.

JWH highlights the proverbial statement that **Past performance is not necessarily indicative of future results.**

JWH's performance shows the reality of this. In their beginning years JWH had 17 out of its first 20 years profitable however this was followed by losing years in 5 out of 7 recent. This would be difficult for any investor to tolerate. One always has to aware of the risks as well as the style of the managers.

Several days ago, JWH made an announcement.

The brief message stated:

*"This is to notify you that JWH has determined to cease managing client assets effective December 31, 2012".*

# CHAPTER 10 SUMMATION

We only deal in uncertainty when we invest. We attempt to make our best decisions. One concept I use is to buy the inevitable drawdown of a world class money manager when they struggle. There are no guarantees with this strategy. The drawdown can worsen and the manager can even close. Buying drawdowns adds to a potential margin of safety.

# CHAPTER 11

# Transparency and Liquidity

I have seen over the years that managers that provide me transparency and liquidity give me somewhat of an additional layer of security. The best source for transparency and liquidity is having a managed account in your name or company's name. You see all the positions as well as you can close the position at your desire. This is the ultimate however in many cases unless you are a large pension plan, the account sizes for established world class managers can be in the tens of millions of dollars. If your account size is not large enough to have a managed account than the route is the manager's fund.

I avoid managers who have lock ups of more than two months; as transparency is an important concept in the unstable trading environment we are located in. I have several managers who send me a daily statement of their positions and profits. When you have this type of transparency you can see exactly what happens intra month. Smart investors always ask to see a daily equity run from a manager. This type of transparency really can give you a good feeling of anticipated volatility. Imagine a manager has swings intra month of 10% on a frequent basis and the end of month does not show that volatility, at some point in the future you might be surprised.

The more informed information you have the better the decision process can be. In the crisis of 2008, imagine seeing the value of your investments plummet and you could not exit due a lock up? Not fun! Actually this happened to countless Hedge funds. The investors did not fully read the subscription documents. You cannot be lazy when investing. Losses will always happen, but having the ability to exit is completely another story.

The reality is that regardless of strategy all managers will experience drawdowns at times (except Bernie Madoff & Allen Stafford). There is no way to avoid losses. Losses are as natural as breathing. It is part of our job as investors to internalize this and take a very long term focus (if we truly want to succeed overtime). Successful investors have internalized that money is made over very long periods of time.

Looking short term is a recipe for disaster. There is no need to ask "How was last month or last year?" For successful managers that understand risk and are world class, these are redundant questions only asked by amateurs. You just need to make your best decision and stick with that plan over long periods of time.

The importance of liquidity is exemplified by managers who might have a great record but if you need or want to exit the investment their great record is not going to help you get your money out. Think in terms of not just "***return on investment***", think in terms "***return of investment***".

*The Bible of Compounding Money*

## *You Cannot Get Your Money Out in Illiquid Strategies!*

There are strategies in which manager's trade in such markets such as mortgages, distressed debt or private placements. These are typical of having impediments of liquidity. Even long short stock managers in times such as 2008 there were gates placed in order to redeem investments.

I focus on commodity trading advisors who have been in business at a minimum of 10 years who give me liquidity and transparency. Liquidity is such an important consideration that most forget about. In times of a crisis liquidity is paramount. Commodity trading advisors have always provided me liquidity. However I am aware that can change and anything can happen. I prefer managed accounts as this offers the greatest possibility of liquidity when I invest with commodity trading advisors.

I believe commodity trading advisers look at the world in a little different manner than most. They have a much broader horizon and trade exchange listed contracts on exchanges throughout the world. There is no counter party risk as with other strategies. These commodity trading advisers look to catch trends not just in the stock market but actually in all markets that we use in our human existence.

World class commodity trading advisers look for moves in everything from sugar to soybeans to the stock market. The concept of being available for any bull or bear market in numerous asset classes I feel I put myself in a position to benefit.

Compare this to just looking at the stock market. With the US stock market, from mid-1960s to 1982, 'buy and hold' lost money. A more outstanding example is the Japanese stock market which went from 39,000 in the late

1980s to today slightly below 9,000. A complete lifetime of investing was lost.

The NASDAQ is another great example. Who would have thought all of these years later that the NASDAQ still has not recovered to the prior highs?

Trend following commodity trading advisors are not the Holy Grail. They do go through drawdowns which can be gut-wrenching even when the manager attempts to manage the risks when trading.

Over the 32-year period ending in 2011, the Barclay CTA Index achieved a compound annualized return of 11.16 per cent versus annualized gains of 11.06 per cent for the S&P 500 Index and 8.69 per cent for the Barclays Capital US Aggregate Bond Index. Bear in mind however during this 32 year period the stock experienced a major bull run.

What stands out is that during the same period the Barclay CTA Index also experienced somewhat less overall volatility and substantially lowers drawdowns than the S&P 500. Take into consideration that the S&P 500 within approximately the last 10 years had two 50% gut-wrenching collapses as well as over that last 10 years earned low, single digit returns.

The Barclays CTA Index showed positive returns during the dot-com crash of 2000-2002 and the financial crisis of 2008, years when the S&P 500 got clobbered.

Despite the above mentioned realities there are those that believe that money managers that are long/short make money regardless of stock market environment. In all of my years investing the vast majority have a high correlation to the stock market. The vast majority do not create Alpha.

*When the stock market retreated they did not create the promised,*
*"All Weather Profits."*

Contrarily when one compares commodity trading advisors they are not correlated to the stock market. More so the world class commodity trading advisors that I look to invest with are not gunslingers. They understand risk and know that anything can happen. They anticipate $6^{th}$ sigma events. They believe they will happen. They have risk controls that many fundamental mutual fund or fundamental hedge funds do not have in place. Even so they are not GD and these money managers will have drawdowns and long periods of elusive profits.

The concept of commodity investing is very tangible. Try to internalize this point. You wake up in the morning and if you are like me, you drink coffee. Coffee is a market in which there are bull markets and bear markets. You might want to add sugar to your coffee or eat a donut in the morning. Sugar is a market again at times with massive moves. You get dressed. Most clothes have cotton. In 2010 the price of cotton almost tripled. Futures were made and lost.

Expert after expert stated that the cotton market could not go any higher.

## IT DID!

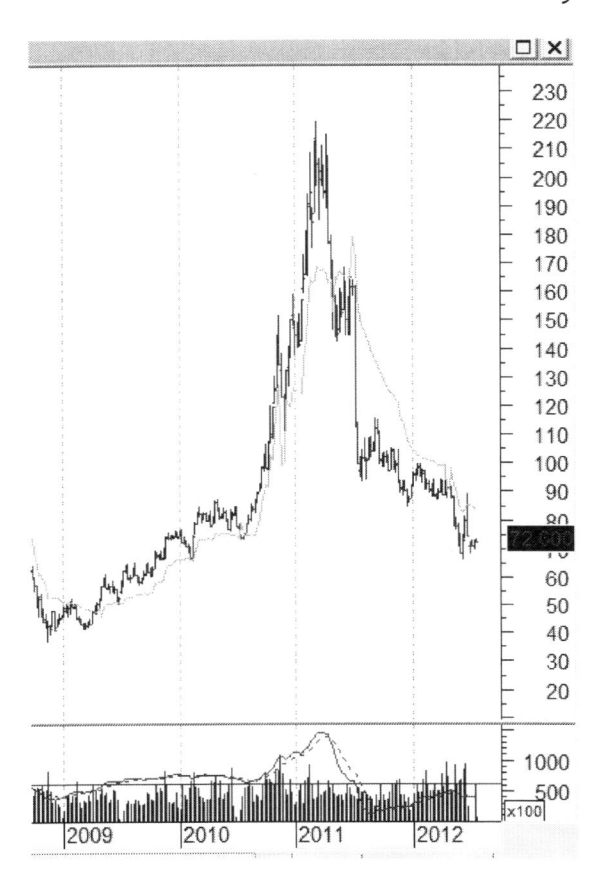

Chart Created in Thomson Reuters MetaStock. All rights reserved. Past Performance is not necessarily indicative of future performance.

Fast forwarding to today, in the US Midwest due to a drought the prices of corn and wheat have jumped in just one month 50%. No one knows if this will continue or end. So far this is one of the worst draughts in US history. A simple question, do you eat pizza or bread? Clearly you do. Due to this drought your sandwich or slice of pizza will get more expensive. Take it to another step. Do you own a car? Most people do. Do you fill your car with gasoline? Clearly you do. In 2008 the price of crude oil went to the $140 a barrel range and then crashed to the mid $30 dollar range. Fortunes were made in both directions and trends. I can continue but I assume you get my point.

These are not esoteric or strange markets. These are things we use in our human existence. These are not complicated derivatives between banks. All of us, regardless where we live on planet earth use these products. In conjunction to food products there are currencies and even bonds denominated in these currencies. Commodity trading advisers can look at more than a 100 or even more markets. These markets move differently. How correlated do you think crude oil is to corn? How about the Australian dollar to US 30 year Treasury bond? Compare this to stocks. When there is a bull market the vast majority of stocks rise and clearly in a bear market it is hard to run against the wind. Even Apple stock is not invincible in a bear market. In 2008 Apple was knocking on the door of $200 only to fall to the $80 range. Believe that anything can happen. The stock market is not the only market.

### *Anything Can and Will Happen - Just Look at Apple Shares*

Who would have really believed the NASDAQ would fall in 2000 and now almost 13 years later it is about half of its value? So much for Buy and Hold!

Chart Created in Thomson Reuters MetaStock. All rights reserved. Past Performance is not necessarily indicative of future performance.

A major example is the Japanese Stock Market. In 1989 the Japanese Stock market was around 39,000 today it is below 9,000. If you did not believe this could happen again even in the US you are deluding yourself.

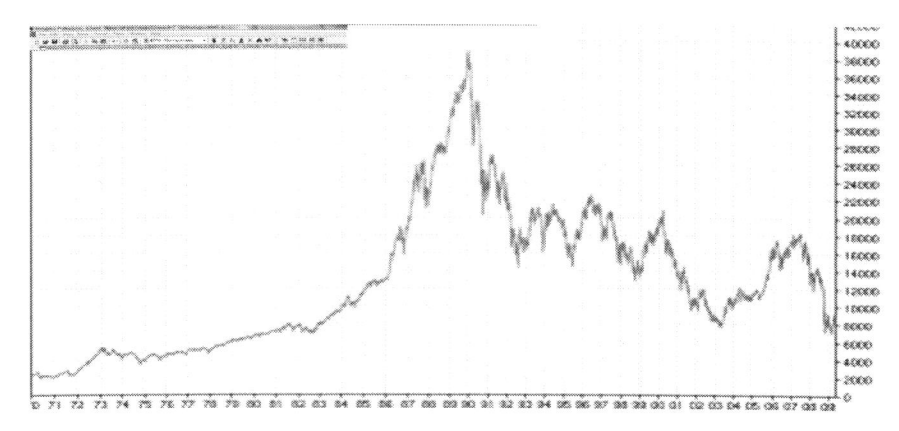

# CHAPTER 11 SUMMATION

During the last financial crisis the importance of liquidity and transparency became evident. One must believe that anything can happen when they invest. Transparency and liquidity is best presented in a managed account.

*Andy Abraham*

CHAPTER 12

# Buying the Drawdowns of Commodity Trading Advisors

I utilize the strategy of buying drawdowns in world class money managers who *understand risk*. This strategy like any investing strategy is far from perfect. I look at historical drawdowns of a particular manager who is on my watch list. As an example, Eckhardt trading program started in 1991 with a CAROR of 14.97% with numerous drawdowns from the mid-teens to the mid twenty percent range. Right off the bat he had his worse drawdown. If you had invested with this manager back in 1991, regardless of his drawdown you could have taken 100,000 to $1,871,000 over 21 years. If you had invested during his inevitable drawdowns you would even have enhanced this amazing return further.

DRAWDOWN REPORT

| Depth | Length (Months) | Recovery (Months) | Start | End |
|---|---|---|---|---|
| -27.11 | 5 | 9 | 12/1/1991 | 5/1/1992 |
| -21.43 | 5 | 3 | 5/1/1995 | 10/1/1995 |
| -21.28 | 7 | - | 4/1/2011 | 11/1/2011 |
| -18.87 | 2 | 13 | 12/1/1993 | 2/1/1994 |
| -17.05 | 4 | 2 | 4/1/1996 | 8/1/1996 |
| -16.88 | 17 | 5 | 2/1/1999 | 7/1/2000 |

PAST PERFORMANCE IS NOT NECESSARILY INDICATIVE OF FUTURE RESULTS. THE RISK OF LOSS IN TRADING COMMODITY FUTURES, OPTIONS, AND FOREIGN EXCHANGE ("FOREX") IS SUBSTANTIAL.

Another world class manager is Abraham Trading Group (no relation) who started his program in 1988. His 25 year record has a CAROR of 18.23% with drawdowns from the mid 20% range up to the low 30% range (so far). If you had invested with Abraham Trading Group $100,000 from the onset in 1988 you would have grown this modest sum to an extreme sum of $6,579,000. If one would have considered buying into one of his numerous drawdowns you could have compounded money in a greater fashion.

DRAWDOWN REPORT

| Depth | Length (Months) | Recovery (Months) | Start | End |
|---|---|---|---|---|
| -31.95 | 3 | 2 | 7/1/1989 | 10/1/1989 |
| -27.18 | 8 | 22 | 11/1/2004 | 7/1/2005 |
| -27.12 | 11 | 4 | 9/1/1990 | 8/1/1991 |
| -26.87 | 4 | 1 | 12/1/1988 | 4/1/1989 |
| -26.55 | 5 | 11 | 12/1/1991 | 5/1/1992 |
| -24.44 | 8 | 9 | 6/1/1995 | 2/1/1996 |

PAST PERFORMANCE IS NOT NECESSARILY INDICATIVE OF FUTURE RESULTS. THE RISK OF LOSS IN TRADING COMMODITY FUTURES, OPTIONS, AND FOREIGN EXCHANGE ("FOREX") IS SUBSTANTIAL.

Clarke Capital has been trading since 1996. Due to a couple of rough years their CAROR fell slightly below 15%. These rough periods are entry points to allocate.

## Clarke Capital Management : Worldwide

**DRAWDOWN REPORT**

| Depth | Length (Months) | Recovery (Months) | Start | End |
|---|---|---|---|---|
| -27.15 | 13 | 4 | 12/1/2010 | 1/1/2012 |
| -26.06 | 36 | 6 | 3/1/2004 | 3/1/2007 |
| -18.46 | 11 | 10 | 3/1/2001 | 2/1/2002 |
| -15.64 | 1 | 0 | 5/1/2012 | 6/1/2012 |
| -13.74 | 1 | 7 | 11/1/2009 | 12/1/2009 |
| -13.65 | 4 | 1 | 12/1/2008 | 4/1/2009 |

PAST PERFORMANCE IS NOT NECESSARILY INDICATIVE OF FUTURE RESULTS. THE RISK OF LOSS IN TRADING COMMODITY FUTURES, OPTIONS, AND FOREIGN EXCHANGE ("FOREX") IS SUBSTANTIAL

Once one accepts the inherent risks they are in a better situation. Regardless if it is the stock market or real estate there will be losses. No way to avoid them. In commodity trading you go through periods of consolidation and expansion. The periods of expansion you can have some huge profits. You just need to be available for them.

## REDUCED FEES

The usual fees on trading accounts are 2% management and 20% incentive fee. When managers are in a drawdown they are more flexible to reduce fees. I always try to reduce fees. Sometimes it works and sometimes it does not. I do not make it a deal breaker if I want to invest with a manager when my goal is to compound money over long periods of time. What I try to do is to negate the 2% management and out of fairness gladly play the 20% incentive fee. I want the manager to make money when he makes me money. This way we both feel good. I hope to stay with the manager for years if not decades. I always think of compounding and that 2% management fee adds up and reduces my compounding.

# MENTORS FROM CHILDHOOD

I was fortunate to have great mentors even from childhood. My grandfather taught me that more people came out of the US Great Depression as millionaires than went in. This reasoning has become part of my psyche. I do not follow the crowd. The investors who bought the proverbial drawdown in the Great Depression were strongly rewarded. The people who did the uncomfortable such as buying depressed real estate or possibly consumer orientated stocks in a bear market put themselves in a position to benefit over time. One cannot follow the herd. The herd gets slaughtered. Be a clear thinker. Be independent and think for yourself.

# CHAPTER 12 SUMMATION

Identify world class managers and in order to give you somewhat of a margin of safely look to invest when they have a drawdown. Realize nothing is perfect and we are dealing with uncertainty. You might miss the opportunity to invest with a manager just by waiting. As well as there will be instances drawdowns continue and even in extreme cases the manager might close. We are dealing with uncertainty and that is why I suggest very strongly only investing 1-5% of your investable assets with any money manager.

## CHAPTER 13

# Due Diligence

Due diligence is one of the most critical aspects of manager selection. All too often this important aspect is negated and simply a manager's returns are chased. There are numerous aspects of due diligence that must be completed in order to attempt to enhance a margin of safety. The due diligence that needs to be ascertained includes the structure of the organization, critical backup policies, the managers and key personal, the methodology, its implementation, how the manager approaches risk, fee structure, high water mark as well as the many other issues regarding the trading itself need to be researched.

Even the simplest of doing a Google search on managers or firms is forgotten all too often. It is unbelievable the amount of free information Google has on money managers. I set up a Google alert to give me a heads up on news articles on managers I am interested in as well as the ones I am invested with. These come right to my Gmail account. ***What a simple start***.

# OPERATIONAL RISKS

I do my own due diligence before I allocate. It takes time however it gives me greater confidence and reinforces my decision when I invest. Inevitably there will be drawdowns and even hard times with world class managers. There is no free lunch when we invest. Doing my own due diligence gives me a greater feeling of certainty of my decisions.

There are firms that perform due diligence services as well. These firms have the ability to do due diligence on the manager or managers themselves as well as evaluate the money management firm as a business concern or operational risk. Operational risk is broadly defined as the risk of loss resulting from inadequate or failed internal processes, people, systems, or external events. It exists for all companies in every field and industry. If operational risk is ignored, unexpected events will occur that may have far-reaching and expensive implications. Operational risk has been shown to lead to financial loss, reputational damage, loss of customers, and even business failure.

It is imperative to understand the manager's infrastructure and his key personal to gain a grasp on operational risk. In the context of operational risk you want to start to obtain a copy of the business continuity plan. This "BCP" needs to describe all the provisions the firm has in place in case of various disasters. Hurricanes or earthquakes are not the only issue. Remember 9/11; can you imagine if your money manager was in the Towers?

You have untold business continuity issues. You would like to make sure the firm has a continuity plan for its computer systems, electricity and internet backup as well as backup brokers to take and execute orders. As an example, for my continuity plan for my trading company, I have a computer on 24 hours a day in another city thousands of miles away in which I have all my trading algorithms backed up and data ready to trade. If I lose power or internet I have a hotel in another city in which I will drive to which gives me the ability either use my laptop to log into that remote computer where all information is backed up.

## HAVING CLIENTS TOO LARGE

I recently had looked to invest in a money manager who has been around for decades who is in an ugly drawdown. They have had great returns over the decades. In the course of conversation with the marketing person at the firm, he told me that one of their clients was a large Sovereign wealth fund who has been with them for numerous years. Upon hearing that I wondered what would happen if the Sovereign fund pulled the plug and exited. The assets under management at the firm had fallen more than 70% already. I thought that if the Sovereign wealth fund left them this event could be devastating. The firm had a relatively large staff and overhead. I was concerned that if the Sovereign left that could impact their operations. Bottom line is investors or are there any clients who comprise more than 25% of the fund?

Regarding clients, you want to know if some of the larger investors are family. You would like to know ahead of time about any potential conflict of interests. On that same tangent you want to know if the manager was seeded and if so how is the relationship between the parties. A seeder is one who makes a substantial initial investment for a share of the future profits of the management fees and incentive fees. It is very similar to a venture capital deal. As in every relationship and marriage, some are wonderful and some are nightmares.

As a personal example, at the Alphametrix convention I spoke to a manager who had possibly too much to drink. He let out all of his disappointments as if I was his therapist. He told me he got involved with a seeding organization and it has been a nightmare. The fund grew assets under management however there was constant conflict between him and his seeding partners. He was extremely unhappy and was very frustrated.

Clearly this would not be a situation I would want to invest with. On the contrary I have a colleague that I met in 2009 at the CTA Expo in Chicago. He had at that time $25 million. He is a complete gentleman as well as a great trader. His firm was discovered by a much larger money manager and that firm opened up a very large managed account and in lieu took an interest in the firm. Their assets under management today are in the mid $300 million dollar range. Their seeded relationship has been a win-win for both parties.

These are the type of details that you want to be aware of when you invest. It takes work but it is much better to know these types of issues before you start as opposed to discovering them and them being a detriment to your investment.

## GROWING TOO FAST?

You will encounter another typical operational risk if a firm grows too quick. You want to know what the maximum assets under management the firm feels they can handle and more so how the firm plans the growth. You would like to get an idea how quickly the firm is raising assets. Are the assets being raised by the money managers themselves or outside 3rd party marketers? You do want your money manager running all over Europe when you want him compounding your money.

Once the firm does start growing many times it is a parabolic move. You are lucky you are reading this book as you know not to chase performance. Once a manager starts having a good run investors throw money very quickly. You want to know at what juncture does the firm expand their location or hire new people and for what tasks. Growth is not always beneficial. In many cases smaller or even emerging managers out perform their much larger peers.

## PROFESSIONAL DUE DILIGENCE OR YOUR OWN

One of the largest firms in investigative due diligence is Kroll. They have been active in the field for decades. I have heard that some fund or funds will use an organization like Kroll because it gives their investors a greater sense of comfort due to the professionalism of an organization like Kroll.

Personally, I prefer to preform my own due diligence once I have decided I am interested in a particular money manager. There are online databases in the US that give full disclosure on numerous levels. These databases are payment based and unbelievably inexpensive for the information they provide. I use a service called Intelius.com. I run a background check on the key personal which includes, property ownership, address history, phone numbers, relatives and associates, neighbors, marriage/divorce records, civil judgments, 7-year criminal database search which covers 43 states and the District of Columbia, including courthouse verification of all potential records associated with the subject, SSN trace, a nationwide search of the National Sex Offender Registry, Federal Criminal Search, Education Verification and Employment Verification. Most important is a Criminal Report which could show criminal convictions, felonies, misdemeanors, and other criminal offenses associated with a name as well as civil judgments.

### *Think about it!*

- Would you want to entrust your money to a money manager who has a record of drunk driving?

- Would you want to entrust your money to a money manager who has been divorced three times?

- Would you want to entrust your money to a money manager who has a record of assault on his ex-wife?

- Would you want to entrust your money to a money manager who hasn't paid his real estate taxes?

- Would you want to entrust your money to a money manager who has been involved in numerous civil judgments?

## PEDIGREE HELPS

Pedigree is just part of the story; you want a biography of each of the key personal. You want to know where they went to school and past work experiences. You want to verify all of these. Sometimes the smallest lie is just the start of bigger lies. A colleague of mine once told me about a prospective manager he was interested in who lied about where he went to school. If a manager would lie about something like this, what else would he lie about?

Pedigree always helps. For example, one of the managers I listed as up and coming called Blackwater, both of the managers worked at Eagle Trading. The principle of Eagle Trading, Menachem Sternberg had worked with Bruce Kovner. There is almost a lineage. You can just imagine all the wisdom passed down over the ages.

The countless other examples but the ones that stand out for me are the offspring of the turtle programs. Jerry Parker from Chesapeake learned under William Eckhardt & Richard Denis. The same can be stated for Howard Siedler of Saxon, Tom Shanks from Hawksbill and Elizabeth Chavel from EMC.

The story continues with the graduates of Commodity Corp. The graduates of Commodity Corporation are many well-known trend followers such as Bruce Kovner, Paul Tudor Jones, Michael Marcus Greenville Craig, Louis Bacon and Ed Seykota. Commodity Corporation was featured in the book, *Market Wizards*, due to the success of its traders from the 1980s. Commodity Corporation was founded by Helmut Weymar and Amos Hostetter with $2.5 million and grew quickly due to the success of its traders. By 1997 they had approximately $2 billion in assets under management and were subsequently sold to Goldman Sachs.

## STICK WITH THE ORIGINAL WINNERS

When you invest in a fund you want to make sure the original people are running it. You do not want a new management group. If you have a new group managing the fund the results could be dramatically different.

I had a situation with one of my first investments in 1994. In retrospect it was more luck than brains when I invested $200,000 with a particular manager. I did not have the knowledge that I am sharing with you in this book at the time. In all truthfulness I was guilty of chasing returns. I had a great run with him however. I compounded the money and when the manager retired my original investment had turned into $1,400,000 over 12 years. When the manager retired, I thought it was prudent to exit and move one even though one of his Lieutenants would be running the program.

## UNDERSTANDING THE ORGANIZATION

You want to understand the organization's structure. Who owns the management company? Who are the principles? Are there any related businesses that can distract the money manager? You want to know if there were there any lawsuits, arbitrations or any disputes against not just the principles, but the firm itself. You want to know if there were prior funds that the management company closed down.

Sometimes in your due diligence you will discover the money manager had a prior fund. You want to know if there were prior funds closed down. What happens then is that funds have high water marks.

The concept of the high water mark is: if a manager loses money over a period, he must get the fund above the high watermark before receiving a performance bonus or incentive fee. For example if a manager loses 10% in one year and the following year he makes 15% he overcame the high water mark and is compensated on that overage. Basically you are not paying a performance fee for substandard returns. You want the manager to be your partner. You want him to have incentive to make you money and when he doesn't he only makes his management fee. What happens with money managers who lack integrity is that instead of grinding back the drawdown they close the fund in order to avoid the high water mark and get compensated with a new fund.

In context of conflict of interest you want to know if the firm allows its employees to trade their own accounts. You do not want employees' front running the trades (placing trades in front of large orders). You want to know what type of restrictions if any are placed on employees trading.

## REGULATORY BODY DUE DILIGENCE

The National Futures Association (NFA) which is a self-regulating body in conjunction with the CFTC, are in charge of the commodities markets. FINRA is the largest independent regulator for all securities firms doing business in the United States and both offer services to run due diligence on their perspective members.

The National futures association has a service called Basic. Using NFA's Background Affiliation Status Information Center (BASIC), you can check the registration status and disciplinary history of any firm or individual that conducts business on the U.S. futures exchanges on behalf of the investing public. Within "BASIC" you can search via NFA ID number, Individual name, Firm name as well as pool name (fund).

You can access BASIC at:
http://www.nfa.futures.org/basicnet/

Finra maintains a service called Broker Check. Broker check monitors Research Brokers, Brokerage Firms, Investment Adviser Representatives and Investment Adviser Firms. From the website of Finra they state" Broker Check is a free tool to help investors research the professional backgrounds of current and former FINRA-registered brokerage firms and brokers, as well as investment adviser firms and representatives. It should be the first resource investors turn to when choosing whether to do business or continue to do business with a particular firm or individual.

http://www.finra.org/Investors/ToolsCalculators/BrokerCheck/

*Through BrokerCheck, investors can:*

*Search for information about brokers and brokerage firms*

*Search for information about investment adviser firms and representatives*

*Obtain online background reports, if available*

The best part of both the NFA and Finra sites is that they are free.

# CHAPTER 13 SUMMATION

Due diligence is a broad process of various qualitative approaches that need to be addressed. This is one of the most important aspects of successful investing as well as one of the most overlooked.

## CHAPTER 14

# The First Question: Are the Returns REAL?

One of my first thoughts always is, are the returns for real? There has been so much fraud in the recent past I am skeptical of everything. Even though I am not from Missouri, I am a huge skeptic. My wife so nicely calls me obsessive compulsive paranoid. I take it is a compliment in this day and age. I want proof that something someone is telling me is real. You also should want proof. This is what an audit of returns should do. However people can even falsify an audit. Many times there is not even an audit.

*Are the returns audited?*
*Who did the auditing?*

If the returns are "real" and audited you need to verify and confirm everything. You want to receive a copy of the audit. You want to review the audit and if you have any questions do not be shy to ask. I go the long step; I want to actually confirm with the person who did the audit. I look at the auditing firms. If I have never heard of them I research them. I speak to the person over the phone and ask them if they did the audit for manager xyz.

This simple step would have avoided the devastation of Bernie Madoff. Would it be logical to you that a multibillion dollar fund would only use a small, three-person accounting firm located in a New York City suburb? Would it have been logical to you that no one had ever heard of Friehling & Horowitz? Would it have been logical that Friehling & Horowitz had no peer reviews for 15 years? How about the icing on the cake, the partner Horowitz was 80 years old and was living in Florida.

Between 1991 and 2008 David Friehling audited Madoff's financial records. When he entered the plea in U.S. District Court in Manhattan he apologized to the thousands of who lost billions of dollars. That and a piece of bubble gum would have made those people feel better after losing everything. Ironically he claimed that "At no time was he ever aware Bernard Madoff was engaged in a Ponzi scheme."

Friehling admitted to failing to independently verify the assets of Madoff's investment company or ensure that his bank account records or charts listing the purchase of securities were accurate.

What do you glean from this? You must use common sense. Probably no one ever checked out Bernie Madoffs auditor/accounting firm. If they did, red flags would have been raised, actually would have been screaming. If one had

# The Bible of Compounding Money

used common sense they would have known that it was impossible not to have losses. The reality is that all of the investors in Madoff did not use common sense. They were simply greedy and chased returns.

The investors burned by Madoff were not stupid people. There were banks in Europe and with their entire institutional due diligence they failed. There were famous people that did not even think to perform any due diligence.

Look at this short list. Wouldn't you have thought someone would have called the auditor? A good question always is to have the manager list all auditors with their contact details since the inception of the fund. If there are changes it would be prudent to know why.

| Investor | Description | Amount of Exposure |
|---|---|---|
| Fairfield Greenwich Advisors | An investment management firm | $7,500,000,000 |
| Tremont Group Holdings | Asset management firm | $3,300,000,000 |
| Bank Medici | Austrian bank | $2,100,000,000 |

|  |  |  |
|---|---|---|
| Ascot Partners | A hedge fund founded by billionaire investor, philanthropist and GMAC chief J. Ezra Merkin | $1,800,000,000 |
| Access International Advisors | A New York-based investment firm | $1,500,000,000 |
| Fortis | Dutch bank | $1,350,000,000 |

| | | |
|---|---|---|
| Union Bancaire Privee | Swiss bank | $700,000,000 |
| HSBC | British bank | $1,000,000,000 |
| Natixis SA | A French investment bank | $554,400,000 |
| Carl Shapiro | The founder and former chairman of apparel company | $500,000,000 |

|  | Kay Windsor Inc., and his wife |  |
|---|---|---|
| Royal Bank of Scotland Group PLC | British bank | $492,760,000 |
| BNP Paribas | French bank | $431,170,000 |
| BBVA | Spanish bank | $369,570,000 |
| Man Group PLC | A U.K. hedge fund | $360,000,000 |

*The Bible of Compounding Money*

|  |  |  |
|---|---|---|
|  |  |  |
| Reichmuth & Co. | A Swiss private bank | $327,000,000 |
| Nomura Holdings | Japanese brokerage firm | $358,900,000 |
| Maxam Capital Management | A fund of funds based in Darien, Connecticut | $280,000,000 |
| EIM SA | A European investment manager with about $11 billion in assets | $230,000,000 |
| AXA SA | French insurance giant | N/A |
| UniCredit SpA | Italian Bank | $92,390,000 |

| | | |
|---|---|---|
| Nordea Bank AB | Swedish Bank | $59,130,000 |
| Hyposwiss | A Swiss private bank owned by St. Gallery Kantonalbank | $50,000,000 |
| Banque Benedict Hentsch & Cie. SA | A Swiss-based private bank | $48,800,000 |
| Fairfield, Conn. | town pension fund | $42,000,000 |
| Bramdean Alternatives | An asset manager | $31,200,000 |
| Jewish Community Foundation of Los Angeles | The largest manager of charitable gift assets for Los Angeles Jewish philanthropists | $18,000,000 |

Source:
http://s.wsj.net/public/resources/documents/st_madoff_victims_20081215.html

## THE EASY 'FOLLOWING THE HERD' WITHOUT DOING ANY DUE DILIGENCE LED TO DISASTER.

If the returns are not audited you should ask for monthly statements. You want these statements to come from the brokerage firm directly (not from the money manager). If the statements come directly from the brokerage company there is less of a possibility any number fudging occurred. In order to be thorough, I would confirm with the actual person at the brokerage company who sent them and confirm verbally. You want to look at the intra month swings. Managers can have seemingly good returns end of month but there are times there are big swings intra month.

Another reason I prefer commodity trading advisors as opposed to other types of money managers—they are audited and regulated by both the National Futures association and the CFTC. Do not simply rely on the regulators as they failed miserably with both MF Global and PFG in which client accounts were pilfered.

I have had money managers tell me that they could not show me their customer account statements for confidentiality reasons. Let me tell you, **that's a HUGE RED FLAG!** All they have to do is "black-out" the names or entity on the customer account statements. If a money manager tells you he can't do this, do not walk, RUN!

*Andy Abraham*

# HYPOTHETICAL RETURNS

Believe it or not, there are managers that will show **hypothetical returns** or **back tested returns**. Clearly we are only interested in an actual track record (one that really happened with real money), preferable to anything hypothetical (a simulation that didn't really happen with real money).

*In over 19 years, I have never seen a hypothetical track record that didn't look phenomenal, outstanding, etc. Why? Who would advertise a bad one? I hold hypothetical returns with less than a grain of salt. They are worthless to me and suggest you the same. I have yet to see a hypothetical track record actually hold up in real time.*

Back testing is another version of hypothetical returns. Back-testing is a process whereby a money manager takes his actual strategy and resulting recommendations and applies those signals to past market data *before* he began to manage real money in real market conditions. **The obvious weakness to back-testing is that it implies that future market conditions will be similar to the past.** We all know that future market conditions are unpredictable. The NFA

(National Futures Association) prime disclaimer is "Past performance is not necessarily indicative of future performance". We would not even be interested in a manager who shows hypothetical returns as one of our prime rules is we want 10 years of real time experience over different market periods.

## THE MEAT AND POTATOES OF DUE DILIGENCE

What I call the meat and the potatoes of due diligence is the strategy, risk management and methodology of the money manager. Some managers are discretionary meaning they decide what positions to take and there are managers who are systematic and running mechanical systems.

Clearly if the manager is discretionary he makes the decisions based on his years of experience. Contrarily if the manager is systematic this adds a level of complexity and necessity to preform greater due diligence. You want to know if at any time the system may be overridden and discretion applied by the manager. You want to know who developed the methodology. You want to understand the inputs of the systematic model.

Does the model have different parameters for different markets? If so I would take this as a red flag. If different markets have different parameters, my first inclination would be that the system was curve fitted. I want a system to be robust and that all markets are traded in the same fashion with the same risk per trade.

Is the model in house or out of house? You want to know how much time and energy the manager applies to trading research. If the methodology is out of house, who does the algorithm belong to? Is it leased? Obviously you want to make sure that the trading program belongs to the money manager and preferably that was developed in house. Along with this you would like to see constant research and testing. *I want the managers to be as passionate as me in my trading. I wake up in the middle of night and write down ideas to test with my programmer. Talk about being passionate.*

Once you determine if the manager is discretionary or systematic you want to get him/ her speaking about the methodology. There are so many questions and probably more I have not thought of:

- Do you utilize a multiple system approach?
- Do you utilize one system?
- What are the time periods traded in the system?
- Is it trend following?
- If it is trend following why is it different from other trend followers?
- Is it counter trend?
- Does the system go equally short and long?
- Is there a bias for either long or short?
- How about what can go wrong?
- Is there an Achilles heel in your program?
- Have you changed strategies?
- Is the current methodology the same as in your past results?
- If the system is mechanical do you discretion or override the system?
- What are the markets you trade and why?
- What are your anticipated draw downs and anticipated returns?
- What do you consider an optimal market environment?

- What do you consider a negative market environment?
- What is the time periods you hold trades?
- How do you get out of trades that are not working?
- What would make you exit a trade that is working?
- How markets are you trading?
- To what degree if any do you leverage?
- What are your average winners?
- What are your average losers?
- What gets you into a trade?
- If anyone particular year was dramatically different to either the positive side or negative side, you want to know why.

# CHAPTER 14 SUMMATION

Verification of returns is an integral aspect of the due diligence process. It is a fantastic learning lesson of the importance of verification of returns from the long list of Madoff investors.

*Andy Abraham*

# CHAPTER 15

# Risk Management

Risk management is what keeps us in the marathon of trading. You want to understand how the manager defines and controls risk. Some managers only look at risk from a portfolio level. However one of my most important questions is:

## WHAT IS YOUR RISK PER TRADE?

You want to know how much of the account size the manager willing to risk on any trade. When trades work, that is great and you make a lot of money. The converse is when the trade does not work, how much of your account do you lose. With all of my years of trading, regardless of research or anything, I know that any trade is 50/50. So if any trade is 50/50 why risk too much of the account on any trade?

My programmer summed it up very clearly with his witty sense of humor. Risk per trade is bites out of the apple.

If you risk 1% of your account you get 100 bites. If you risk 2% you get 50 bites. If you risk 3% you get approximately 32 bites.

In our company we know we do not know the future. We know that any trade is 50/50. We know we want to be around for the next 30 years so we risk on our programs 50 basis points in our Formula72 L program, 75 basis points in Formula 72 M and a whopping 1.25% on our Formula 72H. As you can easily infer the letters L, M and H refer to our risk profile.

We attempt and I put in parenthesis "attempt" to have a Low volatility program, mid volatility program and a High volatility program. The concept is to understand what the investor is looking for and understand his risk profile.

When managers do not know what their risk per trade is—watch out. I have even had the audacity of a manager to tell he does not need to think in those terms as his trades work over time (BTW at the time of this writing he is out of business). A good question to ask the prospective manager is how do they respond when trades start to go against them? Depending on the answer, a great deal of information on how the manager looks at risk can be revealed. For instance if the manager adds to a losing position, WATCH OUT!

## JON PAULSON BIG WINS AND BIG DRAWDOWNS

John Paulson started Paulson & Co in 1994. He became famous for his bets against subprime mortgages. He made billions! Paulson bets big. At times he wins big. However with big bets can be big losses. Before that he was relatively unknown and pursuing a merger arbitrage strategy with mediocre returns.

*The Bible of Compounding Money*

John Paulson is not a great stock picker. His strength is in macro-themed investments. He doesn't pick a single or a couple of stocks from a sector. He picks a bunch of stocks from each sector in which he invests.

During the recent bear market, Paulson was in a class by himself, generating returns of up to 600% by betting against mortgages in 2008 as the market crashed. In 2009, he's placed bets on a U.S. recovery, and his recent results are as dismal as the US economy. Some of Paulson's $30 billion funds have generated losses of roughly 30% after placing big bets on the US banking sector with such stocks such as Bank of America and others.

Paulson had another issue with the <u>Chinese timber company Sino-Forest</u>, which faced fraud allegations. Paulson was a holder of 34.7 million shares of Sino-Forest. Shares were halted <u>after Muddy Waters came out with a report</u> accusing fraud. The shares were at $18 the day prior to the report and afterwards the shares hit $2.45. This generated a loss of over $500 million for John Paulson, who was in addition rumored to be very heavily long in the company's bonds. Even Paulson's primary hedge, gold, has lost its luster.

Big wins and big losses will occur when one does not think of risk per trade

## RISK PER SECTOR

Risk per sector is another one of my hot buttons that gives me a quick idea on how the manager approaches risk. I learned the hard way myself, over my years trading, how important it is to manage the risks on the sector level. There were times in my career in which I thought I was taking low risk bets however these low risk bets were concentrated in a specific sector. On two occasions I woke up to find myself not in the greatest situation. Clearly contracts or shares in the same sector move together.

At one point I had a signal in the interest rates sectors. I bought 30 year bonds, 10 year bonds, 5 year and Gilts and Bunds. Upon waking and checking my screens all of these small risks went against me. These small losses added up and were a bigger risk than I had thought about.

The same issue happened in the grain markets. I had a signal to sell soybeans. That was not enough. I had a signal to sell soybean oil and soymeal. I had the same signal in corn as well as wheat. I took all the low risk signals to my mistake. Clearly all of these were all correlated. Small 1% risks grew and what I thought was a small risk was much greater. This taught me to cap my sector risk to a maximum of 5% of my account size in our trading at our firm.

When I look to invest with other managers I want to know how they approach sector risk. If you get a blind stare you know for sure they are making the same mistake I made when I started 18 years ago.

There are those who say everything is correlated. To some degree I can agree to this statement. When I look at my screen on significant big up days the entire screen might look green to me. Vice versa on huge down days, it looks like everything is selling off. These are the extreme days not the everyday. Risk per sector needs to be addressed and know, otherwise it can come and bite you when you least expect it.

## TOTAL RISK ON THE PORTFOLIO

Running a portfolio is similar in nature to running a business. You need to have an exact business plan. The manager or CEO of a company knows exactly what the expenses are and what the income is. The business plan of a world class money manager is similar. His/ her finger is on the pulse of the portfolio. At every juncture the total risk on the portfolio should be monitored.

If the manager does not know where they are at any point, how do they know where they are going? Smart money managers usually cap the total risk on their portfolio. In my money management firm we cap the maximum open trade equity risk of our positions at 20%. More so we do not take new positions and even tighten up the stops on existing positions. Working in this context lowers risk and volatility.

I want to invest in money managers that think in the same manner as this. What I have seen over the years is that after some of the biggest runs up have been the biggest drawdowns. My goal like yours is to compound money. Giving back profits is not one of my favorite past times. Monitoring the total risk on the portfolio is one way to "try" to mitigate this. A good question to ask is: are there downside risk thresholds such as maximum monthly drawdown or if there is a point when the manager could stop trading?

## RISK LITMUS TEST

Three questions can give you the quick litmus test on how a manager approaches risk. These questions are imperative to your trading success.

1. What is your risk per trade?
2. What is your maximum risk per sector?
3. What is your maximum risk on the entire portfolio?

Another interesting issue was gleaned from the MF Global implosion. Foreign markets were treated dramatically different than US markets. The foreign markets were considered F2 and were locked up in a legal dispute in the UK. Eventually when vulture funds came in and started buying claims they substantially discounted the foreign commodity contracts.

Thus it is a very important issue to understand if the money manager trades in foreign markets. Make sure you are comfortable and aware of this. The real litmus test for liquidity is posed by this simple question: has the manager ever suspended or delayed redemptions? At the height of the 2008 bear market this happened to even some of the biggest and well known managers.

## IMPORTANCE OF ENTRY AND EXIT ORDERS

The more you know about the money manager and how he trades the better off you will be. Today markets almost trade 24 hours a day. Depending on the hour there are different levels of liquidity. You want to know if trading is done during regular market hours or during one of the Globex periods (premarket and aftermarket).

In the currency markets many times money managers will trade EFP's (Exchange for Physicals). You want to know the markets that the manager uses for EFP's as well as who is the counterparty as they are not regulated contracts. All I have to say is one word and that is Lehman Brothers and you will understand my point.

Entry and exit orders are a good way in which you learn to understand how the money manager thinks. Some managers do not make a full investment at the onset of taking a position. Some managers scale in and out of positions. There really is no complete right or wrong and it is more applicable to the manager's style. You do want to know if the manager leverages himself/ herself to much. The amount of risk per trade will give you an indication.

*The Bible of Compounding Money*

There are some managers that pyramid. Pyramiding is adding to an existing profitable position. This use of leverage works both ways. At times it increases the returns of the managers as well as times will lead you to a hefty draw down.

The more you fully understand every aspect of the manager you will avoid unfulfilled expectations or shocks. In order to better fully understand the manager you want to know what type of order entries and exit the managers' use. There are all types of stop orders as well as limit orders. Stops can be price stops, volatility stops, money management stops and even time stops. You want to understand if stops are adjusted. Furthermore you want to understand if entire positions are exited all at once or scaled out of. This will affect the chances of a negative surprise or increase drawdown.

There is nothing perfect when we trade. My firm uses stop orders in our trading as I do not want to miss any trade. I know that if I miss one trade this trade could be the trade of the year. Contrarily, I will have slippage.

There are some money managers that they only want to be filled at a specific price or better. These types of orders are limit orders. The negative is they can miss a trade. You want to know if the actual orders are placed ahead of time with the broker or executed manually upon reaching a certain price threshold. If orders are not placed ahead of time in the market with the broker you run the possibility of orders not being placed. This comes down to the discipline of the trader to react to the price.

Money managers are not gods. I have seen money managers' freeze in fear or panic. One case in particular was a mutual fund manager who in 2008 went short large positions of futures for his personal account. In every bear market you have sharp reverse rallies. This was an experienced money manager. However he did not believe that the SP500 was rallying. He felt he knew better than the market. He was right and the market was wrong. Well he ended up being right several weeks later after losing $5 million dollars. You need to take the type of orders into consideration as part of your due diligence.

## HOW OFTEN DOES THE MANAGER TRADE?

As George Soros has said, "***Boring is good***." You do not want gunslingers or money managers that over trade. The less trading, believe it or not, can be more profitable in many cases. In order to determine the frequency you want to know the roundtrips per million. This gives you a very good idea of how often the manager trades. The lower number of round trips per million shows you frequency of trading.

When there is less trading there is less slippage and reduced commissions. Even when commissions are low priced they add up and eat into performance; the same with slippage. Slippage is: you want to buy at X price on a stop order and you get filled at Y. These slight differences add up over the year and eat into your profits as an investor.

Contrarily there is positive slippage when you get filled on a stop order but in most cases you end up with negative slippage. You would want to look at round turns per million on a rolling basis over numerous time frames. The reason being is when trades are working there should be less trading. Conversely during a period of choppy markets the manager might have a higher round turn per million. The number of round turns per million vary amongst managers. There is really no set number but you want to ask and understand.

As a reference point, in our company on average we have 500 round turns per million. This is considered low. As part of your due diligence in regard to round turns per million you want to know does the frequency of trading increase or decrease during either profitable or unprofitable periods.

## MANAGED ACCOUNTS

Managed accounts are always preferred as they give full transparency and liquidity to the investor. However there are questions needing to be asked as far as managed accounts are concerned. You want to understand how positions are enabled for new accounts. Invariably when you invest there will existing positions the manager has invested in already. You want to know if he will put in all existing positions or if you will only take new signals. There is no free lunch with either approach.

If you take all existing positions you possibly might be increasing your risks. However conversely, one of these existing positions might be the big winner of the year and if you are not in this trade you will underperform the other accounts.

If you take only new signals you might diminish your drawdowns if these positions do not work but if are not in one of the existing positions you can definitely under perform.

In my trading programs I put all trades on for new investors unless one of the existing positions is showing an extreme profit. If I put this trade on for the new investor I would be increasing his risk. You want to understand how the orders are placed for all managed accounts. I place all orders in a group account for my clients. Trading in this fashion ensures fairness and that all investors have approximately the same fills. You want to know if the manager allows notional funding.

## MY FAVORITE QUESTIONS

Every manager would love to tell you about his best trade. I always ask them this question to lower their guard. Everyone likes to talk about themselves. This is the ABC of Dale Carnegie. People like to be accentuated. I want to know what was their best trade and why. I really am interested and hope that can be repeated when I am invested with them.

What I have found is that honest managers are simply consistent and they "stumbled" into their "best trade". They followed their plan. They did not know anything special nor did they do anything special. World class managers are simply consistent, they follow their plan and try to mitigate their losing trades and make themselves available for some market to move much more they expected. The worst trades can be another story. You want to understand this worst trade and what was gleaned from it, if anything.

A great question, in order to enhance your compounding over time is to ask this simple question: do any of your investors have reduced fee structures? If they do, so should you. Lowering management fees or incentive fees increases your potential of compounding. You always want to know if the manager has a high water mark and how it is calculated.

Due diligence is very broad and time consuming. It is a mistake to assume that money managers, or mutual funds for that matter, will provide you with *all* of their pertinent information voluntarily, especially if some of that information is negative. You have to know how to dig for the pertinent information, how to ask the right questions and press until you get the real answers. They won't necessarily lie to you, but you have to ask the right questions to get the whole truth. I have made a business out of asking the tough questions and getting the answers from money managers.

## WORLD CLASS COMMODITY TRADING ADVISORS DO NOT ADVERTISE

World class money managers do not hold themselves out generally. These world class money managers do not advertise nor have the mainstream ever really heard of them.

As I have expressed in this book, I have a preference to commodity trading advisors and managed futures who are trend followers. I believe that investing in this context puts me in the position to benefit from any eventual bull or bear market in a wide range of markets while at the same time providing me liquidity and transparency.

I have experienced the success that trend followers can offer. This small unique group of world class money managers trade without any opinion. They will go long or short without any hesitation. They know they do not know the future nor do they believe it is necessary to compound money. There is nothing perfect and even these world class money managers go through periods of drawdowns and losses. I use these points as allocation points.

## MONEY MANAGER DISASTER STORIES

Contrary to commodity trading advisors who are trend following there are the option sellers in the managed futures space. Many brokers like pushing these types of investments as they generate large commission dollars. I strongly suggest avoiding option sellers. I will not invest in any option writing strategy as enticing in the short run they seem. These option sellers for years look great as they generate a proverbial 1%

per month without a lot of volatility. This is on par with Madoff until there is a $6^{th}$ sigma event and they blow up. I have seen this repeatedly from selling SP 500 options to selling feeder cattle options right before the Mad Cow debacle. I have seen more managers blow up after having sold options more than anything else.

Another niche of managed futures is the counter trend traders. I have learned to avoid these managers like the plague. One of the first conferences I went to featured Victor Niederhoffer as a guest speaker. Niederhoffer was extremely successful and even managed money for George Soros. He had returned in the 30% for more than a decade. In cases such as this, he was showered with money.

Investors were simply blinded by his numbers. Investors only saw the 30%, not how he traded. They did not look at his daily equity curve. Within the month there can be tremendous volatility. Many times this is masked by the monthly numbers. To these foolish investors they did not care how Niederhoffer traded. Niederhoffer even wrote a bestselling book, *The Education of a Speculator*. During the Asian contagion he was hurt badly by his bet in Thai banks as well as his bet on the SP 500. On Oct 27 1997 the SP 500 fell more than 7% or 554 points. Niederhoffer still felt his assumption was correct and the market was wrong. He thought the proverbial, that the market would bounce back! He had nakedly put positions on the Stock indices. As Murphy's Law would have it he ended up being right but his timing was wrong. This was a fatal blow to Niederhoffer. He had to close his fund and left a $20 million dollar debt at his broker.

As usual, greed has a way of making people forget the past. After closing his fund in 1998, Niederhoffer traded his own account. However in 2002 Niederhoffer came back and opened his Matador fund. He was returning 50% per year with his worst year of 40%. Again he was flooded with money and in 2007 at the onset of the credit and housing debacle he closed the Matador fund, after experiencing a 75% drop. Lightening stuck twice with Niederhoffer. Niederhoffer is not the only example.

In 2011 there was a counter trend manager called Dighton, who had a fantastic record. For those who simply chase returns blindly, Dighton would have been a perfect pick. Over the last 6 years or so he compounded money at around a 30% rate. Many naïve investors threw him money and were blinded by his returns. Dighton was managing upwards of $200 million dollars. In July 2011 however Dighton blew up and lost 80% of his fund. Dighton was a counter trend trader who blew up over one trade with the Swiss Franc. **Think about it, 6 years of hard work to be blown up by one trade.**

The potential of these types of blowups are the reasons I avoid counter trend traders. My goal is to compound money. If I have a big loss I inhibit my compounding. Contrarily trend followers grind it out over long periods of time.

## TREND FOLLOWING SUCCESS STORIES

At one point in my investing career, I made a large amount of money with one trend following money manager who traded Malaysian Palm oil. I had never heard of Palm oil before this trade. I would tend to believe that 99% of you have never heard of Palm Oil. However palm oil is common cooking oil through Southeast Asia, Africa and South American. Not just millions of people use palm oil on a daily basis but probably closer to several billion.

Palm oil is a market on its own and there is liquidity. There are periods of shortages and surpluses. These shortages make bull markets and conversely surpluses make bear markets. In both cases potential profits exist.

Think about coffee. The prices fluctuate. Think about gasoline for your car. All the time prices are moving up and moving down. These movements create potential trades for commodity trading advisors. Contrarily a money manager who only trades the stock market or bond market is limited to some degree. It is very difficult for even top tier money managers to generate positive returns solely in bear markets. The greater profits are in bull markets. If you can imagine if you were an investor in Japan and only focused on the Nikkei, since 1989 the Nikkei has been falling. In 1989 the Nikkei was 39,000 and today it is slightly below 9,000. Can you imagine how hard it would have been to profit?

In 2007 and 2008 the prices of wheat and crude oil ranged from extreme bull markets to bear markets. Wheat went from around 500 to the low 1300 dollar range. Everything from pizzas to bread skyrocketed in price. Within a half a year in 2008 wheat crashed back down to $500. Fortunes were made as well as fortunes were lost.

Remember Peak Oil in 2008? We were running out of gas. Sure, prices ran up to $140+ range and then cratered down to $34 a barrel. Again fortunes were made and lost. T Boone Pickens the oil expert lost a great of money. Contrarily Abraham trading group who had no opinions on the markets made in 2007 21.80% and in 2008 28.80%.

## The Bible of Compounding Money

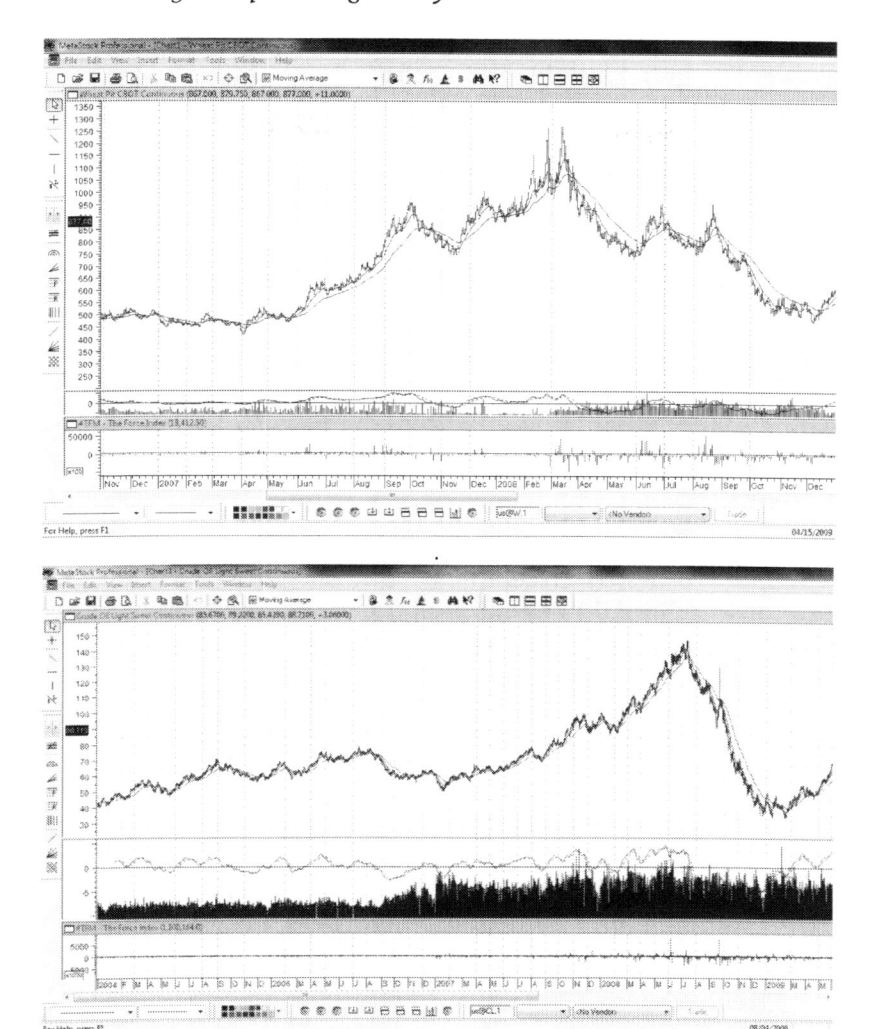

Chart Created in Thomson Reuters MetaStock. All rights reserved. Past Performance is not necessarily indicative of future performance

**THE RISK OF LOSS IN TRADING COMMODITY FUTURES, OPTIONS, AND FOREIGN EXCHANGE ("FOREX") IS SUBSTANTIAL**

# CHAPTER 15 SUMMATION

Successful investing all boils down to risk. Three very simple questions will give you a feel how a manager addresses risk.

Risk per trade

Risk per sector

Risk on open trade equity

## CHAPTER 16

# How to Find the World Class Trend Followers

As trading and investing are my passion, I spend a great deal of time reading and schmoozing. In order to find today's world class money managers there are several things I do. Firstly I study quantitatively the various data bases of money managers. I know that I am seeking a small select group that has generated over 15% CAROR over at least a 10 year period. I have my exact rules as I have exact rules in my money management business. I sit on both sides of the table. I am a commodity trading advisor as well as I invest with commodity trading advisors. This can be seen very clearly when digging in the databases quantitatively. However this is only one step.

I like to meet the money managers first hand, even before doing my qualitative due diligence. I go to various conferences specializing in hedge funds and commodity trading advisors. This maximizes my time. At these conferences you meet firsthand the potential managers you might consider investing with. You will be shocked when you actually meet some managers. There are always happy hours and when the drinks are flowing so are the inhibitions.

I was in London at a conference and after the conference there was a happy hour. My wife met me and we had a glass of wine. We started to speak with a manager. Between his slurring and staggering he told me and my wife about his girlfriend and by the way he was married. Can you imagine investing with him? Guess not!

I make it a point to both attending and presenting my money management firm at the CTA Expo and the Emerging Manager Forum. In addition to the CTA Expo the Alphametrix conventions are fantastic and completely first class.

The CTA EXPO was established in 2008 and their Emerging Manager Forum in London was established in 2010. CTA EXPO was created to help professional capital raisers and allocators identify managed futures trading talent and to promote investing in managed futures. In just over three years CTA EXPO has grown to offering one day conferences in New York, London, Chicago and Miami. What is wonderful is that capital sources, including asset allocators, pool operators and professional clients attend CTA EXPO events for free.

Bucky Isaacson is one of the cofounders of the CTA EXPO and has a long and illustrious career in the field. Bucky has been in the field for decades. He was a partner with Keith Campbell and Chet Conrad in Campbell & Company which was one of the first commodities trading firms from the 1970s. Campbell & Company is a world class money manager with many clients ranging from pension funds and sovereign wealth funds. Today Campbell & Company is considered one of the most successful trend following firms.

Later in his career he was vice president of Lind-Waldock & Company; member of board of directors of Japanese Brokerage firm; president of Interalliance U.S.A., LTD; general partner of AC Private Equity Partners, LP; Marketing director of Florasynth, INC and partner of Lincolnwood, INC; director of Geldermanand Company.

Bucky's partner in the CTA Expo is Frank Pusateri. Frank has been a managed futures consultant and industry leader for over 30 years. He is the president of Adirondack Portfolio Management, a consulting firm that specializes in managed futures, as well as Executive Vice President of Fall River Capital a leading CTA and CPO firm. The two partners make a great duo. The networking at the CTA Expo has been wonderful as growing my money management as well as meeting industry players on a one on one basis.

*The CTA Expo is a must go event.*

## ALPHAMETRIX

Alphametrix is a great source of information for research in the alternative investment sector. Alphametrix has "The Marketplace" which has 100,000 active profiles of pre-qualified industry participants which serves to connect investors, service providers and funds to facilitate research, due diligence and efficient business operations.

In conjunction to Alphametrix's "Marketplace" they host events biannually. The events are located at luxury locations such as the Fountain Blue in Miami Beach and the Grimaldi Forum, an internationally renowned cultural event and conference center located in Monaco.

Alphametrix offers the opportunity for investors to speak face-to-face with money managers in private meetings called an "AlphaSuite". I attended last year's conference in Miami Beach. From this conference I made several allocations to money managers. I was following the managers for quite some time and sat with them in an AlphaSuite to understand further how the manager approaches risk.

Going to the Alphametrix should not be missed. Alphametrix has a diverse and hand-picked group of top hedge funds and investors from around the world all in one place at the same time.

There are other conferences; however I have not attended them:

- Canadian Alternative Investment Forum
- Battle of the Quants
- IIR's 3 Annual Hedge Fund Managed Accounts Conference
- UCITS for Hedge, Mutual & Investment Fund Managers
- Hedge Fund Association's Market & Operational Risks

In the past I have attended the MFA (Managed Funds Association) however I have found the CTA Expo and the

Alphametrix to be much better and a valuable investment of my time.

## DATABASES

There are various databases in which to research manager's returns. Many of the databases below follow managed futures. CogentHedge.com lists numerous sectors such as long/short, real estate, asset backed lending and many more.

I have not found any substantial differences between the paid databases and the free databases. When utilizing the databases you can do all types of searches within their data to define possibly which managers you should continue your due diligence.

In the database www.iasg.com you can sort all types of parameters. You can search by assets under management, annual rate of return, start dates, strategy, and investment size as well as other parameters.

## Managed Futures : Performance

*Source: Chart with permission from lasg.com*

Remember this is not just a quantitative search for returns. The qualitative aspects are equally important as well as your understanding of exactly how the manager trades. I am a big believer in simple robust concepts with a heavy dose of risk management. I am always concerned about ***risk per trade, risk per sector and overall risk on the portfolio***.

Below are some of the databases I report to for my money management or use for my allocation research.

# DATABASE LIST

www.Absolutereturns.com

www.alphametrix.com

www.Altegris.com

www.AutumnGold.com

www.BarclayHedge.com

www.Cogenthedge.com

www.Eurekahedge.com

www.Hedgeco.net

www.Hedgefund.net

www.hedgefundresearch.com/

www.Hedgeworld.com

www.Iasg.com

www.Managedfutures.eu

www.Starkresearch.com

## CHAPTER 16 SUMMATION

Networking is the key to finding world class money managers. Many do not hold themselves out. Conferences are one of the best places to interact and find world class money managers.

*Andy Abraham*

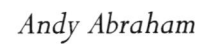

# Conclusion

In conclusion, investing is a marathon. There are no magic bullets or anything simple. In order to succeed long term one must play the defense. This defensive posture starts with your initial allocation. As anything can and will happen, I would not suggest investing more than 5% of your investable assets in any idea regardless how good they are. This is the first step.

I would only look to invest in managers who have in the past endured 10 years in the markets. During this 10 year period it is very fair to assume they have experienced various conditions and survived.

However I am not just looking for survivors, I am looking for the cream of managers. I only want to consider managers that have a compounded rate of return over this period in excess of 15%. This is a tough cut and eliminates the vast majority. But why would I settle for mediocrity? I wouldn't, since my goal is to compound money.

Every percentage point over long periods of time corresponds to large differences in wealth. I want the managers to offer me complete liquidity and transparency. This is achieved by having a managed account with them if I am large enough. Many managers have minimums of several million dollars for managed accounts. My preference is for commodity trading advisors that are not too large. In this context they are available to trade numerous markets. They can trade anything from New Zealand dollars to corn. They can go long as well as go short.

The handful of managers I presented are not gurus. They will have drawdowns and long periods in which they will have elusive profits. The reason I look for smaller managers is that they are flexible to enter and exit that some UBER size commodity trading advisors cannot enter due to their size. Most of the large commodity-trading firms are bound only to financials, due to their size. They can only trade interest rates, stock indices and currencies. This negates my goal of being available for any bull or bear market across a large set of markets. More so the returns of the large or UBER size commodity trading firms have fallen with their large size. I stand potentially to profit greater with smaller and more agile managers.

Now that I have done my simple quantitative screening the real work is the qualitative. In the previous chapters I detailed the entire due diligence process. This process should not be skimped on or negated.

I included the long list of so-called professional institutional investors who simply followed the herd and blindly invested with Madoff. There is a long list as well of both high net worth investors and professional institutional investors who were fleeced by Alan Stanford and his $7 billion dollar scam.

Actually my uncle also lost money with Stanford. He did not want to listen to me. He knew better. You have the tools. You know what you need to do.

*I wish you prosperity, success and good luck...*

*The Bible of Compounding Money*

*but you won't need luck if you work hard and follow the guidelines which I have provided for you.*

*Andrew Abraham can be reached at:*

Abraham Investment Management

www.AbrahamCTA.com

Andrew@AbrahamCta.com

Printed in Great Britain
by Amazon